DARING,
Disreputable, *and*
DEVOUT

DARING,
Disreputable, *and*
DEVOUT

Interpreting the Bible's Women
in the Arts and Music

Dan W. Clanton Jr.

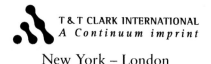

T & T CLARK INTERNATIONAL
A Continuum imprint

New York – London

2009
The Continuum International Publishing Group Inc
80 Maiden Lane, New York, NY 10038
The Continuum International Publishing Group Ltd
The Tower Building, 11 York Road, London SE1 7NX
www.continuumbooks.com

Printed in the United States of America
ISBN (HC) 9780567027474
ISBN (PB) 9780567027016

Library of Congress Cataloging-in-Publication Data

Clanton, Dan W.
  Daring, disreputable, and devout : interpreting the Bible's women in the arts and music / Dan
W. Clanton, Jr.
    p. cm.
  Includes bibliographical references and index.
  ISBN-13: 978-0-567-02747-4 (hardcover : alk. paper)
  ISBN-10: 0-567-02747-3 (hardcover : alk. paper)
  ISBN-13: 978-0-567-02701-6 (pbk. : alk. paper)
  ISBN-10: 0-567-02701-5 (pbk. : alk. paper) 1. Women in the Bible. 2. Bible. O.T.—Criticism,
interpretation, etc. 3. Arts in the Bible. 4. Music in the Bible. I. Title.

  BS575.C543 2009
  221.9'22082—dc22

                                                              2008044628

ℭ CONTENTS

ℭ ACKNOWLEDGMENTS

I AM VERY GRATEFUL to Bonnie Mullin at *Biblical Archaeology Review* for permission to reprint portions of chapter 3; and to Dr. Leonard Greenspoon for permission to reprint material included in chapters 3 and 6. I would also like to thank Andy Weiner, the cofounder of Spaightwood Galleries in Upton, Massachusetts (*http://spaightwoodgalleries.com/index.html*), for his kind permission to reprint the cover image.

As with any research project, I certainly did not work in a vacuum. My general editor at T & T Clark, Burke Gertenschlager, and my production editor, Ryan Masteller, have provided me with valuable suggestions, helpful comments, enduring encouragement, and near-limitless patience. For this, I thank them deeply.

Thanks to Drs. G. Andrew Tooze and Terry Clark for their continued friendship and support through this process, as well as more reasons than I have space to list.

During the process of writing this book, I converted to Judaism. I would like to thank Rabbis Richard Rheins, Susan Miller Rheins, and Jay TelRav of Temple Sinai in Denver for sponsoring me, taking the time to guide me through the process, and serving as my *beit din*. Words cannot describe the debt of gratitude I feel for how you all have enriched my life.

Our family in the south deserve a huge thanks for their love, compassion, and willingness to be there for us, in spirit and in person: Dan and Kaye Clanton; Kristin, Charles, Alex, and Kate Ferryman; Jeff Clanton; Kara Clanton and Justin Harper; Janet Stutsman and Lillian Hudlin; and John and Mary Stutsman. Our family in the west—whom we'll miss so much—also merit a huge *gracias*: Natalie, Ted, Ben, and Lulu Fickes.

Thanks also to our children, Danny and Hannah, for their willingness to let their old, bald papa get his work done, as well as for their empathy, compassion, enthusiasm, and happiness.

No one has done more for me than my wife, Missy. She has always supported my work with her time and love, and I'm simply the luckiest guy in the world to be with her. As Townes Van Zandt wrote, "The blues shall wash me / and sun shall dry me / the world will hide me / but she will find me / and when she finds me / she will take me home." My home is you, and I love you more than I can say.

After becoming a Jew and writing a book about Jewish women, I decided to dedicate this book to two important Jewish women. Suzan Markman and her husband, Allan, have shown me and my family what it means to be responsible and honorable people, as well as good Jews. Suzan, for your teaching, your compassion, and your contribution to our family as well as our community, I dedicate this book to you.

The other Jewish woman to whom I am dedicating this book will only be a few months old when it is published. Her name is Jenna Victoria Leader, and she is the daughter of my best friend of more than twenty-five years, Joe Leader, and his wife, Jeanette. For Israel, for Key West, for your friendship, and for always Keeping the Faith, I dedicate this book to your daughter. May she live long and prosper, and inherit her father's zest for life, love for Judaism, and fierce loyalty to friends.

ℛ INTRODUCTION

THIS BOOK IS AN OUTGROWTH of a long-standing interest in the way(s) in which biblical literature—and specifically narratives about or that include female characters—has been and continues to be interpreted and retold. It also grew out of the pedagogical frustration over finding a text that would address stories of biblical women as well as engage aesthetic interpretations of those characters. Interpretive genres may vary, for example, biblical commentary, art, literature, music, film, and so on, but I have always been fascinated at the way in which many people's understanding of the Bible stems from later renderings or retellings, not the biblical texts themselves. These retellings can be fruitfully engaged in the classroom in order to impress upon students the continuing relevance of biblical narrative in the formation of identity and ideology. For example, one only needs to look at the uproar surrounding Mel Gibson's film *The Passion of the Christ* (2004) and the numerous books and articles that ensued, many of which attempted to disentangle the biblical narratives from Gibson's specific interpretation of them.[1] Even so, many members of the film's audience no doubt took the film's interpretation of the Passion narratives at face value and constructed various discourses—both personal and communal—as a result.

The case of interpretations of biblical women is analogous, as many commonly held assumptions about these characters originate from the layers of retellings, commentaries, and aesthetic renderings, many of which add salacious details or simply invent new stories and associations to augment or

---

1. For example, see Timothy K. Beal, "'The Passion': They Know Not What They Watch," *Chronicle of Higher Education* (19 March 2004), sec. B, pp. 14–15; Philip A. Cunningham, ed., *Pondering the Passion: What's at Stake for Christians and Jews?* (Lanham, Md.: Rowman & Littlefield, 2004); J. Shawn Landres and Michael Berenbaum, eds., *After "The Passion" Is Gone: American Religious Consequences* (Walnut Creek, Calif.: AltaMira Press, 2004); and S. Brent Plate, ed., *Re-viewing "The Passion": Mel Gibson's Film and Its Critics* (New York: Palgrave Macmillan, 2004).

supplant the biblical texts. Put differently, stories of women in the Bible have been interpreted by artists, writers, musicians, filmmakers, and biblical commentators for centuries. However, in many cases, these later interpreters have often adapted and altered the Bible to fit their own views of the stories. Ironically, these later renderings usually serve as the basis for the generally accepted views of biblical women. For example, many readers of the Bible assume that Eve is to blame for the disobedient act in the garden of Eden, or that Delilah seduced Samson and then cut his hair. A closer look at these assumptions, though, reveals that they are not based on the Bible, but are mediated through the creations of later interpreters.

In the chapters that follow, I summarize and analyze selected stories of biblical women as well as discuss how these stories have been mediated in various genres of cultural production, for example, art, literature, music, film, and religious commentary. The word "mediated" is significant as it indicates not only the "media" aspect of the interpretations considered but also my earlier claim that the views many Bible readers hold about biblical women are "mediated" through these later interpretations rather than the biblical text itself. I will not offer systematic or holistic readings of each character, but rather some vignettes from the ways in which later interpreters have read these women. The foci of these vignettes vary in that I have chosen to examine certain historically or ideologically important renderings in great detail (for example, in chapters 3, 6, and 7), but treat others in the context of other interpretations to illustrate trends or themes in the history of interpretation of a given character (for example, in chapters 1, 2, 4, and 5). Some chapters delve into the biblical narrative more deeply than others (namely, chapters 2 and 4), mainly because in those chapters the interpretations I discuss deal more closely with the biblical text than other renderings in other chapters.

I have designed this book for undergraduates and interested lay readers, but it can also be used prosperously by more advanced readers. To facilitate its use in the classroom and in adult study groups, I have included study questions at the end of each chapter. Not specifically a monograph with an overarching argument, the book addresses my two main goals. First, I want to illuminate what the biblical text actually says about major female characters; and, second, I want to highlight how these later interpretations adapt, shift, and sometimes distort the biblical narratives in their attempts to comprehend its vagueness or to resituate its plot in a new time for a new audience with a new purpose. My main goal, though, is simple: I want readers to reengage the biblical text so that the biblical narrative's voice will not be lost in the interpretive layers of the centuries.

1

"A Hard-Headed Woman"?

Eve in the Hebrew Bible and Later Interpretations

THE TITLE FOR THIS CHAPTER comes from *King Creole*, a film starring Elvis Presley that was released in 1958. Unbeknownst to most biblical scholars, this song treats its basic theme, namely, "Ever since the world began / A hard-headed woman been a thorn in the side of man," by using three examples from the Hebrew Bible: Delilah, Jezebel, and Eve. Elvis says, regarding Eve, "Now Adam told to Eve, 'Listen here to me, don't you let me catch you messin' round that apple tree.'" As I will show, this injunction is not recorded in the story of the garden of Eden in Genesis 2–3, but the point I would like to make is that the song was immensely popular *in spite of its addition to the biblical text*. One of the main points I will make in what follows is a related one, namely, that the character of Eve has suffered immensely at the hands of biblical interpreters, and by a close reading of the biblical text we may be able to address some of these more harmful images. My goal then is fourfold: (1) to examine the story of Eve in Genesis 2–3 to assess what it says and does not say about this character; (2) to note ambiguities or questions left unanswered by the Genesis story; (3) to survey briefly how Jewish writers in the Second Temple period and early rabbinic era, as well as Christian writers like Paul and Augustine, tried to concretize these ambiguities and answer these questions; and (4) to see how the issue of blame for the disobedient act in the garden of Eden is dealt with in the tradition of interpretations that has grown up around this story.

EVE IN GENESIS 2–3

To begin, I will focus specifically on the character of Eve as she is treated in the Genesis story. Even though there are many ways to approach the text, for our purposes I will be utilizing a literary-critical approach so that I can highlight issues of plot, characterization, and motivation.

The Creation of Eve

Following the creation of the human/earthling/clod ('*adam*) from the soil/earth ('*adamah*), God decides that the solitary state of the earthling's existence is not good.[1] God decides to make him "a helper as his partner" (NRSV), or a "fitting helper" (JPS).[2] This vocabulary is telling because in the Hebrew Bible, the word '*ezer*, here rendered as "helper," is most often used to refer to God. After an attempt to discover a suitable partner for the earthling, God administers some sort of anesthesia to the earthling and while the earthling sleeps removes one of its ribs and makes it into a woman. At this point in the story, we see the creation of sexual differentiation, because up until this point there has been no knowledge of sexual difference.[3] Now, though, the creature formerly known as the earthling can say, "This at last is bone of my bones / and flesh of my flesh; / this one shall be called Woman ('*ishshâ*), / for out of Man ('*ish*) this one was taken" (2.23). Following this, we have a narrative aside in which we are told the results of this first human speech as well as the resultant sexual differentiation in 2.24–25. The narrator tells us that, just like this first couple, other men and women will be joined into one flesh, thus implying some sort of unity between the man and woman here in the story.

The Interaction with the Serpent and the Tree

We are told in 2.25 that the man and woman were "naked" ('*arummim*), and this characterization immediately leads into the introduction to the serpent in 3.1, because the serpent is "crafty" or "shrewd" ('*arum*). He approaches the woman, although the narrative does not specify why, and asks her a simple question: "Did God say, 'You shall not eat from any tree in the garden'?" (3.1). The woman's reply, her first quoted speech, represents a misquotation of God's command to the earthling in 2.16–17: she adds to the prescription about eating from the tree, "nor shall you touch it,

---

1. For this nontraditional translation of '*adam*, see Carol Meyers, *Discovering Eve: Ancient Israelite Women in Context* (New York: Oxford University Press, 1988), 81–82.

2. In his translation, Robert Alter renders this term as "sustainer beside him," noting, "The Hebrew '*ezer kenegdo* (King James Version 'help meet') is notoriously difficult to translate. The second term means 'alongside him,' 'opposite him,' 'a counterpart to him.' 'Help' is too weak because it suggests a merely auxiliary function, whereas '*ezer* elsewhere connotes active intervention on behalf of someone, especially in military context, as often in Psalms." See *The Five Books of Moses: A Translation with Commentary* (New York and London: W. W. Norton, 2004), 22.

3. This aspect of the text was famously noted and explored in the groundbreaking analysis of Phyllis Trible in her "A Love Story Gone Awry," in *God and the Rhetoric of Sexuality* (OBT; Philadelphia: Fortress, 1978), 80. See also Burton L. Visotzky, *Reading the Book: Making the Bible a Timeless Text* (New York: Schocken Books, 1996), 198–202.

or you shall die" (3.3). Her response is telling because of a rather simple-minded point: she had not been created yet when God gave the earthling the order not to eat from the tree. As such, it is unclear from where the woman would have heard the injunction she repeats to the serpent, although presumably the man told her. The serpent engages the woman in a debate over her amplification and claims, "You will not die; for God knows that when you eat of it your eyes will be opened, and you will be like God, knowing good and evil" (3.4–5). The woman then looks at the tree and comprehends three things about it: (a) it is good for food; (b) it is a delight to the eyes; and (c) the tree "was to be desired to make one wise" (3.6).[4] Following this, we are told that "she took of its fruit and ate; and she also gave some to her husband, who was with her, and he ate" (3.6). This verse has important implications for our purposes, both in what it says and in what it omits. It says that the woman ate the fruit and that she gave some to her husband who was with her, and then he ate as well. We do not know how long the man has been with the woman, and the text omits any mention of the woman tempting, begging, or persuading the man to eat the fruit. We do know what happens next, though: the serpent's claim is at least partially fulfilled. Their eyes are certainly opened, but the knowledge they gain seems to be of their nakedness, because their first act is to clothe themselves.

The Repercussions

The next scene occurs in 3.8–24, in which God discovers that the couple has violated his commandment and eaten of the tree. When God confronts the man in 3.11, the man blames the woman, who in turn blames the serpent. The man says that the woman gave him the fruit and he ate, and the woman blames the serpent's trickery for her actions. In reverse order then, God makes three statements: (1) he first curses the serpent and speaks negatively about the relationship between him and the woman, as well as the woman's offspring; (2) he then makes a pronouncement to the woman about her future role as child bearer and her relation to the man; and (3) he finally speaks to the man and curses the relationship between him and the ground because of his actions.[5]

---

4. Alter, *Five Books of Moses*, 24–25, renders part of this verse, "And the woman saw that the tree was good for eating and that it was lust to the eyes and the tree was lovely to look at," arguing that a term like "delight" is unacceptable for the Hebrew word *ta'awah* in 3.6. In his work, Martin O'Kane builds on Alter's work and stresses the recurrent visual language and imagery found in this section. See "The Bible and the Visual Imagination," in *Painting the Text: The Artist as Biblical Interpreter* (The Bible in the Modern World Series 8; Sheffield: Sheffield Phoenix Press, 2007), 12–13.

5. As Anne Lapidus Lerner notes in her *Eternally Eve: Images of Eve in the Hebrew Bible, Midrash, and Modern Jewish Poetry* (HBI Series on Jewish Women; Waltham, Mass., and London: Brandeis University Press/University Press of New England, 2007), 108: "Contrary to popular opinion, God's responding statements are not curses. The word 'curse' is used in connection with the snake, but neither the woman nor the *adam* is cursed."

After these pronouncements, the man names his wife Eve in 3.20, in much the same way as he named the animals earlier in 2.19–20. In 3.21 we are told that God made clothes for the couple and he clothed them. Finally, God reflects on the man's newly acquired knowledge and decides that the danger of the man becoming immortal too is just too great, so he drives out the man (and presumably the woman) from the garden in 3.24, and our story ends.

AMBIGUITIES AND QUESTIONS

Our story, as presented in Genesis, tells the tale of relationship troubles. The earthling has an ideal relationship with the earth that winds up being ruined. The man and the woman have an equitable, unified relationship that winds up with the man naming her like an animal; in addition, her position of equality has been put into question by God's pronouncement in 3.16. Finally, the human-animal relationship has been put into jeopardy by the actions of the serpent. Because the story is interested in God's command to humans, the disobeying of that command, and the repercussions of that disobedience, we can conclude that the narrative serves an etiological function in that it attempts to explain the origins of the human situation in the author's time. However, it also addresses questions of identity and behavior; that is, it was written in the hopes of establishing an identity for the writer's audience and followers that would regulate and control behavior. The triple emphasis on etiology, identity, and theology marks this text as a sacred myth insofar as myths shape our sense of self by sanctioning certain types of behavior, explaining the origin(s) of evil, and providing a moral order to our surroundings, as well as by the fact that this story performs these functions within a religious context.

However, our story is also tantalizingly ambiguous about certain important questions. As any good Bible teacher will tell you, knowing the content of the story is key, but it is also important for us to be aware of the responses to and interpretations of texts because often these renderings and readings attempt to fill in lacunae or interpretive gaps in the text as well as to retell or resituate stories in different times for different purposes. In this way, interpreted biblical texts become ciphers for attitudes and identities, and if we are able to pay attention to these interpretations, as well as examine them critically, we will not only be honing our exegetical skills; we will also be more aware of the enduring impact biblical literature has had on our cultures. In the case of Genesis 2–3, there are many questions that puzzled and fascinated later readers of the story. Because of the enormous number and variety of the responses to and interpretations of this story, our focus will be narrow. I will only discuss four major questions associated with Eve and how later readers of Scripture attempted to answer them. I will also attend to the interpretation of these issues, particularly the issue of blame, in popular culture. Following are the four main questions we will examine:

1. What are the implications of Eve's status as "helper" and "taken from the man"?
2. Why did the serpent approach the woman and not the man?
3. Where was the man during the woman's exchange with the serpent?
4. Who is to blame for the disobedient act in the garden?

LATER READINGS

What follows will not be a comprehensive survey of every Jewish or Christian reading of Genesis 2–3. As I said, we are focusing on four main questions and I will discuss what select representative texts did with the story. Even so, my purpose is not only to indicate the pregnancy of our text, but also to demonstrate the immense creativity with which biblical interpreters work(ed).

Eve as "Helper" and "Taken from the Man"?

For centuries, many biblical interpreters have seen Eve's condition of being created from Adam's rib as implying some sort of subordination, especially when paired with God's description of her as a "helper" in 2.18.[6] As we have seen, neither of these in and of itself implies a secondary or submissive status for the woman. In general, Jewish interpreters have not spilled much ink on proving that Gen. 2.18–23 means that women are inferior to men, even though not all of their comments are what we might call "feminist." In fact, they have been much more interested in discussing how and why God chose to create the woman as he did.

One of the most interesting attempts to explain why God created the woman is found in the *Sibylline Oracles*, a collection of oracular materials usually dated to around the turn of the era. In the first book, the Sibyl tells us that the man,

> being alone in the luxuriant plantation of the garden / desired conversation, and prayed to behold another form / like his own. God himself indeed took a bone from his / flank and made Eve, a wonderful maidenly / spouse, whom he gave to this man to live with in the garden. / And he, when he saw her, was suddenly greatly / amazed in spirit, rejoicing, such a corresponding / copy did he see. They conversed with wise words / which flowed spontaneously, for God had taken care of everything. (Book 1, lines 26–34)[7]

---

6. See Trible, "Love Story Gone Awry," 90: "According to [God], what the earth creature needs is a companion, one who is neither subordinate nor superior; one who alleviated isolation through identity."

7. John J. Collins, "Sibylline Oracles: A New Translation and Introduction," in *The Old Testament Pseudepigrapha*, vol. 1, *Apocalyptic Literature and Testaments* (ed. James H. Charlesworth; New York: Doubleday, 1983), 335.

In this retelling, then, not only is there no subordination, but also we see the image of perfect complementarity between the man and woman, both in form and in intellect. Specifically, the woman here is portrayed as being wise, a characterization that will echo in later retellings and feminist readings of the text.[8]

In the Babylonian Talmud (or *Bavli*)—the encyclopedic collection of Jewish biblical and legal interpretations from circa the sixth century C.E.—the following exchange is recorded:

> R. Simeon b. Menasia expounded: What is meant by the words, "*And the Lord God built the rib*"? It teaches that the Holy One, blessed be He, plaited Eve's hair and brought her to Adam; for in the seacoast towns "plaiting" is called "building" . . . *And he brought her to the man.* R. Jeremiah b. Eleazar said: This teaches that [God] acted as best man to Adam. (*Ber.* 61a)[9]

In these interpretations, the confusion over why God chose to build the woman out of the rib is explained by a linguistic analogy that allows the image of Eve the bride to be proffered. Note, though, that we have no mention of any lessening of Eve's status here.

Finally, in the fourteenth century C.E., the *Chronicles of Jerahmeel* records that the creation of Eve was necessitated by the man's grandiose stature in the eyes of the animals:

> All the creatures saw him and were afraid of him; they thought he was their creator, and prostrated themselves before him. . . . Now Adam walked about the Garden of Eden like one of the ministering angels. God said, "Just as I am alone in My world, so is Adam; just as I have no companion, neither has Adam. Tomorrow the creatures will say, 'He does not propagate, he is surely our creator.' It is not good for man to be alone, I will make a helpmeet for him." (6.12–13)[10]

Thus, Eve's creation was occasioned by the animals' miscomprehension of the man's identity as well as God's fear of Adam infringing on his domain of divinity, as in Gen. 3.22–24.

Thus, in these three readings Eve is not viewed as "less" than Adam, nor is she viewed as being a subordinate to a master. However, in other readings, Eve is linked to less than desirable qualities because of her creation as well as her sex. Writing in the first century C.E., the famous Jewish exegete Philo of Alexandria discusses Eve in several of his writings but comments on her creation in a particularly interesting passage in his *Questions and Answers on Genesis* (*QG*). In book 1, he delivers some of his harshest pronouncements on the first woman, especially with regard to the

---

8. In her work, Meyers argues that the genre of Genesis 3 is that of wisdom literature, with the woman being the seeker of wisdom, not the man. See *Discovering Eve*, 90–92.
9. Quoted in J. M. Evans, *Paradise Lost and the Genesis Tradition* (Oxford: Oxford University Press, 1968), 45. See also A. Lerner, *Eternally Eve*, 56–60.
10. Quoted in Evans, *Paradise Lost and the Genesis Tradition*, 43.

question of why Eve was not formed from the ground, but rather from the man: "First, because woman is not equal in honour with man. Second, because she is not equal in age, but younger" (*QG* 1:27). He also notes that the woman is the "softer" of the two (*QG* 1:33) and that her place is in the domestic sphere, not the public, active sphere of men (*QG* 1:26). In his work *On the Account of the World's Creation Given by Moses*, Philo discusses the implications of Eve's creation with an eye toward the future disobedient act. He writes, "And woman becomes for him the beginning of blameworthy life," because of the pleasure they both felt when they saw each other, that is, "that pleasure which is the beginning of wrongs and violation of law, the pleasure for the sake of which men bring on themselves the life of mortality and wretchedness in lieu of that of immortality and bliss" (151–52). Thus, the creation of woman brought about a sense of pleasure that ultimately led to the disregarding of God's commandments. These comments on Eve reflect Philo's context as a male exegete in the first century, especially as a follower of Plato, and we should also note that these comments represent Philo's attempt to discern the "literal" meaning of the story prior to the more important "allegorical" meaning, which was his favored purview. As such, these comments, while not complimentary, certainly do not represent a comprehensive summary of Philo's view of Eve.[11]

At the end of the fourth century, and possibly at the beginning of the fifth, a collection of rabbinic comments on Genesis was compiled and came to be known as *Genesis Rabbah*.[12] In this compilation, which represents one of the best examples we have of rabbinic interpretation, the issue of Eve's creation is addressed twice, and in both cases the rabbis take a dim view of the first woman.

First, in *parashah* 17, Gen. 2.21 is commented upon, and one of the preserved sayings notices an important grammatical point. In 17.6.2, Rabbi Hinena notes that up until Gen. 2.21 the letter *samech* has not been used. Since *samech* is also the first letter in the word for Satan, Hinena concludes, "When woman was created, Satan was created with her."[13] There is no elaboration on this point, though, and as such we do not necessarily need to view this as a degrading statement about the woman. That is, we can view this statement as a comment on the coterminous creation of Satan and

---

11. For a fuller survey of Philo on Eve, see Dorothy Sly, *Philo's Perception of Women* (BJS 209; Atlanta: Scholars Press, 1990), 91–110.

12. For a general introduction to this text, see Jacob Neusner, "*Genesis Rabbah*," in *Introduction to Rabbinic Literature* (ABRL; New York: Doubleday, 1994), 355–81. For an examination of the interpretation of Genesis in this text, see Neusner, "Genesis in *Genesis Rabbah*: Recasting the Patriarchs into the Models for Israelite Conduct," in *Judaism and the Interpretation of Scripture: Introduction to the Rabbinic Midrash* (Peabody, Mass.: Hendrickson, 2004), 30–45.

13. Jacob Neusner, *Genesis Rabbah: The Judaic Commentary to the Book of Genesis; A New American Translation*, vol. I, *Parashiyyot One through Thirty-three on Genesis 1:1 to 8:14* (BJS 104; Atlanta: Scholars Press, 1985), 185. See A. Lerner's comments on this text in her *Eternally Eve*, 44–47.

the woman without imputing any sort of pernicious connections between the two.

However, the next *parashah* addresses the same question the *Bavli* does, namely, what is meant by the phrase "God built the rib"? In the *Bavli*, as we saw, the question is used as an opportunity to discuss marriage, but here in *Genesis Rabbah*, the question is used to speculate on why God chose that specific place on the man from which to begin building woman. As R. Joshua said in the name of R. Levi, God

> thought to himself, "We should not create her beginning with the head, so that she not be frivolous, nor from the eye, that she not be a starer [looking at men], nor from the ear, that she may not be an eavesdropper, nor from the mouth, that she not talk too much [gossip], nor from the heart, that she not be jealous, nor from the hand, that she not be light-fingered, nor from the foot, that she not be a gadabout, but from a covered up place on man. For even when a man is standing naked, that spot is covered up." (*Parashah* 18.2.1)[14]

Unfortunately, the plan does not work and R. Joshua goes on to delineate how women still embody all of the above negative attributes by appealing to select examples of biblical females. In *Genesis Rabbah*, then, we see the adoption of a view of Eve as the ancestress of all women, and as such she must embody the distasteful traits the various rabbinic contributors find in women of their own time.

In sum, Jewish tradition is decidedly mixed on what Genesis 2 means when it says that Eve was created from Adam to be a fitting helper. As we have seen, some interpreters view the story as implying something important about God, or Adam, or even Eve, but the tradition is not in agreement that Eve should somehow be subordinate to Adam because of the mode of her creation.

The Serpent + the Woman – the Man?

Interpreters of Scripture have always pondered why the serpent approached the woman and not the man. As we shall see, in answering this question the tradition is as multivocal as it is regarding our above question. Some interpreters use this question to denigrate Eve and her sex, but others use it to make a comment on the serpent.

We will begin with Philo, who again has some interesting comments on this question. He responds specifically to our question by noting:

> Woman is more accustomed to be deceived than man. For his judgment, like his body, is masculine and is capable of dissolving or destroying the designs of deception; but the judgment of woman is more feminine, and because of softness she easily gives way and is taken in by plausible falsehoods which resemble the truth. (*QG* 1:33)

---

14. Neusner, *Genesis Rabbah*, 1:191.

Seeing this defect in woman, the serpent, who "adjusts himself to different times," approached her instead of the man. Again we see Philo's assumptions regarding the female sex, and that his interpretation is still at the "literal" level, and we see as such perhaps is not representative of his reading of Eve elsewhere.

The most complete interpretation we have in antiquity of Genesis 2–3 is a text creatively titled *The Life of Adam and Eve*. Probably composed between the first century B.C.E and the second century C.E., the story is preserved in two different versions: one in Greek (cited as *Apoc.*) and one in Latin (cited as *Vita*). In the Latin version, Satan explains to Adam why he hates him: when Adam was created, Michael brought him to all the angels and commanded them to worship him, but Satan refused along with all the angels in his charge, and thus they were expelled from the "presence of God and the fellowship of the angels" (13.2). Thus, Satan recounts, "With deceit I assailed your wife and made you to be expelled through her from the joys of your bliss, as I have been expelled from my glory" (16.3). There is also an implication that Eve is somewhat gullible in the Latin version because in chapters 9–11 Satan manages to deceive her a second time.

The rabbinic compendium of *Genesis Rabbah* also discusses this issue twice and comes to two very different conclusions. In *parashah* 18, R. Joshua b. Qorha comments on the description of the serpent as "subtle" (*'arum*) as follows: "It serves to let you know the sin that that wicked [creature] had got them to do. When he saw that they were having sexual relations, and he lusted after the woman [he tried to kill Adam by getting him to sin]" (18.6.2).[15] Thus, the serpent approaches Eve not because he senses in her some sort of defect, but rather because he lusts after her and desires to ruin Adam through her.[16]

Parashah 20, however, makes a more definitive, if grammatically based, connection between the woman and the serpent. In commenting on 3.20, the naming of Eve, the rabbis noticed that the same consonants in the name Eve can be used for the word *snake*. Thus, "R. Aha said, 'The snake was your snake, and you were the snake for man'" (20.11.2).[17] Thus, the snake in some way belonged to Eve, and so it would have naturally come to her with its question.

Somewhere between 400 and 600 C.E., a rabbinical commentary on the tractate *Pirke 'Avot* in the Mishnah—the third-century collection of oral commentary on legal matters—was compiled. In this commentary, called *The Fathers According to Rabbi Nathan*, R. Nathan focuses on God's command to the earthling in Gen. 2.16–17 and makes a simpleminded comment on the serpent's decision to approach Eve: "At that time the wicked serpent

---

15. Ibid., 196.
16. See also Wisdom of Solomon 2.24: "Through the devil's envy death entered the world."
17. Neusner, *Genesis Rabbah*, 1:226.

said to himself: 'As it is impossible for me to make Adam stumble [for he himself received the words from the Lord], I will make Eve stumble.'[18] The assumption is clear from our reading of Genesis earlier: since Eve had not been created when God told Adam not to eat from the tree, presumably Eve did not hear the command, and as such she would be the more vulnerable party.

What these interpretations tell us about Eve is that some interpreters do see in her some fault that was exploited by the serpent, but many others see the serpent's personal motivation as more determinative for his decision to approach her.

Where Was the Man?

As I noted earlier in our reading of the text, the Hebrew seems fairly clear: in 3.6 we are told, "She also gave some to her husband, with her, and he ate."[19] Because of the seeming clarity of the text, speculation was not as rampant on this issue as on others we have examined. Even so, the literal translation I provide here is not the only option when rendering the Hebrew in 3.6. Gary A. Anderson comments on this verse and notes the translational ambiguity:

> Our problem is one of translation. The original Hebrew could also be rendered, "she also gave some of the fruit to her husband and he ate along with her . . ." In this translation, the emphasis is on the fact that both ate, not on physical proximity at the time of eating. The text does not explicitly say that Adam was beside the tree as Eve consumed the fruit. Because of this ambiguity, a rather large stream of interpreters preferred to understand the transgression as a two-part process. First Eve ate while standing beside the tree, talking with the snake; then, at a later time in an undisclosed place, Eve fed the fruit to Adam.[20]

Given this ambiguity, the importance of this question is paramount in the discussion of who should bear the lion's share of blame for the disobedient act; that is, if Adam was "with her" while she was conversing with the serpent, then he could have said or done something to prevent her from eating, but he did not. As such, he could be implicated as well. As Anderson notes, though, the Hebrew is not clear how long he was "with her," or even when he was "with her," and many interpreters take this indeterminacy and use it to place Adam somewhere else while Eve is conversing with the serpent.

---

18. Quoted in Evans, *Paradise Lost and the Genesis Tradition*, 48.
19. There is some confusion over the correct translation of the Hebrew word *'immāh* here. The NRSV and NIV include the phrase "who was with her"; the KJV, NKJV, NASB, and ASV include "with her," but the RSV and JPS translations don't render the word *'immāh* in English.
20. Gary Anderson, "The Culpability of Eve: From Genesis to Timothy," in *From Prophecy to Testament: The Function of the Old Testament in the New* (ed. Craig A. Evans; Peabody, Mass.: Hendrickson, 2004), 242.

In his discussion of this issue, Philo finally reveals his larger, allegorical understanding of the garden story. Adam, Eve, and the serpent all represent larger traits of humanity: Adam represents mind, Eve sense-perception, and the serpent pleasure. As such, when it comes time to address the question of Adam's location, Philo relies on this interpretation: "In the allegorical sense . . . woman is a symbol of sense, and man, of mind. Now of necessity sense comes into contact with the sense-perceptible; and by the participation of sense, things pass into the mind; for sense is moved by objects, while the mind is moved by sense" (QG 1.37). Thus, where was Adam? He was right there with Eve when she beheld the fruit because "at the same time sense-perception is received from objects . . . the mind is impressed by sense-perception" (QG 1.38). However, now that Philo is exegeting the story allegorically, he offers no comment that we can construe as negative toward Eve. In fact, his reading here is remarkably free of such concerns.

In *The Life of Adam and Eve*, the Latin version answers this question in a straightforward manner. When Adam speaks to his sons about the garden, he tells them, "God gave a part of paradise to me and (a part) to your mother" (32.2). As such, the man and woman had their own allotments of land, so that Adam could have been in his section of the garden when the conversation took place.

Once again proving the saying that if you get two rabbis in a room you will have three opinions, *Genesis Rabbah* offers two distinct answers to the question of Adam's location:

B. Where was the man when this conversation was going on?

C. Abba Halpurn bar Qoriah said, "He had earlier had sexual relations, and now he was sleeping it off."

D. Rabbis say, "God had taken him and was showing him the whole world, saying to him, 'This is what an orchard looks like, this is an area suitable for sowing grain.' So it is written, 'Through a land that no man had passed through, and where Adam had not dwelt' (Jer. 2:6), that is, Adam had not lived there [but there were lands Adam had seen on his tour]."[21]

So either Adam was fast asleep in his newfound conjugal bliss, or else God was taking him on a tour of his new domain. Either way, Adam was not present for the conversation, but presumably he returned or woke up in time to eat of the fruit.

As I said earlier, the tradition is, by and large, unconcerned about Adam's location, in my opinion because the Hebrew seems clear that he was with Eve during the conversation. If this is correct, then it has certainly been underplayed in both ancient and modern readings of the story.

---

21. Neusner, *Genesis Rabbah*, 1:201.

Who's to Bless and Who's to Blame?

In any discussion of the character of Eve, the central issue is that of blame; that is, if Eve is to blame for the disobedient act in the garden, then the usual assumption is that somehow her actions reflect badly on other women.[22] This assumption has in fact been the operative premise behind many of the negative assumptions about women in later Jewish, Christian, and Islamic theology. However, as we shall see, the sources I have been discussing are far from unanimous on who exactly should be blamed for the act of disobedience. One thing that almost all the sources have in common is that they include the serpent in the figuring of blame. Because we are interested in the characters of Eve and Adam, though, we are going to focus on how texts imagine the blame with regard to the humans. For clarity's sake, I will divide them up into four main categories of blame: Eve and the serpent; Eve alone; Adam alone; and Adam and Eve. Within the sources that blame Adam alone, there are sources that simply mention the story in passing and others that analyze the story in more detail. We will obviously spend more time on the latter.

Eve and the Serpent

First, several exegetes allow for a complementary blaming of both Eve and the serpent, with no culpability assigned to Adam. We will begin with the first-century retelling of the creation by Flavius Josephus, who wrote his works under the auspices of the courts of Titus and Vespasian following the first Jewish revolt against Rome (66–70 C.E.). Josephus writes in the first book of his *Antiquities*:

> The serpent, living in the company of Adam and his wife, grew jealous of the blessings which he supposed were destined for them if they obeyed God's behests, and, believing that disobedience would bring trouble upon them, he maliciously persuaded the woman to taste of the tree of wisdom, telling her that in it resided the power of distinguishing good and evil, possessing which they would lead a blissful existence no whit behind that of a god. By these means he misled the woman to scorn the commandment of God: she tasted of the tree, was pleased with the food, and persuaded Adam also to partake of it. (1.41–43)

Here we see Josephus picking up on the theme of the serpent's envy to supply him with the motivation to approach Eve, who in turn persuades Adam to eat of the tree. Once God finds out what has happened, though, Adam does not come off too well:

> Adam then began to make excuse for his sin and besought God not to be wroth with him, laying the blame for the deed upon the woman and saying that it was

---

22. See Anderson, "Culpability of Eve," 245: "In order to assess blame for the fall, one must determine exegetically the level of culpability for the transgression. According to Jewish legal tradition, one could sin either with full cognizance of the misdeed or inadvertently. To sin knowingly was, of course, the more serious breach of responsibility."

her deception that caused him to sin. . . . Thereupon God imposed punishment
on Adam for yielding to a woman's counsel. (1.48–49)

Josephus's emphasis on Adam's weakness in listening to his wife does not
obscure the fact that it was Eve who persuaded him to eat the fruit.

In *The Life of Adam and Eve*, the author lays the blame for the disobedient act in the garden on both the serpent, here imagined as the vessel for
Satan's revenge, and Eve. This narrative seems quite specific as to who
should be blamed for the disobedient act: in the Latin recension alone, Eve
is blamed nine times either by the narrator or by her own admission. In
fact, in her second speech, Eve says to Adam, "My lord, would you kill me?
O that I would die! Then perhaps the Lord God will bring you again into
Paradise, for it is because of me that the Lord God is angry with you. . . . I
have brought toil and tribulation upon you" (*Vita* 3.1 and 5.2). At the
same time, the narrative implicates Satan. In *Vita* 12–16, Satan tells Adam
that he is responsible for their expulsion from Eden. When God created
Adam, the angel Michael brought him before the angels and told them all
to worship this new image of God. Satan refused and was thus expelled
from the "presence of God and the fellowship of the angels" (13.2). Thus,
Satan recounts, "With deceit I assailed your wife and made you to be
expelled through her from the joys of your bliss, as I have been expelled
from my glory" (16.3). This motivation is highlighted by the inclusion of a
peculiar request on the part of the serpent in the Greek version: he tells Eve,
"Swear to me that you are giving (it) also to your husband" (*Apoc.* 19.1).
Later in the Greek version, Eve comments to her children that after she ate
of the fruit, she sought out their father, saying, "I spoke to him unlawful
words of transgression such as brought us down from great glory. For
when he came, I opened my mouth and the devil was speaking" (*Apoc.*
21.2–3). Since this version of the story is included in the earlier Greek version, but not in the later Latin version, we may assume that it possibly
reflects a view of the story in which blame is shared between the
serpent/devil and Eve. Over time, though, it is Eve who begins to bear the
brunt of the blame, as evinced by the Latin version.

We find a later instance of this trend in the York Cowper's Mystery
Play. In the fifteenth century there began in England a tradition of public
performance of religious, specifically biblical dramas in the "vulgar" tongue.
One of the only complete cycles still in existence stems from the town of
York, and it treats forty-eight specific scenes from the creation of the world
to the Last Judgment. In the extant section dealing with the fall of man, the
medieval poet tells his audience that Satan, still bitter over being cast out of
heaven, decides to take the likeness of a "worm" to deceive Eve: "In a
worm's likeness will I wend, / And try to feign a likely lie."[23] Here, as in the
biblical text, Satan/the worm tries to convince Eve of the knowledge she

---

23. All quotations are from E. Martin Browne, ed., "The Fall of Man, from the York Cowper's Play," in *Religious Drama 2: Mystery and Morality Plays* (Cleveland: Meridian Books,
1958), 37–44.

would gain from eating of the tree: "For wilt thou see? / Who eats the fruit of good and ill / Shall have knowing as well as he [God]." However, in the Mystery Play, Satan presents another motive for Eve to eat the fruit. When she asks why the worm is telling her all of this, he replies, "That ye may worshipped be. . . . To greater state ye may be brought, / If ye will do as I shall say." Thus, the worm makes Eve believe that she and Adam will not only be as knowledgeable as God, but will be worshipped as gods as well: "For right as God shall ye be wise, / And peers to him in everything. / Ay, great gods shall ye be, / Of ill and good to have knowing, / For to be all as wise as he." In fact, after Eve eats the fruit, she repeats the worm's promises to Adam twice. After hearing her words, Adam says, "To win that name / I shall taste it at thy teaching. / Alas! What have I done? For shame! / Ill counsel! Woe worth thee! / Ah Eve, thou art to blame; / To this thou enticed me." Even though Adam expressly blames Eve, the dramatist lays a heavy burden on the worm as well, all the while excusing Adam's role in the act entirely.

In the artistic tradition, Eve is usually assigned the guilt, but this complementary blaming of the serpent and Eve is found in the Western artistic tradition as well. A good example is Raphael's fresco of 1517 entitled *Original Sin*. In this piece, the scene is the garden and the focus is on the tree. Eve is standing, handing an apple to a seated and reclining Adam, while the serpent—complete with a female's head—is wrapped around the tree gazing at Adam as he takes the fruit. The serpent assumes a more prominent role in this work and even seems to be watching over Eve to ensure she carries out her role. There are also similarities between Eve's face and that of the serpent's; this is a common way of representing the serpent in the artistic tradition, and it serves to link the serpent and Eve, both representationally and symbolically. That is, by rendering the serpent's head as a female's, and by making it look like Eve, Raphael is connecting the two characters in appearance and purpose. In contrast to Eve, Adam's posture is passive, as if he is performing no overt action to receive the fruit. He is merely reclining, and Eve is giving him the fruit. All of these characteristics point to a reading of this work in which the serpent and Eve are to blame, while Adam is merely a passive bystander.

Eve Alone

There are obviously numerous sources that lay the blame squarely on the shoulders of Eve. *The Life of Adam and Eve* is quite specific in its story as to who should be blamed for the disobedient act. As I discussed above, in the Latin recension it is clear that Eve is to blame. In the Greek version of *The Life of Adam and Eve*, though, this guilt is tempered somewhat by the inclusion of the serpent's request that Eve swears she will give some of the fruit to Adam (*Apoc.* 19.1). Also in the earlier Greek version, Eve notes that the devil spoke "unlawful words of transgression" through her (*Apoc.* 21.2–3). In the later Latin version of *The Life of Adam and Eve*, this edition of the story is omitted as a reflection of a more general trend of interpretations that lay all the blame for the disobedient act on Eve.

In contrast to this line of argument, some sources are very straightforward in their assignment of blame. In the *Sibylline Oracles*, the Sibyl tells us that

> a very horrible / snake craftily deceived them not to go to the fate / of death and receive knowledge of good and evil. / But the woman first became a betrayer to him. / She gave, and persuaded him to sin in his ignorance. / He was persuaded by the woman's words, forgot / about his immortal creator, and neglected clear commands. (Book 1, lines 42–45)

Here there is no doubt that Eve both betrayed and persuaded Adam to eat the fruit.

A text from the second century B.C.E., *Jubilees*, retells the story of Genesis 2–3, highlighting Eve's guilt in a subtle fashion. In 3.20–22, the text tells us:

> And the woman saw the tree that it was pleasant and it was pleasing to the eye and its fruit was good to eat and she took some of it and she ate. And she first covered her shame with a fig leaf, and then she gave it to Adam and he ate and his eyes were opened and he saw that he was naked. And he took a fig leaf and sewed it and made an apron for himself. And he covered his shame.[24]

Because Eve took the time to cover herself prior to giving Adam the fruit, we can assume that she would have had the requisite time to apprehend her change of status, and as such would have given the fruit to Adam fully aware of the consequences of her actions. Conversely, though, if Adam were indeed "with her," as we see in Genesis, then he too would have been able to detect some sort of difference in Eve's choice to cover herself.[25]

An example from the New Testament in which blame is laid on Eve is 1 Timothy. Most scholars think that even though this letter is ascribed to Paul, it is pseudonymous; that is, it was written in Paul's name by someone else, probably early in the second century. In this text, women figure prominently. More specifically, the author is concerned to regulate women and their sexuality in order to make the fledgling Christian movement appear more in line with Roman views on women and society. Thus, in 2.9–15, the

---

24. O. S. Wintermute, "Jubilees: A New Translation and Introduction," in *The Old Testament Pseudepigrapha*, volume 2 (ed. James L. Charlesworth; New York: Doubleday, 1985), 60.

25. Another important text in this regard is the *Similitudes of Enoch*, which was probably composed early in the first century. In the context of listing the fallen angels after the delineation of the judgment in chapters 61–62, Enoch mentions an angel named Gadre'el in 69.6, "who showed all the blows of death to the sons of men, and he led Eve astray, and he showed the shield and the coat of mail and the sword for battle and all the implements of death to the sons of men" (George W. E. Nickelsburg and James C. VanderKam, trans., *1 Enoch: A New Translation* [Minneapolis: Fortress, 2004], 89).

author discusses the proper attire and attitude for women. In the midst of this discussion, the author lays out the basis for his dictum that women should have no authority over men. He writes, "For Adam was formed first, then Eve; and Adam was not deceived, but the woman was deceived and became a transgressor. Yet she will be saved through childbearing, provided they continue in faith and love and holiness, with modesty" (2.13–15). It seems obvious that this reading of Genesis 2–3 is designed to lend credence to the author's more practical concerns, but it is important to note that it lays *all* the blame on Eve and reserves no guilt for either the serpent or Adam.

For a curious intertextual reading of Eve's participation in the disobedient act, let us examine *Genesis Rabbah*. Here, the rabbis comment on Gen. 3.6 in the following manner:

A. "She took of its fruit and ate" (Gen. 3:6):

B. Said R. Aibu, "She squeezed some grapes and gave him the juice."

C. R. Simlai said, "She approached him fully prepared [with strong arguments], saying to him, 'What do you think? Is it that I am going to die, and that another woman will be created for you?' [That is not possible:] 'There is nothing new under the sun' (Qoh. 1:9).

D. "Or perhaps you think that I shall die and you will live all by yourself? 'He did not create the world as a waste, he formed it to be inhabited' (Is. 45:18)."

E. Rabbis say, "She began to moan and weep to him" (19.5.2).[26]

This interpretation is extremely interesting because it provides us with a fuller glimpse of the conversation between Adam and Eve. In "B" above, there is an allusion to Adam drinking wine that Eve provided for him, which certainly could have impaired his judgment. In "C" and "D" we see Eve coming to Adam with scripturally based arguments as to why he should eat of the fruit. Presumably she already has and is now arguing with him to convince him not only that he will not die if he eats, as God told him, but also that he has no choice but to do so. He will not be given another wife, nor will he be allowed to live alone, so he might as well eat. In the end, though, these arguments evidently are not persuasive, so she approaches him with what the rabbis feel is that most feminine of arguments: moaning and crying. Following this, he acquiesces and eats.[27]

In addition to other sources that rewrite Genesis 2–3 such as Josephus and *Jubilees*, we also must consider the two great Targums that represent Aramaic translations of the Hebrew text of Genesis, namely, *Targum Onkelos* and *Targum Pseudo-Jonathan*. The former was most

---

26. Neusner, *Genesis Rabbah*, 1:203–4. For a commentary on this text, see Gerald J. Blidstein, "Eve: The Fear and the Loneliness," in *In the Rabbis' Garden: Adam and Eve in the Midrash* (Northvale, N.J.: Jason Aronson, 1997), 43–51.

27. See A. Lerner's comments on this text in her *Eternally Eve*, 99–101.

likely completed by the third century C.E., and the latter was in existence prior to circa 600. *Targum Onkelos* represents a very literal translation of the Hebrew text, and the differences between the two are negligible. For example, in 3.6 the text reads, "And when the woman saw that the tree was good for eating, and that it was a cure for the eyes, and that the tree was desirable to become wise therewith, she took of its fruit and ate; and she gave also to her husband (who was) with her, and he ate."[28] However, *Targum Pseudo-Jonathan* is more expansionistic and adds several intriguing details to the story in Genesis. When the serpent confronts Eve in 3.5, he tells her that if they eat the fruit, they will be "like the great angels."[29] Following this, Eve saw "Sammael the angel of death and she was afraid. . . . And she took of its fruit and ate; and she also gave to her husband (who was) with her, and he ate." After they sew themselves girdles of figs, they attempt to hide from the Lord God. Here, though, God admonishes Adam prior to any conversation, both for thinking he could hide from him and for breaking the "commandments that [God] commanded you" (3.9). Also, Eve's response to God's query is expanded: "The serpent lured me with his cleverness and led me astray in his wickedness, and I ate" (3.13). In fact, in 3.23, God tells the angels:

> If he [Adam] had kept the commandments (which) I commanded him he would have lived and endured like the tree of life forever. But now, since he has not observed what I commanded him, let us decree against him, and let us banish him from the Garden of Eden, before he puts forth his hand and takes (also) from the tree of life.

In the textual sources from religious interpreters we have surveyed thus far, there seems to be little ambiguity as to the assignment of blame: Eve persuaded Adam to eat the fruit, and as such she is to blame.[30] This blame on Eve is also found in the modern era in the realm of popular culture. In 1892, Mark Twain wrote his "Extracts from Adam's Diary," in which he details Adam's internal feelings toward Eve and how he perceives

---

28. Moses Aberbach and Bernard Grossfeld, *Targum Onkelos to Genesis: A Critical Analysis Together with an English Translation of the Text* (Denver: KTAV Publishing and Center for Judaic Studies, University of Denver, 1982), 32.

29. Translation taken from Kristin E. Kvam, Linda S. Schearing, and Valarie H. Ziegler, eds., *Eve and Adam: Jewish, Christian, and Muslim Readings on Genesis and Gender* (Bloomington: Indiana University Press, 1999), 105–6.

30. There are obviously many more sources that discuss Eve's role in the disobedient act in the garden. One of the most famous is found in the wisdom text of Sirach from the second century B.C.E. In 25.24, Ben Sira notes, "From a woman sin had its beginning, and because of her we all die." The difficulty with associating the claim in this text with the story in Genesis 2–3 is noted admirably by John J. Collins in his "Before the Fall: The Earliest Interpretations of Adam and Eve," in *The Idea of Interpretation: Essays in Honor of James L. Kugel* (ed. Hindy Najman and Judith H. Newman; JSJSup 83; Leiden and Boston: Brill, 2004), 298: "It is possible that Ben Sira was laying the blame for sin and death on woman in general than on Eve in particular. . . . The statement in Sir 25:24 seems to arise from his distrust of women than from his exegesis of Genesis."

the disobedient act in the garden. Twain's Adam seems annoyed by Eve and bitter over losing his solitude. He reports:

> She says the snake advises her to try the fruit of that tree, and says the result will be a great and fine and noble education. I told her there would be another result, too—it would introduce death into the world. . . . I advised her to keep away from the tree. She said she wouldn't. I foresee trouble.[31]

The next day, Adam reports that in order to avoid the coming disaster, he rode away as far as he could. He wound up in a luscious field with all sorts of frolicking animals, when

> all of a sudden they broke into a tempest of frightful noises, and in one moment the plain was in a frantic commotion and every beast was destroying its neighbor. I knew what it meant—Eve had eaten that fruit. And death was come into the world. . . . The tigers ate my horse, paying no attention when I ordered them to desist, and they would have even eaten me if I had stayed—which I didn't.

Eve then joins Adam outside the garden, and Adam is finally happy to see her because "there are but meagre pickings here, and she brought some of those apples. I was obliged to eat them, I was so hungry. It was against my principles, but I find that principles have no real force except when one is well fed." Thus, even though Adam consciously eats the fruit out of hunger, the narrative asserts that Eve is responsible for the disobedient act, especially since Adam was far away when the event occurred! However, as I mentioned earlier, there are also sources that point the finger at Adam.

Adam Alone

To begin, I will examine some sources that blame Adam in passing, without analyzing the story in any detail. From the late first century C.E. we have a text titled *4 Ezra*. At one point, this work is interested in claiming that the inhabitants of Babylon are burdened with an evil heart. To do so, the author makes the following claim: "For the first Adam, burdened with an evil heart, transgressed and was overcome, as were all who descended from him" (3.20). The author of *4 Ezra* seems concerned with God's perceived injustice toward Israel, and through Ezra, here an apocalyptic seer, relates time and time again that it is through Adam that sin became a human trait and that people began to die.[32]

---

31. All quotations are taken from Howard G. Baetzhold and Joseph B. McCullough, eds., *The Bible According to Mark Twain* (New York: Simon & Schuster, 1996), 8–16.
32. In addition to 3.20, see also 3.7 ("And you laid upon him [Adam] one commandment of yours; but he transgressed it, and immediately you appointed death for him and his descendants"); 4.30 ("For a grain of evil seed was sown in Adam's heart from the beginning, and how much ungodliness it has produced until now—and will produce until the time of threshing comes!"); 7.11 ("For I made the world for their [Israel's] sake, and when Adam transgressed my statutes, what had been made was judged"); and 7.48/118 ("O Adam, what have you done? For though it was you who sinned, the fall was not yours alone, but ours who are your descendants").

The apocalyptic text *2 Baruch* of the early second century mentions the story five times in its eighty-seven chapters, and each time the blame is laid squarely on Adam. For example, "For what did it profit Adam that he lived 930 years and transgressed that which he was commanded?" (17.2; cf. 48.42–43); "For when Adam sinned and death was decreed against those who were to be born, the multitude of those who would be born was numbered" (23.4); "For, although Adam sinned first and has brought death upon all who were not in his own time, yet each of them who has been born from him has prepared for himself the coming torment" (54.15; cf. 56.5–6).[33] Additionally, *3 Baruch*, a work that most likely was written in the first two centuries of the Common Era, mentions a tree planted by an angel named Satanael that deceives Adam (4.6), and later it mentions that after Adam sinned, he used the serpent as a garment (9.7), presumably one that would be replaced by the garments made by God (Gen. 3.21).

The *Testament of Adam* of the third century C.E. contains an extended speech by Adam to his son Seth. Even though many Christian interpolations have been made to the text, it seems clear that this work, too, blames Adam for the disobedient act in the garden. Adam tells Seth that God spoke to him in the garden "after [he] picked some of the fruit in which death was hiding," and told him that he was going to die. Adam asks why, and God tells him, "Because you listened to the words of the serpent, you and your posterity will be food for the serpent" (3.2–3).[34] Not only does Adam take responsibility for the act of disobedience, but Eve is not even mentioned here.

There are also sources that interpret the story with more detail. For example, in Rom. 5.12–21, Paul argues that since sin and death were introduced through one man, that is, Adam, "justification and life for all" will come through one man as well, that is, Jesus. In Gal. 3, Paul takes pains to establish that Jesus is the "seed" (sing.) of Abraham and thus gentiles can be incorporated into the family of God via baptism into Christ. However, in Romans 5, Paul switches the analogy to include a comparison with Adam, "who is a type of the one who was to come" (5.14). As such, Paul holds here that Adam is responsible for the introduction of sin into the world, not Eve.

The other main source that blames Adam for the disobedient act is an apocalyptic text titled *Apocalypse of Sedrach*, in which the title character wishes to debate God face-to-face regarding the punishment humanity must endure because of the disobedient act.[35] God says to Sedrach that he created

---

33. A. F. J. Klijn, "2 (Syriac Apocalypse of) Baruch: A New Translation and Introduction," in *The Old Testament Pseudepigrapha, volume 1*, 627, 629, 640.

34. S. E. Robinson, "Testament of Adam: A New Translation and Introduction," in *The Old Testament Pseudepigrapha, volume 1*, 994.

35. This text is reminiscent of *4 Ezra* in tone, especially *4 Ezra* 3.28–4.3. The date of *Apocalypse of Sedrach* is disputed, but S. Agourides claims that "it appears that the Apocalypse was originally composed between A.D. 150 and 500, and that it was joined together with the sermon on love [chap. 1] and received its final form shortly after A.D. 1000" ("Apocalypse of Sedrach: A New Translation and Introduction," in *The Old Testament Pseudepigrapha, vol. 1*, 606). All quotes from Apocalypse of Sedrach are taken from Agourides' work.

Adam and placed him in the garden with only one requirement: not to eat of the tree of life. But, says God, "He disobeyed my commandment and having been deceived by the devil he ate from the tree" (4.5). Sedrach is not to be placated, though. He tells God:

> It was by your will that Adam was deceived, my Master. You commanded your angels to worship Adam, but he who was first among the angels disobeyed your order and did not worship him; and so you banished him, because he transgressed your commandment and did not come forth (to worship) the creation of your hands. If you loved man, why did you not kill the devil? (5.1–2)

God replies that everything he required of Adam was within his reach, but claims, "Having received my gifts . . . he became an alien, an adulterer and sinner" (6.3). Sedrach tells him, "You, Master, created man; you know the low state of his will and his knowledge and you send man into punishment on a false pretext; so remove him" (7.1). Eventually, Sedrach is moved into paradise to be with the saints, but his Joban arguments with God presume that Adam is the one who committed the disobedient act, even if there is some question as to what we might call "diminished capacity."

Both Paul and *Apocalypse of Sedrach* assume, then, that not only is Adam to blame for the act in the garden, but he is also to blame for the resultant condition of humanity, which is less than desirable. As we have seen, the sources that blame Adam tend either to downplay or to ignore the character of Eve altogether and focus on the behavior of Adam as the moving force behind the disobedient act.

One very important text to mention in any discussion of the history of interpretation of Adam's role in Genesis 2–3 is *The Fathers According to Rabbi Nathan*. In chapter 1, the author comments on the admonition to "make a fence around the Law" (1:1) and mentions Adam as an example of someone who carried out this exhortation.[36] The proof of this claim is Eve's quotation of Adam in Gen. 3.3, and the author tells us, "Adam, however, did not wish to speak to Eve the way the Holy One, blessed be He, had spoken to him."[37] According to the author, this amplification of God's command to Adam in Gen. 2.16–17 gives the serpent the opening he desires in order to convince Eve:

> At that time the wicked serpent thought in his heart as follows: Since I cannot trip up Adam, I shall go and trip up Eve. So he went and sat down beside her, and entered into a long conversation with her. He said to her, 'If it is against touching the tree thou sayest the Holy One, blessed be He, commanded us—

---

36. See Herbert Danby, trans., *The Mishnah* (Oxford: Oxford University Press, 1933), 446; R. Travers Herford, trans., *Pirkē Aboth: The Tractate "Fathers," from the Mishnah, Commonly Called "Saying of the Fathers"* (New York: Jewish Institute of Religion, 1945), 19; and Leonard Kravitz and Kerry M. Olitzky, *Pirke Avot: A Modern Commentary on Jewish Ethics* (New York: UAHC Press, 1993), 1.

37. Judah Goldin, trans., *The Fathers According to Rabbi Nathan* (New York: Schocken Books, 1955), 8.

behold, I shall touch it and not die. Thou, too, if thou touch it, shalt not die!' What did the wicked serpent do? He then arose and touched the tree with his hands and feet, and shook it until its fruits fell to the ground."[38]

Following this, Eve took the fruit, ate, and gave it to Adam. Commenting on this interpretation, Anderson notes that

> Adam, [the rabbis] surmised, was suspicious of Eve's moral scruples. In order to protect her from any inkling of temptation, he decided "to hedge in" the original command with a protective fence. . . . Eve's sin was the result of Adam's *condescending attitude* toward her. . . . Had Adam not patronized Eve with his beefed-up version of the command, history might have taken a different course. Surprisingly, Eve is not the one to blame. Adam is.[39]

As with sources that blame Eve, we also have evidence that this interpretive trend of blaming Adam has survived into the modern period as well. One of the most well-known examples of this trend is found in the animated television series *The Simpsons*. In the tenth season, an episode entitled "Simpsons Bible Stories" aired around Easter 1999. In the first segment of the show, the garden is portrayed, with Homer as Adam and Marge as Eve. Knowing what we know of Homer and his appetites, it makes sense that when the snake (voiced by Snake) tries to get the couple to eat some of "God's private stash," Homer/Adam would succumb first, despite Marge's/Eve's protestations. In fact, here it is Homer/Adam who entices Marge/Eve to eat the apple in a wonderfully inventive exchange in which Marge/Eve tries to get Homer/Adam to stop eating all the fruit. He, in response, criticizes her for being so uptight in spite of the fact that she is naked. After convincing her to eat the fruit because it is something they can do together as a couple, Marge/Eve takes a bite. She initially responds positively, noting that the fruit will surely add some spice to her pies, but her excitement is short-lived, as God's divine hand (which looks and sounds suspiciously like Ned Flanders) reaches from the sky to accuse her of eating the forbidden fruit. As Homer/Adam hides all his eaten apple cores, Ned/God banishes Marge/Eve from the garden. All Homer/Adam can say in the way of a response is that they both should see other people.

Even though it is Homer/Adam who eats the fruit first and who blatantly tempts Marge/Eve to eat the fruit, it is Marge/Eve who is punished by Ned/God and expelled, leaving Homer/Adam alone in the garden. Thus, the story places the blame primarily on Homer/Adam, which makes sense given the story-world of the show.[40]

---

38. Ibid., 8–9.

39. Gary A. Anderson, *The Genesis of Perfection: Adam and Eve in Jewish and Christian Imagination* (Louisville, Ky.: Westminster John Knox Press, 2001), 77–78.

40. For more information on this episode, see the entry in The Simpsons Archive, online at *http://www.snpp.com/episodes/AABF14*, as well as Dan W. Clanton Jr. and Mark Roncace, "Animated Television," in *Teaching the Bible through Popular Culture and the Arts* (ed. Mark Roncace and Patrick Gray; SBLRBS 53; Atlanta: Society of Biblical Literature, 2007), 345–46.

Adam and Eve

Finally, there are some readers of the story who implicate both Adam and Eve for their dual role in the disobedient act. In his insightful work on Adam and Eve, Gary Anderson discusses the interpretation of Augustine.[41] Unlike some modern readers—who do not find coherence in biblical writings and who therefore are comfortable in treating disparate texts separately— Augustine viewed the Bible as being divinely revealed in its totality. Therefore, everything must cohere, and he must find a way to hold both the blaming of Adam in Romans and the blaming of Eve in 1 Timothy in check. He writes, "Eve accepted the serpent's statement as the truth, while Adam refused to be separated from his only companion, even if it involved sharing her sin" (City of God 14.11).[42] As such, his solution is to assert that both Adam and Eve sinned by consuming the fruit, but Eve's sin is tied to her deception by the serpent, whereas Adam sinned by his own free will. Thus, Adam shares the guilt for the disobedient act, but he does so out of love for Eve.

Anderson also addresses Michelangelo's The Fall of 1509–10.[43] In this piece, we see almost a mirror image of the Raphael fresco I mentioned above. The scene is again the garden, and specifically the tree. Instead of Eve standing, though, Adam is erect with an outstretched arm reaching for the fruit. Eve is seated and reclining, but she too is reaching for the fruit, which the serpent is offering her. Anderson notes that here we see Adam taking, even seizing, the fruit independently of Eve, whose body posture suggests passivity. Furthermore, as I note above, the serpent is often linked to Eve, but here the serpent resembles Adam more than Eve. As such, unlike in the painting by Raphael, here the serpent and Adam are linked together. Thus, Michelangelo portrays Adam's initiative and guilt as compared to Eve's passivity in what appears to be an indictment of his role in the disobedient act.

Finally, the seventeenth-century epic poem Paradise Lost by John Milton blames both Adam and Eve. The transgression in the garden is narrated in book 9, and as in the fathers according to Rabbi Natham, the serpent persuades Eve that the fruit is both safe and beneficial by touching and tasting it, thereby gaining both speech and reason (9.684–90). Through this reason, the serpent convinces Eve that "God cannot therefore hurt ye and be just" (9.700).[44] Milton then provides a long musing by Eve in which she thinks God's "forbidding / commends thee more while it infers the good / By thee communicated and our want" (9.753–55). Finally, assuring herself of the benefits of eating, "Her rash hand in evil hour / Forth reaching to the fruit, she plucked, she eat: / Earth felt the wound and Nature

---

41. See Anderson, Genesis of Perfection, 105–7. Some Jewish writings, too, embrace the idea of a complementary blaming of Adam and Eve. See the Apocalypse of Abraham, 23.

42. Quoted in Anderson, Genesis of Perfection, 106.

43. See ibid., 111–16 and passim.

44. All quotes from Milton are taken from Paradise Lost (Norton Critical Edition; ed. Gordon Teskey; New York and London: W. W. Norton, 2005).

from her seat / Sighing through all her works gave signs of woe / That all was lost" (9.780–84). Following this, Eve is conflicted about whether she should keep this new knowledge to herself (9.819–25), but she decides that she cannot bear to be without Adam:

> What if God have seen / And death ensure? Then I shall be no more / And Adam wedded to another Eve / Shall live with her enjoying, I extinct: / A death to think! Confirmed then I resolve / Adam shall share with me in bliss or woe. / So dear I love him that with him all deaths / I could endure, without him live no life. (9.826–33)

As such, she sets out to find Adam.

Adam is nowhere near Eve while she is conversing with the serpent or eating the fruit. He is actually weaving a garland of flowers for her when he sees her coming toward him. When they meet, she explains what she has done as well as her reasons for doing so (9.863–78). Her words beseech him: "Therefore also taste that equal lot / May join us, equal joy as equal love, / Lest thou not tasting, different degree / Disjoin us and I then too late renounce / Deity for thee when fate will not permit" (9.881–85). Adam makes the error of thinking that because of Eve's act he already shares her state; that is, he feels that he is already in what Milton would call a fallen state because of his relationship with Eve. This interior monologue is followed by a speech to Eve in which Adam speculates on their new knowledge; if the serpent gained the reason of humans by eating, then perhaps they can become as "gods or angels, demigods" (9.937). Finally, Adam says:

> I with thee have fixed my lot / Certain to undergo like doom. If death / Consort with thee death is to me as life, / So forcible within my heart I feel / The bond of nature draw me to my own, / My own in thee, for what thou art is mine. / Our state cannot be severed. We are one, / One flesh: to lose thee were to lose myself." (9.952–59)

Adam, "not deceived / But fondly overcome with female charm" (9.998–99), then eats the fruit, and, as when Eve ate, there are similar signs that the natural order has been disrupted. Immediately following his eating, they both feel an immense sense of lust, and they have sex. However, this lust, this carnal desire, soon gives way to a loss of innocence. Adam blames Eve because she listened to "that false worm" (9.1068), and he notes that "our eyes / Opened we find indeed and find we know / Both good and evil: good lost, and evil got!" (9.1070–72). In turn, Eve blames Adam for not being with her to prevent her from listening to the serpent and eating the fruit: "Being as I am, why didst not thou, the head, / Command me absolutely not to go" (9.1155–56). Adam retorts that he did everything he could short of force, and book 9 ends with Adam ruminating openly: "Thus it shall befall / Him who to worth in women overtrusting / Lets her will rule! Restraint she will not brook / And left t' herself if evil thence ensue / She first his weak indulgence will accuse" (9.1182–86).

In sum, Milton renders both Adam and Eve culpable for the disobedient act in the garden. Eve is obviously responsible because she listens to the serpent, eats the fruit, and then seeks out Adam to invite him to share the fruit out of concern for her own loneliness. That is, she cannot bear the thought of losing Adam, so she must make him eat the fruit. Adam is guilty as well, though, because he ignores his reason and listens to Eve, eating the fruit because of her persuasive words and charm. Eve even blames Adam because she, as a female who evidently does not possess enough reason and self-control, should have been looked after better. Adam should not have let her near the tree because he should have known she did not have the restraint and logic needed to withstand the entreaties of the serpent. Both are culpable, and as such, both suffer.

This abbreviated survey of exegetical readings should reinforce one clear fact: the responsibility for the disobedient act in the garden is both contested and ambiguous. Not all sources agree on who is to blame for what happens in the garden, and some of them posit very different reasons for what does happen.

CONCLUSIONS

There is no question that the story of the garden, and Eve's role in it, has been used throughout history to prescribe or mandate certain attitudes toward and thoughts about women. This story, perhaps more than any other, has served for many interpreters as proof that women are devious, scheming things, and as such deserve the presumed second-place role in society that Gen. 3.16 seems to mandate. However, as we have seen and as many feminist critics have shown, the biblical text itself does not seem to support these assumptions. So where do they come from? Many of them stem from the interpretive tradition I survey above. It may seem that many of these texts have some sort of special grudge against Eve, or that many of these men simply did not like women all that much. However, as James Kugel reminds us, even if it seems that a particular ideology, say, that women are "softer" than men, shows up in an interpretation, that does not mean that all of these interpretations are strictly ideological. He notes that interpretation in antiquity was concerned mainly with elucidating what the text says; but of course scriptural interpretation is much more important than that. Interpreting "ancient texts was a matter of more than merely antiquarian interest: the interpretation of Scripture could lend support for this or that political program or leader, and it determined as well the significance of divine law and its application to daily life."[45] As such, scriptural interpretation has a pragmatic goal: to illuminate the relevance of sacred texts for the modern practitioner. The reason, then, it is important to look at these interpretations is that they, along with the biblical text, form the building blocks of a tradition that serves to promulgate what I

---

45. James L. Kugel, *The Bible as It Was* (Cambridge, Mass., and London: Harvard University Press, 1999), 10–11.

consider to be a harmful image of woman, and not just any woman, but Eve.[46] In his work on Eve, John A. Phillips comments on her importance for Western culture:

> The story of Eve is, in a sense, at the heart of the concept of Woman in Western civilization. . . . [She is] Everywoman, the prototypical woman, all of her sex who are yet to come. And, as Everywoman, her actions in Genesis cause her to be regarded in Western religions as a special problem, requiring special measures for the working out of her salvation. Eve is thus a living part of the cultural and social histories of the people touched by her characterization in Genesis. Her story, along with other stories, other images, other ideas, shapes a Western ideology of women. Through the developing history of this theme, continually reworked and retold not only in theology but also in art, music, literature, law, and social custom, the nature and destiny of Woman in the Western world is disclosed. To follow the path of Eve is to discover much about the identity that has been imposed upon women in Western civilization. If one would understand Woman, one must come to terms with Eve.[47]

In essence, what I have been doing in this chapter is coming to terms with Eve in a specific textual repository in the hopes that by doing so I have shown that many of the assumptions and cultural givens with which Eve has been saddled simply are not found in the biblical text. Hopefully, this will allow us to reencounter Eve as she is presented in the narratives of Genesis: as the man's *'ezer kenegdo*, the one who serves to vanquish his loneliness, his sense of alienation. It is only with Eve that his destiny is enlarged and his future will be shared.

STUDY QUESTIONS

1. In this chapter I focus on the woman in the second recounting of creation in Genesis 1–3. However, there is also the story of creation in Gen. 1.1–2.4a, which can be viewed as either a separate literary account of creation or as a more general description that is given more specificity in 2.4b-3.24. If we assume that the former is true—as do many biblical scholars—then it appears we have two separate accounts of the creation of woman (1.27 and 2.21–24). Compare these accounts of the creation of woman: What are the differences? What conclusions can you draw based on the methods of creation as well as the language used to describe the relationship between the first two humans?[48]

---

46. Meyers comments on this harmful image of Eve in her *Discovering Eve*, 75–76.
47. John A. Phillips, *Eve: The History of an Idea* (San Francisco: Harper & Row, 1984), xiii.
48. For this question, readers can consult Rabbi Elyse Goldstein, "Male and Female Were They Created: Eve, Lilith, and the Snake," in *ReVisions: Seeing Torah through a Feminist Lens* (Toronto: Key Porter Books, 1998), 44–58; as well as Gerard P. Luttikhuizen, *The Creation of Man and Woman: Interpretations of the Biblical Narratives in Jewish and Christian Traditions* (Themes in Biblical Narrative 3; Leiden and Boston: Brill, 2000). My above question does not address the issue of the identity of the first human female, whom many Jewish interpreters name Lilith.

2. Obviously, Eve is an important figure for Jews and Christians, but she is important to Muslims as well. Compare and contrast the account in Genesis 2–3 with the versions of the events in the Qur'ān, especially 4.1; 7.11–25; and 20.115–28.[49] How does the Qur'ān imagine the scene in the garden? Is Eve blamed? Is the expulsion viewed negatively?[50] How does the version in the Qur'ān compare with Genesis 2–3 in terms of characterization, motivation, and action? Keep in mind that as we have seen in this chapter and will see in the next, sacred texts are always filtered through the practices, beliefs, and interpretations of the traditions that hold them to be sacred. As such, just as the Hebrew Bible and New Testament are interpreted by, in, and through communities of faith, so too is the Qur'ān interpreted through Muslim communities around the world.

3. After reading Genesis 2–3, watch the appropriate segment of John Huston's film *The Bible: In the Beginning* (1966). How does Huston retell/adapt this story from Genesis? What changes did he make? Is it significant that Huston himself voices the characters of both God and the serpent?[51] How is Eve rendered here? Is there a difference in the way(s) in which you understand the story when you read it, as opposed to when it is shown to you with sound and music?

4. Listen to the relevant portions of Joseph Haydn's oratorio of 1798, *The Creation (Die Schöpfung)*, Hob.XXI:2.[52] How does Haydn imagine the relationship between Adam and Eve? How does this differ from the narrative in Genesis 2–3? As you cogitate on Haydn's version of creation, think also about what music you hear when you read or think about these chapters in Genesis. What do you hear, if anything, and why?

5. While you are thinking of music, listen also to Gabriel Fauré's song-cycle *La Chanson d'Eve* (op. 95; 1907–10).[53] How is Eve presented in these pieces? Pay special attention to the first song, "Paradise." How does this image of Eve differ from the image in Genesis 2–3? Is it more positive? If so, why?

6. Eve has been extremely popular in the history of art. Using websites like the Web Gallery of Art (*http://www.wga.hu*) and Artcyclopedia (*http://www.artcyclopedia.com/*), find images that correspond to the

49. These and other readings from the Qur'ān on this issue are conveniently located in Kvam, Schearing, and Ziegler, *Eve and Adam*, 178–85.

50. For help with these issues, see Amina Wadud, "In the Beginning, Man and Woman Were Equal: Human Creation in the Qur'ān," in her *Qur'ān and Woman: Rereading the Sacred Text from a Woman's Perspective* (New York and Oxford: Oxford University Press, 1999), 15–28.

51. This question stems from Nicola Denzy and Patrick Gray, "The Bible in Film," in Roncace and Gray, *Teaching the Bible through Popular Culture and the Arts*, 97–98.

52. See Dan W. Clanton Jr. and Bryan Bibb, "Classical Music," in Roncace and Gray, *Teaching the Bible through Popular Culture and the Arts*, 56–57.

53. See ibid., 58–59.

categories of blame I examine above and try to determine why the artist(s) chose to render Eve in such a way. I suggest preparing a brief PowerPoint presentation with both the images and some general information about the images so that you can have easy access to them. After hunting and gathering, compare your images to the story in Genesis 2–3: What similarities or differences do you see? Do any of these images affect the way(s) you read Genesis? If so, why?

7. In Douglas Rushkoff's comic series *Testament*, events narrated in the Bible are juxtaposed with modern-day situations, allowing Rushkoff to draw parallels and analogies between paradigmatic events and modern realities.[54] In the second graphic novel collection, he deals with Genesis 2–3 and parallels it with the creation of AI (artificial intelligence) today.[55] How does Rushkoff imagine Genesis 2–3 in this story? He draws a distinction between creation from words and creation from nature, and he associates the female with the latter. Is this a distinction you see in Genesis? Do you find his modern parallel convincing? Are there other analogies you can draw between the events in Genesis 2–3 and contemporary realities?

---

54. See my "Cartoons and Comics," in Roncace and Gray, *Teaching the Bible through Popular Culture and the Arts*, 333–34.

55. Douglas Rushkoff, *Testament: West of Eden* (New York: DC Comics, 2007).

2

"Two Fires Burning"

SARAH AND HAGAR
AND THE HISTORY OF INTERPRETATION

IT IS DIFFICULT TO THINK of two more important women than Sarah and Hagar for the millions of Jews and Muslims in our world today.[1] In Judaism, Sarah is looked upon as perhaps *the* matriarch of the people. Of the *parashot* (the weekly divisions of Torah readings), there is only one named after a woman: *parashah* "Chayyei Sarah" (Gen. 23.1–25.18). In the Amidah, one of the main prayers recited on Shabbat, many Jewish congregations (especially Reform congregations) recite the words, "Praised be our God, the God of our fathers and our mothers: God of Abraham, God of Isaac, and God of Jacob; *God of Sarah*, God of Rebekah, God of Leah, and God of Rachel" (italics mine). In fact, Sarah is so important to Jewish identity that on 17 August 1938 the Nazi German government passed a law requiring that Jewish women add the middle name "Sarah" to their given names in all legal documents in order to better identify Jews. Similarly, Islam views Hagar as the mother of the progenitor of the Arab tribes, Ishmael. One of the most important rituals in Islamic praxis is the *hajj*, or the annual pilgrimage to Mecca. During this ritual, pilgrims walk back and forth between the Hills of Hagar, imitating her search for water to sustain her dying son, Ishmael, after they had been expelled from the family of Abraham (Gen. 21). The pilgrims are thus reenacting a mother's quest to find life for her son and as such are ritually seeking salvation in the steps of Hagar.

In recent years, more attention has been paid to the function(s) of these women in the monotheistic traditions originating in the Middle East,

---

1. In contrast, these two women play a smaller role in Christian thought and practice, the only textual reference in the New Testament being a mention in Paul's letter to the Galatians.

but many strange details and enticing questions remain.[2] In this chapter, I will examine the stories of Sarah and Hagar in the book of Genesis; identify some of these details and questions; and then examine how scholars—particularly Jewish readers—have addressed these issues and understood these central characters.[3] Unlike chapter 1, then, this chapter focuses more on how these stories in Genesis have been received in both academic and religious circles, as opposed to the arts and popular culture. This focus is intentional in that not only is this domain of interpretation essential for understanding the development of various views of Sarah and Hagar, but also there is a decided paucity of aesthetic renderings of these stories.[4]

SARAH AND HAGAR IN GENESIS 11–23

Sarai begins her textual existence in Gen. 11.29–30, embedded in a larger section delineating the genealogy from Shem down to Abram.[5] Based on this brief notice, we know several important facts about Sarai: she is married to Abram (and may be related to him); she is barren and has no children.[6] The fact that Sarai is barren is very important both to the development of her character and to the unfolding plot of Genesis. A woman unable to bear children would have been looked upon as virtually worthless within the economic structure of ancient Near Eastern society.

---

2. See, for example, Hibba Abugideiri, "Hagar: A Historical Model for 'Gender Jihad,'" and Amy-Jill Levine, "Settling at Beer-lahai-roi," both in *Daughters of Abraham: Feminist Thought in Judaism, Christianity, and Islam* (ed. Yvonne Yazbeck Haddad and John L. Esposito; Gainesville, Fla.: University Press of Florida, 2001), 81–107 and 12–34 respectively; and more recently Phyllis Trible and Letty M. Russell, eds., *Hagar, Sarah, and Their Children: Jewish, Christian, and Muslim Perspectives* (Louisville, Ky.: Westminster John Knox Press, 2006).

3. For a lucid and informative survey of the treatment of Hagar by Christian writers, see John L. Thompson, "Hagar: Abraham's Wife and Exile," in *Writing the Wrongs: Women of the Old Testament among Biblical Commentators from Philo through the Reformation* (Oxford and New York: Oxford University Press, 2001), 17–99. Thompson does mention some Jewish readings, but his overarching focus is on Christian interpreters.

4. Outside of a few novels (for example, Orson Scott Card's *Sarah* [Women of Genesis Series; New York: Forge Books, 2000]) and one film that deals only tangentially with our characters (namely, the 1994 made-for-TV movie *Abraham*), there are only scattered artistic images available to the historian of interpretation. Some work in this area has been done, though. See, for example, Zefira Gitay, "Hagar's Expulsion: A Tale Twice-Told in Genesis," in *Abraham and Family: New Insights into the Patriarchal Narratives* (ed. Hershel Shanks; Washington, D.C.: Biblical Archaeology Society, 2000), 73–91; and Phyllis Silverman Kramer, "The Dismissal of Hagar in Five Art Works of the Sixteenth and Seventeenth Centuries," in *Genesis: A Feminist Companion to the Bible* (ed. Athalya Brenner; Sheffield: Sheffield Academic Press, 1998), 195–217.

5. The names Sarai and Abram will be changed to the more familiar Sarah and Abraham in chapter 17.

6. I will discuss the issue of the biological relationship between Abram and Sarai below in the section titled "The Biological Relationship between Sarah and Abraham."

Almost all of the roles and functions of women during this time (somewhere in the early second millennium) revolved around bearing, raising, and socializing children. Because of the high infant mortality rate, women were expected to have a large number of children to ensure that at least some—hopefully male—children would survive. By revealing to us Sarai's barrenness at her textual introduction, the narrator is telling us that we can expect little in terms of this character's contribution to the family highlighted in this genealogy. We will see just how wrong this assumption will be.

Chapter 12 begins with the Lord telling Abram to go on a journey away from his father's house and everything he knows to "the land that [God] will show you" (12.1).[7] Thereafter, in 12.2, we encounter the first adumbration—vague though it is—of the covenant between the Lord and Abram. The Lord says, "I will make of you a great nation, and I will bless you, and make your name great, so that you will be a blessing." Implicit in these verses is the two-part promise of land and progeny. Obviously, Sarai's barrenness now becomes a troublesome issue, for how can the Lord make a great nation of Abram if his wife is barren?[8] Nevertheless, Abram takes Sarai with him as he sets forth to Canaan.

Beginning in 12.10, problems arise for Abram and his family. A famine occurs, and they are all forced to go down to Egypt to seek refuge.[9] Perhaps already concerned about living as an alien in Egypt, Abram delivers his first quoted speech in the narrative, an urgent plea to Sarai:[10]

---

7. All biblical quotes are taken from the NRSV.

8. Katheryn Pfisterer Darr notes, "Infertility jeopardizes the divine pledge at its most basic level because, without progeny, the land cannot be retained beyond a single lifetime. . . . Barren Sarai is the potential undoing of the promise, the obstacle to its fulfillment" ("More Than the Stars of the Heavens: Critical, Rabbinical, and Feminist Perspectives on Sarah," in *Far More Precious Than Jewels: Perspectives on Biblical Women* [Gender and the Biblical Tradition Series; Louisville, Ky.: Westminster John Knox Press, 1991], 94).

9. Many biblical interpreters have noted the foreshadowing in this chapter of later trips to Egypt, including the mention of plagues in 12.17. For example, it is already noted in the fourth- to fifth-century collection of rabbinic commentary on Genesis known as *Genesis Rabbah* (40.6.1). See Jacob Neusner, *Genesis Rabbah: The Judaic Commentary to the Book of Genesis; A New American Translation*, vol. 2, *Parashiyyot Thirty-four through Sixty-seven on Genesis 8:15 to 28:9* (BJS 105; Atlanta: Scholars Press, 1985), 83–85.

10. See Tammi J. Schneider, *Sarah: Mother of Nations* (New York and London: Continuum, 2004), 31–32. In 12.10–13.1 we have the first of three instances (see also chapters 20 and 26) in which a Hebrew tells a foreign king that his wife is his sister for various reasons. In his work, David L. Petersen analyzes the form, or genre, of these chapters as well as recurring and overlapping motifs found therein; see "A Thrice-Told Tale: Genre, Theme, and Motif," *Biblical Research* 18 (1973): 30–43. For an advanced analysis of these chapters using the theory of folklore, see Susan Niditch, "The Three Wife-Sister Tales of Genesis," in *A Prelude to Biblical Folklore: Underdogs and Tricksters* (Urbana: University of Illinois Press, 2000), 23–69. I will survey opinions about Abram's plan below in "Abram's Plan in Genesis 12."

I know well that you are a woman beautiful in appearance;[11] and when the Egyptians see you, they will say, "This is his wife"; then they will kill me, but they will let you live. Say you are my sister, so that it may go well with me because of you, and that my life may be spared on your account. (12.11–13)

There is no recorded response from Sarai in the narrative, but given their reception in Egypt in 12.14–16, Sarai must have acquiesced to Abram's plan. In fact, in 12.16, we are told that Pharaoh "dealt well with Abram," exactly as Abram hoped he would in 12.13. However, things go awry quickly for Abram in Egypt, as we hear that because of Sarai "the LORD afflicted Pharaoh and his house with great plagues" (12.17). Pharaoh then reproaches Abram, asking him why he told everyone that Sarai was his sister, which resulted in Pharaoh taking Sarai for his wife. With no reply from Abram, Pharaoh orders his men to expel Abram and Sarai, along with all their possessions.

This chapter contains a number of interesting ambiguities. First, at no point does Abram or Sarai ever tell any of the Egyptians that they are brother and sister. As such, Pharaoh's question in 12.19 seems odd. Second, in 12.19 Pharaoh claims that he took Sarai as his wife, but what exactly does this mean? Since the narrator provides no chronological indicators, we do not know how much time has passed, so we are unsure as to how long Sarai has been with Pharaoh. We are also unsure if we should take the text at face value, that is, that Pharaoh had sexual relations with Sarai.[12] We are sure, though, that when Abram leaves Egypt at the end of chapter 12, Sarai is with him even though we do not encounter her again until chapter 16.

---

11. The issue of Sarai's beauty has long fascinated readers. *Genesis Rabbah* contains an interesting comment (40.4.2) on Sarai's beauty. Evidently the reason Sarai's beauty is such an issue for Abram now that they are traveling to Egypt is that "now we are going to a place in which the people are ugly and swarthy" (Neusner, *Genesis Rabbah*, 2:81). As such, because of the horrid nature of the Egyptians' appearance, Sarai's beauty is likely to get the couple in trouble. According to a talmudic interpretation (*Bava Batra* 58a), Sarai was so beautiful that "in comparison with her, all other beauties were like apes compared with men. She even excelled Eve herself" (quoted in Darr, "More Than the Stars of the Heavens," 96; see also *Genesis Rabbah* 40.5.2 in Neusner, *Genesis Rabbah*, 2:82).

12. Jewish commentators worked hard to assure their readers that Sarai's chastity was intact after her sojourn in Egypt. For example, Rabbis Nosson Scherman and Meir Zlotowitz paraphrase Rashi in their commentary on 12.17: "God smote Pharaoh and his household with a debilitating skin disease that made cohabitation impossible, thus assuring that Sarai's chastity would be safeguarded" (*The Chumash* [Artscroll Series Brooklyn: Mesorah Publications, 2001], 58). Robert Alter (*Genesis: Translation and Commentary* [New York and London: W. W. Norton, 1996], 53) also mentions Rashi's suggestion. Similarly, *Genesis Rabbah* not only notes that the skin disease was specifically lupus (41.2.1; Neusner, *Genesis Rabbah*, 2:88–89), but also contains an amusing story of how Sarai's chastity was safeguarded. According to Rabbi Levi, an angel stood by Sarai all night and would whip Pharoah if he tried to come near Sarai. For this story, see Neusner, *Genesis Rabbah*, 2:89.

The issue of an heir for Abram as well as the matter of inheritance is addressed again in chapter 15. Therein, the Lord appears to Abram in a vision and promises him that his reward will be great. Despondent, Abram replies, "O Lord GOD, what will you give me, for I continue childless, and the heir of my house is Eliezer of Damascus [Abram's eldest servant]? . . . You have given me no offspring, and so a slave born in my house is to be my heir." The Lord then responds to Abram's plea by telling him not only that he shall have his own flesh-and-blood heir, but that his descendents will be as numerous as the stars in the heaven. Following this promise, the Lord makes a second covenant with Abram in 15.18 (compare with 12.1–9), in which again land and offspring are promised to Abram. In 16.1, the narrator immediately complicates this promise and moves the action along by stating, "Now Sarai, Abram's wife, bore him no children." Already the reader knows that Sarai is barren and thus has no children, but once again it seems as if her barrenness will interfere with the divine promises made to Abram. However, this time Sarai decides to take the initiative and try to solve the problem of finding an heir for Abram.

Also in 16.1, the narrator tells us that Sarai "had an Egyptian slave-girl whose name was Hagar." As with Sarai's introduction in 11.29–30, we can glean several important facts from this introductory information about Hagar. First, she is Egyptian. Her ethnicity is of prime importance, given the treatment of Egypt already in Genesis and how central Egypt will be in the future of Abram's descendents. Second, we are told that she is a *shifkhah*, which the NRSV translates as a "slave-girl." There is a significant debate over whether or not this is an adequate translation,[13] but for our purposes it suffices to note that this term and its narrative context imply that in some sense Hagar is in Sarai's power.[14]

This power over Hagar is illustrated in 16.2, when Sarai delivers her first speech in the narrative. She tells Abram, "You see that the LORD has prevented me from bearing children; go in to my slave-girl; it may be that I shall obtain children by her." Her near command to Abram may strike some modern readers as odd, but given the social realities of the time, her appeal is understandable. That is, as many interpreters note, this practice of using substitute wives in order to ensure the safe transmission of inheritance was

---

13. This issue will be explored below in the section titled "Who Is Hagar?"

14. John W. Waters, in "Who Was Hagar?" in *Stony the Road We Trod: African American Biblical Interpretation* (ed. Cain Hope Felder; Minneapolis: Fortress, 1991), 187–205, brings up the question of how wandering farmers like Abram and Sarai would have obtained a slave (if we presume that Hagar is in fact a slave in chapter 16) from Egypt, the most powerful country in this region. *Genesis Rabbah* (45.1.5) has an interesting explanation: "Said R. Simeon b. Yohai, 'Hagar was daughter of Pharaoh. When he saw the wonderful deeds that were done for Sarah when she was in his house, he took his daughter and gave her to Sarai, saying, "It is better that my daughter should be a servant girl in this household, rather than a matron in some other house"'" (Neusner, *Genesis Rabbah*, 2:146).

common in the ancient Near East.[15] It is especially important in the midst of this proposal for us to consider the social status of Hagar at this point in the narrative: she is a childless, unmarried, foreign female servant. As such, she would be considered to be at the bottom of the social scale of worth during this time period—especially being a foreigner in the context of Abram's household—except for the simple fact that she, unlike Sarai, is able to have children. Sarai even acknowledges this fact in 16.2 when she says that it is possible that she "shall obtain children by her."[16]

Sarai's plan is enacted very quickly in the narrative, as we read that "Abram listened to the voice of Sarai . . . [who] took Hagar the Egyptian, her slave-girl, and gave her to her husband Abram as a wife." Abram here shows no hesitation in his acceptance of Sarai's plan, but the narrator seems to indicate that the statuses of the women involved will be significant due to the repeated mention of Hagar's status as a foreign servant and Sarai's status as Abram's wife. It is also significant that Sarai gives Hagar to Abram as an *ishshah*, a wife, not a concubine.[17] This specific status of Hagar will be the root of the ensuing conflict between the two women.

---

15. See, for example, E. A. Speiser, *Genesis: A New Translation with Introduction and Commentary* (AB 1; Garden City, N.Y.: Doubleday, 1977), 119–21; Claus Westermann, *Genesis 12–36: A Commentary* (trans. John J. Scullion, S.J.; Minneapolis: Augsburg, 1985), 238–39; Nahum M. Sarna, *Genesis* (Jewish Publication Society Bible Commentary Series; Philadelphia: Jewish Publication Society, 1989), 119; and Naomi Steinberg, *Kinship and Marriage in Genesis: A Household Economics Perspective* (Minneapolis: Fortress, 1993), 61–65. In their interpretation of this story, Danna Nolan Fewell and David M. Gunn astutely note the parallels between Sarai's action here and Abram's action in chapter 12: "We find her [Sarai's] mode of operation to be not unlike Abram's. As Abram traded the sexuality of a woman in his possession for the sake of his security, so too Sarai trades the sexuality of a woman in her possession for the sake of her own security. Hagar, like Sarai in Egypt, is confined to powerless silence" (*Gender, Power, and Promise: The Subject of the Bible's First Story* [Nashville: Abingdon Press, 1993], 45).

16. Most of the major commentaries note the pun in Hebrew in 16.2. When Sarai says, "I shall obtain children," the verb used is *'ibbaneh*, which literally means "I shall be built up." However, the Hebrew word for "son" (*ben*) is phonetically implied here, and so the verb seems to mean "I shall have a son," which is in fact what occurs. See Speiser, *Genesis*, 117; Sarna, *Genesis*, 119; and Alter, *Genesis*, 67. Alter notes that this phrase also means "I shall be sonned through her."

17. As Schneider, *Sarah*, 48–49, notes, some interpreters prefer to translate *ishshah* here as "concubine." The Jewish Publication Society's translation uses "concubine," as does Speiser, *Genesis*, 116–17. However, a large number of translations also use "wife," such as Gerhard von Rad, *Genesis: A Commentary* (rev. ed.; trans. John H. Marks; Old Testament Library; Philadelphia: Westminster, 1972), 190; Westermann, *Genesis 12–36*, 233; and Alter, *Genesis*, 68. Even *Genesis Rabbah* 45.3.3 notes that Hagar was given "'as a wife' (Gen. 16:3)—and not as a concubine" (Neusner, *Genesis Rabbah*, 2:148). The conservative New International Version and Rabbis Scherman and Zlotowitz, *Chumash*, 71, also use "wife." W. Gunther Plaut, ed., *The Torah: A Modern Commentary* (rev. ed.; New York: Union for Reform Judaism, 2005), 99, adopts a middle ground, using the term "wife" in his translation, but noting in his commentary that "though she is called 'wife,' she is in fact a concubine and remains Sarai's slave." See also Dora Rudo Mbuwayesango, "Childlessness and Woman-to-Woman Relationships in Genesis and in African Patriarchal Society: Sarah and Hagar from a Zimbabwean Woman's Perspective (Gen 16:1–16; 21:8–21)," *Semeia* 78 (1997): 30.

This conflict begins quickly, as Abram and Hagar have sex and Hagar becomes pregnant immediately. She then "looked with contempt on her mistress" (16.4). This verse can also be translated as "her mistress was lowered in her esteem," but it seems clear that as a result of her conceiving a child, Hagar now views her status as being heightened, and as such Sarai's status has been lowered.[18] This change of status for the two women would make sense given the importance of fertility for wives during this period. That is, if Hagar is able to bear children when Sarai is not, then it would be culturally appropriate for Hagar to assume the primary wifely role in the household. Sarai is quick to respond to Hagar's new attitude and perhaps her new status. She tells Abram in 16.5, "May the wrong[19] done to me be on you! I gave my slave-girl to your embrace,[20] and when she saw that she had conceived, she looked on me with contempt. May the LORD judge between you and me!" In speaking thus to Abram, Sarai is attempting to appeal not only to her husband, but also to the Lord. In effect, she is pleading for her previous status based not on the success of her plan, but on the attitude and action(s) of Hagar in usurping her role as number one wife.[21] Abram, who has been quite passive throughout the enacting of Sarai's plan, remains passive in his response to her in 16.6: he tells her, "Your slave-girl is in your power; do to her as you please." Effectively removing himself from the power struggle between his wives and paying no heed to Sarai's appeal to the Lord in 16.5, Abram opens the door to Sarai's actions in the

---

18. The alternative translation is that of the Jewish Publication Society. Schneider, *Sarah*, 49–50, notes the severity of the verb translated here. *Genesis Rabbah* 45.4.3 paints a picture of a haughty Hagar, one that would resonate with modern audiences of soap operas. Therein, Hagar says, "My mistress, Sarai, is not on the inside what she is on the outside. She looks like a righteous woman, but she really isn't. For if she were a righteous woman, look how many years have passed and she has not become pregnant, but I got pregnant in a single night. [She must have displeased God.]" (Neusner, *Genesis Rabbah*, 2:149). Scherman and Zlotowitz, *Chumash*, 71; Shera Aranoff Tuchman and Sandra E. Rapoport, *The Passions of the Matriarchs* (Jersey City, N.J.: KTAV Publishing House, 2004), 16; and Nehama Leibowitz, *Studies in Bereshit (Genesis) in the Context of Ancient and Modern Jewish Bible Commentary* (2nd rev. ed.; trans. Aryeh Newman; Jerusalem: World Zionist Organization Department for Torah Education and Culture, 5734/1974), 155, all attribute a very similar comment to Rashi. For the impact of this change in statuses, see Trible, "Ominous Beginnings for a Promise of Blessing," in *Hagar, Sarah, and Their Children*, 39.
19. Sharon Pace Jeansonne, in her *The Women of Genesis: From Sarah to Potiphar's Wife* (Minneapolis: Fortress, 1990), 20, notes correctly that the word the NRSV translates as "wrong" actually has a much stronger meaning of violence. That is, Sarai claims that violence has been done to her as a result of Hagar's change in attitude. *Genesis Rabbah* 45.5.3 seems to have this meaning in mind when it claims Sarai scratched Abram across the face as she spoke these words in 16.5 (Neusner, *Genesis Rabbah*, 2:150).
20. As Alter, *Genesis*, 68, notes, the term "your embrace" is literally "your lap." This term is "often a euphemism for the genital area. The emphasis is pointedly sexual."
21. See Tuchman and Rapoport, *Passions of the Matriarchs*, 17: "Sarai obviously is feeling betrayed. Her intention in introducing Hagar's surrogacy was that she would retain her position as matriarch, while Hagar would function solely in a reproductive capacity. Instead, Sarai feels she has lost her status as mistress of Abram's house, and her hope to nurture Hagar and Abram's child as her own."

remainder of 16.6: "Then Sarai dealt harshly with her, and she [Hagar] ran away from her."[22]

The narrative then shifts to focus on Hagar and her actions. After Sarai's harsh, violent actions, Hagar runs away from her and the security of Abram's family. Readers might be surprised by the narrative focus on Hagar, since so much of the story up to this point has centered on Abram and Sarai and the narrator has taken pains to emphasize Hagar's status as a foreigner. However, in 16.7 something unexpected occurs, the first of a number of firsts in this chapter: "The angel of the LORD found her by a spring of water in the wilderness."[23] This is the first mention of an angel in the Hebrew Bible.[24] The angel then speaks to Hagar—becoming the only character to address her by name—inquiring as to her situation, to which Hagar replies that she is running away from Sarai. The angel then commands Hagar, "Return to your mistress, and submit to her."[25] Lest Hagar balk at this seemingly awful command, the angel then provides Hagar with a familiar-sounding promise: "I will so greatly multiply your offspring that they cannot be counted for multitude." This promise is almost exactly like the ones given to Abram in chapters 12 and 15, making Hagar the first female character in the Bible to have both a theophanic experience and a promise of progeny.[26] Unfortunately, the promise made to Hagar is not as positive as it might seem at first glance, as the angel continues:

---

22. Varying views of what exactly Sarah does to Hagar in this verse will be discussed below in "Sarah's Treatment of Hagar in 16.6."

23. As Jeansonne, *Women of Genesis*, 45, notes, this could be a veiled allusion to the type-scene of having future couples meet at wells in order to indicate their capacity to give life. Alter notes that, two of the most obvious examples of this type-scene occur in Genesis 24 and 29 (see "Biblical Type-Scenes and the Uses of Convention," in *The Art of Biblical Narrative* [New York: Basic Books, 1981], 47–62).

24. See Alter, *Genesis*, 69.

25. The verb used by the angel here, namely, "submit," is based on the same verb used in 16.6 to describe Sarai's violent treatment of Hagar earlier. In effect, then, the angel is instructing Hagar to return to Sarai and to submit to more abuse at her hands. In her work, Phyllis Trible claims, "Without doubt, these two imperatives, return and submit to suffering, bring a divine word of terror to an abused, yet courageous, woman. . . . [God] here identifies with the oppressor and orders a servant to return not only to bondage but also to affliction" ("Hagar: The Desolation of Rejection," in *Texts of Terror: Literary-Feminist Readings of Biblical Narratives* [OBT; Philadelphia: Fortress, 1984], 16). In contrast, Mbuwayesango, "Childlessness," 32, disagrees with Trible, writing that Hagar's return has more to do with "the restoration of Sarai and Hagar's relationship to the state it was before she became Abram's wife, i.e. Hagar as Sarai's [*shifkhah*]."

26. A theophany is when someone encounters the divine, or the divine makes itself present in the human realm. Elie Wiesel, "Ishmael and Hagar," in *Wise Men and Their Tales: Portraits of Biblical, Talmudic, and Hasidic Masters* (New York: Schocken Books, 2003), 16, notes the parallels between the promises made to Abram and the promise to Hagar here, just as Trible notes that "while all the patriarchs of Israel hear such words, Hagar is the only woman ever to receive them" ("Hagar," 16). Trible's comment reminds us of the fact that nowhere does the biblical text specify that either God or Abram ever mentioned the covenantal promise to Sarai. This is a major point in the analysis of Fewell and Gunn in their *Gender, Power, and Promise*, 39–55, especially 44.

Now you have conceived and shall bear a son;
    you shall call him Ishmael,[27]
    for the LORD has given heed to your affliction.
He shall be a wild ass of a man,
    with his hand against everyone,
    and everyone's hand against him;
    and he shall live at odds with all his kin. (16.11–12)

Hagar seems unaffected by this prediction, though, as she proceeds to become the first, and only, character to name God in the Hebrew Bible.[28] In 16.13, the narrator tells us, "So she named the LORD who spoke to her, 'You are El-roi'; for she said, 'Have I really seen God and remained alive after seeing him?'"[29] Following this experience, Hagar evidently does return to Abram's household—even though we are not told that she does—because

---

27. Ishmael's name literally means "God hears," although in the pronouncement of the angel it is linked to God's attention to Hagar's sufferings at the hands of Sarai. Sarna correctly notes that "the image of Ishmael in the Bible, as distinct from later Jewish literature, is by and large not a negative one" (*Genesis*, 122). As an example of these later interpretations, see *Genesis Rabbah* 45.9.1–3, wherein we hear that, among other things, Ishmael is a murderer ("R. Simeon b. Laqish said, "'A wild ass of a man' is meant literally, for most people plundered property, but he plundered lives" [Neusner, *Genesis Rabbah*, 2:54]).

28. See Katheryn Pfisterer Darr, "More than a Possession: Critical, Rabbinical, and Feminist Perspectives on Hagar," in *Far More Precious Than Jewels*, 147.

29. The meaning of this name in Hebrew is variously rendered, but it probably means something like "God Who Sees Me" (Alter, *Genesis*, 71). As such, it represents a play on her following question, which assumes an element of danger in seeing God. For the range of meanings this term has, see Sarna, *Genesis*, 121. In this verse, then, Hagar names God, but there is controversy over whether or not she actually talks to God or is still talking to the angel of the Lord. The text uses the same Hebrew word in 16.13 to refer to the "Lord" as it does in 16.7 to refer to the "angel of the Lord." Because of this, most commentators assume that, in some way, either Hagar is speaking with the Lord (in which case the angel of the Lord either becomes the Lord in some way or else manifests the Lord), or she interprets the being who is speaking to her as being the Lord. Sarna seems to advocate the latter position when he writes, "Hagar gives expression to her personal discovery by designating God after the particular aspect of His providence that she has experienced. . . . When Hagar 'sees,' she experiences God's self-manifestation" (*Genesis*, 121). Alter notes the ambiguity in the fact that "the divine speaker here begins as an angel but ends up (verse 13) being referred to as God Himself" (*Genesis*, 69). He also points out that many interpreters have attempted to explain this ambiguity by positing changes in the text (emendations) over the years, but he sagaciously concludes, "It is anyone's guess how the Hebrew imagination conceived agents of the Lord three thousand years ago, and it is certainly possible that the original traditions had a blurry notion of differentiation between God's own interventions in human life and those of His emissaries" (69). *Genesis Rabbah* 45.10.1 attempts to solve this problem by denying that Hagar encountered the Lord: "On no occasion did the Holy One, blessed be he, ever find it necessary to enter into conversation with a woman, except with that righteous woman [Sarah] alone, and even on that occasion there was a special reason" (Neusner, *Genesis Rabbah*, 2:155). As such, Hagar was definitely not talking with God, but only with an angel, because the only woman who was worthy enough to talk with God was Sarah, and even then the encounter was an exceptional situation (chap. 18).

we hear in 16.15 that "Hagar bore Abram a son; and Abram named his son, whom Hagar bore, Ishmael." Even though we expect to hear more about the complications that undoubtedly occurred due to Ishmael's birth, we will have to wait until chapter 21 for the continuation of Hagar's story.

In chapter 17 we have another telling of the covenant between God and Abram, and most commentators agree that this version stems from the Priestly (P) source. In it, Abram is required to circumcise all the males in his kin group (17.9–14) in order to receive the promise of land and progeny recounted in 17.4–8. To signify their relationship, God changes Abram's name to Abraham in v. 5, as Sarai's name will be changed to Sarah in v. 15.[30] However, in this chapter a new wrinkle is presented. In 17.15–16, not only is Sarai's name changed, but God speaks to Abraham about her, saying, "I will bless her, and moreover I will give you a son by her. I will bless her, and she shall give rise to nations; kings of peoples shall come from her." Abraham is understandably skeptical, as the narrator tells us that he "fell on his face and laughed,[31] and said to himself, 'Can a child be born to a man who is a hundred years old? Can Sarah, who is ninety years old, bear a child?'"[32] It is important to note that here the narrator reveals Abraham's doubts via the use of interior monologue. Giving voice to his disbelief, Abraham then wishes aloud that Ishmael could be the one to receive the covenantal promise.[33] God reassures Abraham on two fronts: first, Sarah will indeed bear him a child who will be named Isaac; and second, Ishmael too will be blessed with progeny and will be the progenitor of a great nation.[34] Following these guarantees, Abraham then circumcises "every male among the men of [his] house," including Ishmael.

---

30. The rabbis, in *Genesis Rabbah* 48.1–2, interpret Sarah's name change in several quite complementary ways. In 48.1.1, R. Aha, using the art of gematria (the science of Hebrew numerology in which letters are ascribed numerical values), argues that since Sarai's name lost a "y" in Hebrew (which corresponds to the number ten), but that both she and Abram gained an "h" (which has a value of five), the "y" must have been split in two. Thus, "her husband was crowned through her, but she was not crowned through her husband" (Neusner, *Genesis Rabbah*, 2:169). Similarly, in 48.1.1 it is recorded, "She was master of her husband. In every other context the man gives the orders, but here: 'In all that Sarah says to you, listen to her voice' (Gen. 21:12)" (169). Also, in 48.1.2, in reference to the fact that both Sarai and Sarah can mean "princess," R. Mana says, "In the past she was princess for her own people, now she shall be princess for all humankind" (169).

31. The verb used in this verse for "laughed" is the same word that will be used for the name Isaac in 17.19. As with Ishmael in 16.11, here the name of the son is connected phonetically and thematically with the events that surround his birth.

32. A different view of/for Abraham's laughter will be examined below in "Abraham's Laughter in 17.17."

33. Commenting on the status of Ishmael in chapter 17, Schneider notes, "All signs promote the idea that, in the eyes of both the Deity and Abraham, Ishmael is the intended heir" (*Sarah*, 57). Specifically focusing on 17.15, she writes, "Abraham's statement clearly indicates that Abraham considers Ishmael his descendent and heir to the promise" (59).

34. This view of Ishmael is in contrast to later Jewish interpretations, which view Ishmael most often as a negative figure.

Chapter 18 opens with Abraham receiving a visit from three men. He runs out to greet them and offers them rest and food.[35] After eating, they reveal to him that Sarah will have a child. Following this, the narrator tells us, "Now Abraham and Sarah were old, advanced in age; it had ceased to be with Sarah after the manner of women" (18.11). In other words, Sarah is postmenopausal and as such is unable to conceive physically. Abraham had noted as much to himself in 17.17 after laughing and falling on his face. This time, as then, a character laughs and voices disbelief: "Sarah laughed to herself, saying, 'After I have grown old, and my husband is old, shall I have pleasure?'" Sarah's laughter and comment raise a number of interesting issues.[36] First, she seems more focused on the act of sexual procreation and the pleasure she could have during that process.[37] Second, her laughing does not seem to indicate doubt as much as Abraham's did in chapter 17.[38] After all, why would Sarah believe such a strange tale from a traveling stranger when Abraham doubted God's own message?[39] Also, nowhere is it recorded that Abraham revealed the promise made to him by the Lord in chapter 17 to Sarah.[40] As such, Sarah could be hearing this information for the first time, which could certainly have heightened her incredulity. Nevertheless, "The LORD said to Abraham, 'Why did Sarah laugh, and say, "Shall I indeed bear a child, now that I am old?" Is anything too wonderful for the LORD? At the set time I will return to you, in due season, and Sarah shall have a son'" (18.13–14). In this dialogue, the Lord speaks directly to Abraham and curiously misquotes Sarah's question.[41] In her original question in 18.12, there is

---

35. Abraham's hospitality to these visitors is often cited as paradigmatic by Jewish interpreters. The best example of this occurs in chapter 7 of *The Fathers According to Rabbi Nathan* (ca. 400–600 C.E.), a commentary on tractate *Pirke 'Avot* in the Mishnah (third century C.E.). In this chapter, Abraham's concern for his visitors and the poor is compared with Job's, with Job's found to be inferior. See Ronald H. Isaacs, "Hospitality," in *A Taste of Text: An Introduction to the Talmud and Midrash* (New York: UAHC Press, 2003), 15–21.

36. Sarah's laughter, and the possible reasons behind it, will be dealt with in "Sarah's Laughter and Her 'Enjoyment' in 18.12" below.

37. See "Sarah's Laughter and Her 'Enjoyment' in 18.12."

38. For this issue, see "Sarah's Laughter and Her 'Enjoyment' in 18.12."

39. According to Tuchman and Rapoport, Sforno reads the problem of Sarah's laughter in a similar way. That is, he "interprets Sarah's laughter as incredulity at the angel-messenger's blessing of fertility. . . . Sarah likened the possibility that she would give birth at the age of ninety to God's ability to resurrect the dead. This is a miraculous feat which only God—and not even His messenger-angel—could accomplish. It is precisely because the prediction came from the angel, and not from God, that Sarah allowed herself to laugh" (*Passions of the Matriarchs*, 32).

40. See Jeansonne, *Women of Genesis*, 24: "It is obvious from this account that this is the first time Sarah has learned about God's promise to her."

41. Generally speaking, interpreters have not been willing to acknowledge that the Lord made a mistake here, so they proceed from the assumption that the Lord must have misquoted Sarah on purpose for some reason. In *Genesis Rabbah* 48.18.1, we are told that "Bar Qappara said, 'The greatness of peace is shown in the fact that even Scripture told a lie so as to bring peace between Abraham and Sarah'" (Neusner, *Genesis Rabbah*, 2:192). That is, the Lord deliberately told a lie in order that Sarah's original dialogue in 18.12—which contains the phrase "now that my husband is old"—might not be the source of marital discord between her and Abraham. The new speech that the Lord attributes to Sarah in 18.13 removes that phrase as well as the mention of sexual enjoyment, which, according to Bar Qappara, serves to

no mention of Sarah doubting God's ability to cause her to conceive, but rather some uncertainty over whether or not she will experience the physical pleasure of sexual intercourse. However, the Lord interprets her question differently and reassures Abraham that when he returns, Sarah shall have a son.[42] Sarah evidently is privy to this conversation, as she interjects, "'I did not laugh'; for she was afraid" (18.15). However, a male speaker—whom most commentators take to be the Lord—rejects what appears to be an outright lie and tells her, "Oh yes, you did laugh" (18.15).[43] At this point, the focus of the narrative abruptly shifts, and we do not return to the conclusion of the story of Sarah's impending pregnancy until chapter 21. In the intervening chapters, we hear of the destruction of Sodom and Gomorrah, as well as a familiar-sounding story in chapter 20.

After Abraham's encounter and disputation with God in chapter 18, the destruction of Sodom and Gomorrah, and the curious adventures of Lot and his family in chapters 18–19, Sarah resurfaces in chapter 20.[44] We are told that Abraham is residing in Gerar as a resident alien, and that he says Sarah is his sister.[45] Obviously, this chapter is connected to chapter 12, in which Abram tells the Egyptians that Sarai is his sister because he is afraid of what could happen to him if they believed her to be his wife.[46]

---

establish peace between the couple. Tuchman and Rapoport, *Passions of the Matriarchs*, also note that both Rashi and the Talmud (*Bava Metzi'a* 87a) interpret this story similarly as an attempt on the part of the Lord not to remind Abraham of his advanced age (33–34). For the talmudic story, see Avraham Yaakov Finkel, *The Torah Revealed: Talmudic Masters Unveil the Secrets of the Bible* (San Francisco: Jossey Bass, 2004), 40–41.

42. The repetition between the Lord's statement in 18.14 and the visitor's statement in 18.10 obviously lends credence to the widely held belief that these visitors are angels (see *Genesis Rabbah* 48.9.2 [Neusner, *Genesis Rabbah*, 2:183]). However, to my knowledge, angels are not normally portrayed as consuming human food (see Judg. 13.16 and Tob. 12.19). As such, the connection here may have more to do with the destruction of Sodom and Gomorrah in 18.16–19.38 and the role of the angels therein.

43. For more information on 18.15, see the section titled "Sarah's Laughter and Her 'Enjoyment' in 18.12" below.

44. Obviously, these are important chapters for understanding the developing narrative of Abraham and his descendents, but for the sake of space I am only focusing on the narratives in which Sarah and/or Hagar appears. The story of Lot and his daughters in 19.30–38 is certainly interesting for an appraisal of female characters in Genesis, and for more information on this story, readers should consult Jeansonne, *Women of Genesis*, 31–42.

45. For opinions on whether or not Sarah agreed to this plan, see "Sarah's Complicity in Abraham's Plan" below.

46. Many scholars explain the repetition of the same motif by arguing for multiple sources behind the final text of Genesis. In this case, chapter 12 is usually assigned to the Yahwist source (signified by the letter J) and chapter 20 is thought to be the work of the Elohist writer (E). See Speiser, *Genesis*, 147–52; and von Rad, *Genesis*, 225–30. For this issue of sources in Genesis, or more broadly, different authors or literary sources in the Torah, see Richard Elliott Friedman, *Who Wrote the Bible?* (New York: Summit Books, 1987). For more advanced analyses and surveys of scholarship, see Douglas A. Knight, "The Pentateuch," in *The Hebrew Bible and Its Modern Interpreters* (ed. Douglas A. Knight and Gene M. Tucker; Philadelphia: Fortress; Decatur: Scholars Press, 1985), 263–96; and Jon Van Seters, "The Pentateuch," in *The Hebrew Bible Today: An Introduction to Critical Issues* (ed. Steven L. McKenzie and M. Patrick Graham; Louisville, Ky.: Westminster John Knox Press, 1998), 3–49.

Here, though, we are told of no threats, no danger to either him or Sarah. In fact, we are told of no reason why Abraham would or should have felt the need to try to pass Sarah off as his sister. The results of his speech are immediate: "King Abimelech of Gerar sent and took Sarah" (20.2).[47] Just as immediate is God's reaction to this situation: God appears to Abimelech in a dream. In the ancient world, dreams were imagined to be messages from the gods, and so Abimelech has no reason to doubt the veracity of God's message to him in 20.3–7.[48] The exchange between God and Abimelech includes several important pieces of information: (1) God reveals to Abimelech that Sarah is married and threatens to kill him because of his actions with her; (2) Abimelech protests and notes his innocence, noting that Abraham told him that Sarah was his sister, and that Sarah confirmed this claim;[49] (3) God agrees that Abimelech is innocent, takes credit for him not touching her, and instructs him to return Sarah to Abraham, whom God refers to as a "prophet" and whom God says will pray for Abimelech and his people.[50]

In 20.9, Abimelech calls Abraham out in front of all his people and asks him why he perpetrated this dishonesty against him and his people. The exchange that occurs in 20.10–13 reveals much about Abraham's character:

> And Abimelech said to Abraham, "What were you thinking of, that you did this thing?" Abraham said, "I did it because I thought, There is no fear of God at all in this place, and they will kill me because of my wife. Besides, she is indeed my sister, the daughter of my father but not the daughter of my mother; and she became my wife. And when God caused me to wander from my father's house, I said to her, 'This is the kindness you must do me: at every place to which we come, say of me, He is my brother.'"

---

47. See the section titled "Sarah's Beauty or Abimelech's Aspirations?" below for views on why exactly Abimelech would have taken Sarah.

48. For example, see Tablet 4 of *Gilgamesh*. Sarna also mentions this in his *Genesis*, 142.

49. See the interpretation of Abimelech's protest in 20.4 in *Genesis Rabbah* 52.6.1: "Said R. Berekhiah, 'If you kill this gentile [namely, me], you kill a righteous man [namely, Abraham, who misled me]'" (Neusner, *Genesis Rabbah*, 2:236). R. Berekhiah here is personalizing Abimelech's protest. Since the Hebrew word for "nation" can also mean "non-Jew" or "gentile," he is making a specific comparison between two men, one Jewish (Abraham) and one gentile (Abimelech), and arguing that if God kills Abimelech, then Abraham deserves to die as well, since it was his dishonesty that led to Abimelech's actions. Similarly, regarding Abimelech's claim in 20.5 that Sarah corroborated Abraham's claim that she was his sister, *Genesis Rabbah* notes that not just Sarah but also "her ass drivers, her camel drivers, her household" agreed with this claim (52.6.2 [236]). As such, Abimelech looks less guilty here, since he sought additional confirmation of Abraham's claim. At the same time, Tuchman and Rapoport argue that Abimelech's claim that Sarah substantiated Abraham's claim shows that he "is not being truthful" (*Passions of the Matriarchs*, 40). That is, Abimelech is lying to God in 20.5, since the narrator does not mention any such statement by Sarah.

50. For more information on Abraham being called a "prophet" here (the first such usage in the Bible), see Sarna, *Genesis*, 142.

In his response, Abraham relates his rationale for claiming that Sarah was his sister, but his claims ring somewhat hollow. First, the reader knows by now that Abimelech certainly has "fear of God," as shown in his exchange with God in 20.3–7. Second, the claim in 20.12 is not supported by the genealogy given to us in 11.29–30 and may be an attempt on the part of the biblical writer to create an excuse for Abraham's seemingly immoral behavior here and in chapter 12.[51] Finally, we have no evidence that Abraham ever asked Sarah to claim him as her brother in perpetuity whenever they traveled. The net result of this exchange is noted by Jeansonne: "Abraham's excuses arouse skepticism, whereas Abimelech appears trusting, honest, and legitimately angry with Abraham's lies."[52]

After Abraham's somewhat sketchy speech, Abimelech again appears to be the more honorable of the two, as he not only returns Sarah to Abraham, but also gives slaves and animals to Abraham and allows him to settle wherever he chooses in Gerar. To make absolutely certain that everyone present knows that he has not had sexual relations with Sarah,[53] he tells her publicly that he has given Abraham a thousand pieces of silver.[54] He then says of this monetary gift, "It is your exoneration before all who are with you; you are completely vindicated" (20.16). As is evident from the final verses of this chapter, even though God did not kill Abimelech for taking in Sarah, the Lord "had closed fast all the wombs of the house of Abimelech because of Sarah, Abraham's wife" (20.18).[55] However, once Abraham prays for Abimelech (as God had told Abimelech he would in 20.7), God heals them all so that they are fertile once again. This emphasis on fertility is especially important, as it

---

51. This confusion could be a result of the presence of two different sources in chapters 11 and 20. The genealogy found in chapter 11 is thought to be the work of the Priestly writer ("P"), save the notice in 11.28–30, which most scholars ascribe to the "J" source. At the same time, most commentators find chapter 20 the work of the Elohist, or "E" writer. See Speiser, *Genesis*, passim, as well as Friedman, *Who Wrote the Bible?*

52. Jeansonne, *Women of Genesis*, 26. In contrast, Sarna refers to Abraham as the "injured party" (*Genesis*, 144) because "by forcibly abducting Sarah, Abimelech has made Abraham an aggrieved party" (142). This view does not seem to take into account Abraham's own deception of Abimelech. In his commentary, von Rad takes a more nuanced view of the ancient and modern understandings of Abimelech's guilt versus Abraham's deception (*Genesis*, 228).

53. This issue of whether or not Sarah has had sexual relations with Abimelech would be a large concern, since this occurs right after the promise of Isaac and right before his birth, so Abimelech must be shown not to be the father of Isaac. Jeansonne notes as much: "If she [Sarah] had stayed with Abimelech, the father of her child [Isaac] would have been in doubt. In order to remove any question, the narrator must stress that Sarah was never approached sexually by Abimelech" (*Women of Genesis*, 27). As we will see, the issue of Isaac's heredity also feeds into interpretations of what exactly occurs in 20.17–18.

54. It seems obvious that Abraham and Abimelech are being contrasted in this chapter; see the section titled "Abraham versus Abimelech" below.

55. For more on this odd verse and its implications, see "Abraham versus Abimelech" below.

provides a segue into chapter 21, where Sarah's promised fertility finally comes to fruition.[56]

Chapter 21 opens with the Lord remembering the promise made to Sarah. The Lord then causes Sarah to conceive and bear a child, whom Abraham names Isaac and circumcises.[57] Sarah's first speech following the birth of Isaac seems exultant and gives us a window into her jubilant mood: "God has brought laughter for me; everyone who hears will laugh with me."[58] And she said, "Who would ever have said to Abraham that Sarah would nurse children? Yet I have borne him a son in his old age" (21.6–7).[59] However, the happiness of Sarah soon gives way to misery. The narrator relates that "Sarah saw the son of Hagar the Egyptian, whom she had borne to Abraham, playing with her son Isaac.[60] So she said to Abraham, 'Cast out this slave woman with her son; for the son of this slave woman shall not inherit along with my son Isaac'" (21.9–10). There are several important issues raised by these verses. First, this narrative is obviously reminiscent of chapter 16, but there are also important differences, which I will discuss below.[61] Second, the text is not specific as to what the boys are doing together, if anything, that would cause Sarah such consternation.[62] Finally, in her speech the focus seems to be on the issue of inheritance. That is, since Ishmael was Abraham's eldest son, he would be the one to whom the patrimony (the lands, monies, and property of the father) would pass upon Abraham's death. God's promise to both Abraham and Sarah that *their* offspring (Isaac) would be the child of the covenant complicates the usual

---

56. Building on the theme of the sexual and reproductive incapacity of Abimelech and his people, the Talmud (*Bava Kamma* 92a) links the intercessory prayer of Abraham for Abimelech and his people to Sarah's conception of Isaac: "Rava said, 'From where do we know that a person who prays for his neighbor while he himself needs the same thing, he will be answered first? For it says "Abraham prayed to God and God healed Avimelech, as well as his wife"; and immediately after that, it says, "God remembered Sarah as he had . . . said," that is, as Abraham had prayed and said concerning Avimelech. And the next verse says "And Sarah became pregnant"'" (quoted in Finkel, *Torah Revealed*, 42).

57. As Tuchman and Rapoport note, the issue of Isaac's paternity is still addressed here: "Verses two through five in this episode refer *eight* times either to the fact that Isaac is Abraham's son, or to the fact that Isaac is the son that Sarah bore to Abraham" (*Passions of the Matriarchs*, 53).

58. Speiser notes that the repetition of the word "laughter" in this verse is "a double allusion . . . to the name Isaac" (*Genesis*, 155). There is no mistaking Sarah's joy in 21.6, and commentators have delighted in explaining the meanings and implications of her elation (see Tuchman and Rapoport, *Passions of the Matriarchs*, 54–55).

59. For readings that deal with Sarah's and Abraham's advanced ages, as well as the issue of Sarah nursing "children," see "Sarah and Abraham: Parents at Their Age?" below.

60. As Schneider, *Sarah*, 93, notes, the phrase "with her son Isaac" is not present in the Hebrew text. Rather, it is added in the Greek (Septuagint) and Latin (Vulgate) translations, presumably to clarify the action of the verb.

61. As with the previous chapter, the similarities are usually thought to be the result of having two different literary sources telling a similar story. See Speiser, *Genesis*, 156.

62. For more information on how commentators have understood 21.9, see "'Playing' with Ishmael" below.

distribution of the patrimony.[63] Perhaps Sarah is concerned that with Ishmael still active in the family unit, Isaac will not be able to fulfill the plan God has in mind for him.[64] As such, she commands Abraham to send both Hagar and Ishmael into exile.

Curiously, Abraham is characterized as being "distressed" over Sarah's command "on account of his son" (20.11). Abraham has never been one to value family members over himself, so this distress is unexpected.[65] God notices his distress and reassures him that a nation will be made out of Ishmael, a promise similar to the one God made to Abraham concerning Ishmael in 17.20. Here, though, God instructs Abraham to do whatever Sarah tells him to do,[66] and so "Abraham rose early in the morning, and took bread and a skin of water, and gave it to Hagar, putting it on her shoulder, along with the child, and sent her away" (21.14).[67]

The following scene in 21.15–19 is wrenching, as we watch Hagar and Ishmael run out of water in the wilderness.[68] Hagar then casts or throws Ishmael under a bush, presumably for the shade it offers, and moves away from him. Her desperation is palatable, as she says, "'Do not let me look on the death of the child.' And as she sat opposite him, she lifted up her voice and

---

63. For more information on the legalities of inheritance in the ancient Near East, see Sarna, *Genesis*, 146–47. Schneider, *Sarah*, 95–97, reproduces and discusses texts from the ancient Near East that discuss the legal issues of brothers and inheritance. Westermann claims that Sarah's motivation goes beyond the issue of inheritance:

> It is rather an uncompromising and relentless intervention on behalf of her son and his future that moves her. . . . This is full of meaning for such an early form of society: the future of a woman lay with her own son and nowhere else. Hagar's son, "whom she had borne to Abraham," threatens both her son's and her own future, even though he is also Abraham's son. And so he must go. The question of "inheritance" is merely symptomatic. What Sarah is providing for is her son's future. To censure Sarah's demand from the point of view of individual ethic or our own religious attitude is to fail to see that Sarah is engaged in a struggle for her very existence. (*Genesis 12–36*, 339)

64. Alter sees the verb "laughing" as a possible pun on the name of Isaac. He writes, "Given the fact . . . that she [Sarah] is concerned lest Ishmael encroach on her son's inheritance, and given the inscription of her son's name in this crucial verb, we may also be invited to construe it as 'Isaac-ing-it'—that is, Sarah sees Ishmael presuming to play the role of Isaac, child of laughter, presuming to be the legitimate heir" (*Genesis*, 98).

65. But see Schneider, *Sarah*, 98–99.

66. This command to Abraham has led several Jewish readers to consider Sarah as a prophetess. Rashi claims that in this verse "God tells Abraham that Sarah's voice is the voice of prophecy. Furthermore, that her prophetic ability exceeds Abraham's" (noted in Tuchman and Rapoport, *Passions of the Matriarchs*, 64). In his *Ohr HaChaim* Rabbi Chaim ibn Attar argues that "God's amazing statement to Abraham to heed Sarah's voice validates her directive to send away Ishmael and Hagar" (*Passions of the Matriarchs*, 64). According to this line of thought, "God's instruction to Abraham to obey Sarah is His explicit acceptance of Ishmael and Hagar's banishment" (*Passions of the Matriarchs*, 64–65). As such, the characterization of Sarah as a prophetess, based on 21.12, serves to excuse Sarah's order to Abraham to send Hagar and his son Ishmael into exile.

67. Sarna notes that the Hebrew verb translated here as "sent her away" "is used for divorce as well as for the emancipation of slaves" (*Genesis*, 147). As such, Hagar is being formally dismissed from any wifely duties she may have had as well as all her obligations as a slave.

68. See Westermann, *Genesis 12–36*, 341–42.

wept" (21.16). If we calculate Ishmael's age using the chronological indicators in the narrative, he would be about sixteen years old at his point, which is evidently old enough to cry out to God on his own. The next verse tells us that God heard Ishmael's cry,[69] and an angel addresses Hagar from heaven, saying, "'What troubles you, Hagar? Do not be afraid; for God has heard the voice of the boy where he is. Come, lift up the boy and hold him fast with your hand, for I will make a great nation of him.' Then God opened her eyes, and she saw a well of water. She went, and filled the skin with water, and gave the boy a drink" (21.17–19). This nourishment rejuvenates mother and son, and Ishmael grows up to be strong, an expert with the bow, as we are told in 21.20. The last we hear of either Ishmael or Hagar in this chapter is that Hagar obtained a wife for her son from Egypt, which connects her son to her heritage and probably was meant to cast a negative shadow on Ishmael, given the common view of Egypt in the Torah.[70]

As I note above, this chapter shares a number of parallels with the story of Hagar's flight in chapter 16. In examining that chapter, I noted that there is some confusion over what exactly Hagar's status was, but here there is no such ambiguity: she is referred to as an 'amah, a female slave. As such, she would be totally subject to the whims of Abraham and Sarah. Unlike in chapter 16, here Hagar does not run away because of abusive treatment; instead, she is driven into exile by Abraham acting on Sarah's orders and God's recommendation.[71] Again, the initial problem Sarah has with the two boys playing is ambiguous, but it seems that the issue is probably related to inheritance, as shown in 21.10. After Hagar is exiled, she is again alone in a vast wilderness, but this time there is no spring of water, as in 16.7, nothing to vouchsafe the security and survival of her son. She is in danger, and her son is on the verge of dying. Once again, though, Hagar is addressed by a divine intermediary, but here the message is much more positive than the

---

69. As Sarna notes, "The phrase [God heard] is equivalent to the meaning of the name Ishmael" (Genesis, 147). The narrative says Hagar cried in 21.16, but it does not mention Ishmael's cry until 21.17, when we hear that God heard Ishmael's voice. In the Septuagint translation, this problem is resolved by changing the text so that it is Ishmael who cries in 21.16, not Hagar. See Westermann, Genesis 12–36, 341. However, in her work Trible argues against such an emendation of the text, claiming that altering the text in this way silences Hagar's grief over her child (see "Hagar," 24–25).

70. Speiser correctly points out that "in ancient Near Eastern society the father had to obtain a wife for his son and assume the costs involved; here it is Hagar who takes over the responsibility" (Genesis, 156).

71. Even though it is Abraham who ultimately drives her away, Genesis Rabbah does not judge him too harshly. Instead, these interpreters praise Abraham's generosity in providing water for Hagar and Ishmael (53.13.1), and even go so far as to say that when God took notice of Hagar in the wilderness, it was "on account of the merit accumulated by Abraham" (53.14.2; Neusner, Genesis Rabbah, 2:256). In his writing, though, Elie Wiesel criticizes Sarah roundly: "It is sad to say—and even sadder to repeat—but a possible villain in this story is Sarah, our beautiful and noble matriarch, so warm toward strangers, so hospitable to the needy, so welcoming to all women seeking faith. Too intense, too jealous a mother? Of course she desired a glorious future for her son! But she was wrong to do so at the expense of another mother, another son" ("Ishmael and Hagar," 20).

one recounted in 16.11–12, where Ishmael is characterized as a "wild ass of a man, with his hand against everyone, and everyone's hand against him." Here the promise echoes the promise God made to Abraham regarding Ishmael in 17.20, that he will become a "great nation." Finally, the results of the theophany in chapter 21 are different than in chapter 16. In the latter, Hagar is instructed to return to Sarah, to the abuse that had caused her to flee in the first place. Here, God opens her eyes and she sees a well of water, a symbol of life, from which she procures sustenance for Ishmael. The narrator then relates to us the growth and marriage of Ishmael. Thus, Hagar is subject no more to Sarah's abuse, nor is Ishmael to live in Isaac's shadow anymore. Both mother and son fade from the narrative as autonomous characters, free to realize their own blessed destinies.

Chapter 22 is almost universally regarded as one of the most impressive literary achievements of the Bible, as well as one of the most discussed and controversial statements of human-divine interaction in the history of religion.[72] In this chapter, often referred to as the Akedah (the "binding," a reference to the binding of Isaac by Abraham) in Jewish tradition, Abraham is tested by God when God orders him to sacrifice his beloved son Isaac. Abraham is in the process of obeying God when at the last second God relents and tells Abraham to belay God's order. Instead, a ram is provided to serve as a sacrifice. Curiously, this chapter never mentions Sarah, even though by now Sarah is a major character in the book of Genesis. Phyllis Trible has famously argued that on the basis of the characterization and rhetoric thus far in the story of Abraham, Sarah should have been the one tested here, not Abraham.[73] Focusing on the theme of attachment and the "mother-son" dynamic present thus far, Trible claims that by including Abraham as the subject of the test, the story undercuts its own narrative logic. Trible's claim is persuasive, especially given the fate of Sarah in 23.1–2.[74] The narrative presents us with a stark, brief notice: "Sarah lived

---

72. Aside from the major commentaries I have mentioned, some of the key sources the reader should consult for a greater understanding of this chapter include James L. Crenshaw, "A Monstrous Test: Genesis 22," in *A Whirlpool of Torment: Israelite Traditions of God as an Oppressive Presence* (OBT; Philadelphia: Fortress, 1984), 9–29; Edward Kessler, "The Sacrifice of Isaac (the *Akedah*) in Christian and Jewish Tradition: Artistic Interpretations," in *Borders, Boundaries, and the Bible* (ed. Martin O'Kane; JSOTSup 313; Sheffield: Sheffield Academic Press, 2002), 74–98; idem, *Bound by the Bible: Jews, Christians, and the Sacrifice of Isaac* (Cambridge: Cambridge University Press, 2004); Jo Milgrom, *The Binding of Isaac: The Akedah—A Primary Symbol in Jewish Thought and Art* (Berkeley: BIBAL Press, 1988); Ed Noort and Eibert Tigchelaar, eds., *The Sacrifice of Isaac: The Aqedah (Genesis 22) and Its Interpretations* (Leiden and Boston: Brill, 2002); Shalom Spiegel, *The Last Trial: On the Legends and Lore of the Command to Abraham to Offer Isaac as a Sacrifice; The Akedah* (trans. Judah Goldin; Jewish Theological Seminary of America, 1950; repr., Woodstock, Vt.: Jewish Lights Publishing, 1993); and Elie Wiesel, "The Sacrifice of Isaac: A Survivor's Story," and "Parables and Sayings III," in *Messengers of God: Biblical Portraits and Legends* (trans. Marion Wiesel; New York: Summit Books, 1976), 69–102.

73. Phyllis Trible, "Genesis 22: The Sacrifice of Sarah," in *Women in the Hebrew Bible: A Reader* (ed. Alice Bach; New York and London: Routledge, 1999), 271–90.

74. Ironically, as Schneider, *Sarah*, 113, notes, the weekly Torah reading that begins at Genesis 23.1 is titled "Chayyei Sarah," or "The Life of Sarah."

one hundred twenty-seven years; this was the length of Sarah's life. And Sarah died at Kiriath-arba (that is, Hebron) in the land of Canaan; and Abraham went in to mourn for Sarah and to weep for her." There is no fanfare, no comments from the narrator on Sarah's faithfulness. Instead, the story moves ahead quickly with details as to how Abraham acquired a burial plot for her located in the Cave of Machpelah.[75] With the report of Sarah's burial in 23.19, she too fades from the biblical narrative.

Sarah and Hagar have shared a husband, similar experiences as women, the births of beloved sons, and important relationships with God. In conclusion, I should note two important facts about these central characters. First, both women are highly regarded in both biblical and religious contexts. In Jewish tradition, Sarah is looked upon as being not only the spiritual ancestress of all Jews, but the physical mother as well.[76] In her work, Trible aptly states the view of many feminist biblical scholars as to the status of Hagar:

> Hagar is a pivotal figure in biblical theology. She is the first person in scripture whom a divine messenger visits and the only person who dares to name the deity. Within the historical memories of Israel, she is the first woman to bear a child. This conception and birth make her an extraordinary figure in the story of faith: the first woman to hear an annunciation, the only one to receive a divine promise of descendents, and the first to weep for her dying child. Truly, Hagar the Egyptian is the prototype of not only special but all mothers in Israel.[77]

This high view of Hagar is shared by Muslims as well.[78] Second, it is one of the hallmarks of the Torah that the matriarchs and patriarchs are presented as fully human figures, with all their foibles and faults on public display. Many of the interpretations we will survey next stem from these two facts, as Elie Wiesel observes:

> [Sarah] loved her husband and therefore gave him Hagar; she believed in God and in His Promise, therefore she suffered for her own kindness. And because she suffered, she inflicted suffering. Was she wrong? Maybe, but we love her nonetheless. In fact, I would say that we love her even more. In other words: Because she was wrong and knew it but could not help it, it becomes our duty to do the impossible and correct her fault without diminishing her. We are her children; that is the least we can do for our mother.[79]

So Sarah's and Hagar's stories become fodder for centuries of interpretation because of the paucity of information we are given in the biblical text as well as the centrality of these two women. In what follows, I will point out

---

75. Sarah's death is examined below in "Sarah's Death and the Akedah."
76. Adin Steinsaltz, "Sarah," in *Biblical Images* (Northvale, N.J., and London: Jason Aronson, 1994), 31.
77. Trible, "Hagar," 28.
78. See, for example, Abugideiri, "Hagar."
79. Wiesel, "Ishmael and Hagar," 21.

several questions raised but not answered by the text and then assess some of the ways later commentators—mostly from the Jewish tradition—have responded to these gaps and ambiguities.

AMBIGUITIES AND QUESTIONS

As with the story of Adam and Eve in Genesis 2–3, the overlapping stories of Sarah and Hagar contain numerous gaps in what the narrator tells us, as well as many questions that are raised by the narrative but that never get answered therein. In this section of the chapter, then, I list thirteen questions that have enthralled interpreters of Scripture for hundreds of years:

1. Are Abram and Sarai related?
2. Why does Abram say that Sarai is his sister in chapter 12?
3. Who is Hagar?
4. What does Sarai do to Hagar in 16.6?
5. Why does Abram laugh in 17.17?
6. Why does Sarah laugh in 18.12?
7. Did Sarah agree with Abraham's plan to pass her off as his sister again in chapter 20?
8. Is Sarah still desirable now that she is ninety years old (17.17)?
9. If Abraham is the carrier of the covenant, how come Abimelech seems so nice (chap. 20)?
10. What does it mean that God closed all the wombs of Abimelech's people because of Sarah (20.18)?
11. Could Abraham and Sarah *really* have had Isaac at their age?
12. What did Ishmael do to upset Sarah so much in 21.9?
13. Why did Sarah die so abruptly in 23.2, and did the Akedah have anything to do with it?

The Biological Relationship between Sarah and Abraham

The issue of Sarai's familial relationship to Abram is convoluted. In Gen. 11.29, no mention is provided of Sarai's father; rather, the reader is provided with more information about Milchah, who is the "daughter of Haran the father of Milchah and Iscah." However, in Gen. 20.12 (which I will discuss below), Abraham specifically refers to Sarah as "indeed my sister, the daughter of my father but not the daughter of my mother." Because of this claim (which some interpreters claim to be false given Abraham's fear of punishment in chapter 20), many readers of the Bible have been content to read Gen. 11.29 as referring to Sarai, not Milchah. Rabbi Adin Steinsaltz simply writes that "Sarah was the daughter of Haran, Abraham's elder brother."[80] Similarly, Nahum Sarna argues that the omission of the

---

80. Steinsaltz, "Sarah," 22.

name of Sarai's father "is so extraordinary that it must be intentional. The Narrator withholds information so as not to ruin the suspense in chapter 20 when Abraham, in order to extricate himself from an embarrassing predicament, reveals that Sarai is his half-sister."[81] Gerhard von Rad posits that the author does not mention Sarai's father because "perhaps the Yahwist too knew her as Abraham's sister . . . but does not want to state it."[82] We also know that early Jewish readers of the text tried hard to justify the view that Sarai was Abraham's half sister, most likely in an attempt to cast Abraham in a better light in chapter 20, as well as establish a greater coherence between the two accounts. In Gen. 11.29, the name Iscah is mentioned, and according to one tradition in the Talmud (the encyclopedic compilation of law, interpretation, and story produced in the sixth and seventh centuries C.E.), Sarai is to be identified with Iscah (b. Meg. 14a). According to Shera Aranoff Tuchman and Sandra E. Rapoport, Rashi (a very important medieval French commentator on Torah and Talmud) also "identifies Sarai as Yiscah."[83] In fact, in their Orthodox Jewish translation of and commentary on the Torah, Rabbi Nosson Scherman and Rabbi Meir Zlotowitz simply state that "Iscah was Sarah" when commenting on Gen. 11.29.[84] In contrast, Claus Westermann disagrees with these interpreters and notes, "There is no justification for the view . . . that the name of [Sarai's] father was later struck out because of Gen. 20:12; rather it is a sign that this genealogy is not complete because the names were no longer known."[85] Finally, there are modern interpreters who simply follow the plain meaning of the text in Gen. 11.29 and argue that "where their names first appeared in the genealogy of Genesis 11, there was no hint that Abram and Sarai were siblings."[86]

Abram's Plan in Genesis 12

Responses to Abram's plan in chapter 12 have varied over the years. Generally speaking, though, most commentators have viewed his plan negatively. The great medieval Spanish Jewish commentator Rambam (Moses Maimonides) wrote:

> Know that Abraham our father committed a grave sin, in error, by placing temptation in the way of his saintly spouse, because he was afraid they [the Egyptians] might kill him. On the contrary, it was his duty to have trust in God to save him and his wife and all his possessions.[87]

---

81. Sarna, *Genesis*, 87.
82. Von Rad, *Genesis*, 158.
83. Tuchman and Rapoport, *Passions of the Matriarchs*, 3.
84. Scherman and Zlotowitz, *Chumash*, 52.
85. Westermann, *Genesis 12–36*, 137–38.
86. Darr, "More Than the Stars of the Heavens," 104. Schneider agrees with Darr on this point; see her *Sarah*, 15–17.
87. Quoted in Leibowitz, *Studies in Bereshit*, 157.

Tuchman and Rapoport add that

> the Zohar [the medieval mystical commentary on Torah] (*Tazriya* 52a), also
> incredulous that Abram places Sarai in a life-threatening situation to save him-
> self, asks: "Can we believe that a God-fearing man like Abram should speak
> thus to his wife in order that he may be well-treated?!" The Zohar resolves this
> issue by explaining that at the gates of Egypt Abram saw a guardian angel
> accompanying Sarai. The Zohar elevates Sarai to such a high plane that *her*
> *own merit* summons a guardian angel to watch over her in Egypt. Faced with
> the text's grim fact that Abram has placed his wife in jeopardy, the commen-
> taries justify his behavior by explaining Abram's expectation that Sarai's
> guardian angel would save her from harm.[88]

Sharon Pace Jeansonne writes, "As the narrative progresses, the reader's
sympathies are drawn increasingly toward Sarai and less toward Abram. . . .
He surprisingly shows no concern for Sarai's welfare. . . . Abram's language
demonstrates his concern for himself, with no regard for Sarai."[89] Along
these same lines, Danna Nolan Fewell and David M. Gunn roundly criticize
Abram in their work. Commenting on Abram's plan, they note:

> Certainly he values her beauty (though a liability as well as an asset) and (we
> presume) their previous years together, but her chief value now lies in his safety
> and his wealth. Besides, she is barren. Fidelity to her would certainly mean the
> end of his line. If he is giving any thought at all to God's promise that *he* will be
> a great nation, that *he* will be blessed, that *his* name will be great, that *his*
> descendents will have land, he realizes that Sarai is hardly likely to be of help. . . .
> Thus Abram sacrifices his wife, for his safety perhaps, but assuredly for eco-
> nomic gain. As for God's call and promise, it is clear that he sees himself as the
> sole subject. If God is interested in blessing *him*, then he must be the one to
> succeed. Sarai is expendable.[90]

In contrast to these negative opinions of Abram's plan, several interpreters
refuse to see Abram in a negative light. In his *Reading the Book: Making
the Bible a Timeless Text*, Burton L. Visotzky illuminates the process of
employing "some form or other of midrashic hermeneutic to make this narrative into the story of St. Abraham."[91] For example, Steinsaltz takes a
much more positive view toward Abram's plan, as well as Sarai's place
within it:

> [Sarai's] acquiescence to Abraham's suggestion was not an expression of pas-
> sivity or surrender. Her behavior can be explained as the implementation of a

88. Tuchman and Rapoport, *Passions of the Matriarchs*, 9.

89. Jeansonne, *Women of Genesis*, 16–17.

90. Fewell and Gunn, *Gender, Power, and Promise*, 43. See also their treatment of this text in
David M. Gunn and Danna Nolan Fewell, *Narrative in the Hebrew Bible* (New York and
Oxford: Oxford University Press, 1993), 91–93.

91. Burton L. Visotzky, *Reading the Book: Making the Bible a Timeless Text* (New York:
Schocken Books, 1996), 63.

joint decision. They had decided, despite the shame and humiliation involved, that it was preferable to preserve the whole of Abraham's camp—representing, as it did, the new ideal—even at the cost of Sarah's honor. They felt it was better to pay this awful price, jeopardizing her own happiness and well-being, with all that was here implied, because she and Abraham were working together toward a specific common goal.[92]

Rabbis Scherman and Zlotowitz argue in their commentary that

the Egyptians were notorious for their immorality. Now Abraham and Sarah would be at the mercy of the Egyptians, who might lust after her and kill him. Knowing that he and Sarah would be in grave danger in Egypt if they came as man and wife, Abraham concocted the claim that she was his sister. The honesty of the Patriarchs makes it impossible to believe that Abraham would have told an outright lie, which is why the Sages wonder: was she then his sister? She was really his niece! (11:29).[93]

They continue, "The sense of Abraham's statement [in Gen. 12.13] was that if the nobles of Egypt were to shower him with gifts to win his 'sister's' hand, the masses would be afraid to harm him, and Sarah's safety would be assured."[94] This claim, of course, assumes that Abram and Sarai were in some sort of danger as they traveled to Egypt as husband and wife. However, Tammi J. Schneider notes that the actions taken against Abram and Sarai in Egypt only occur because the Egyptians assume that they are, in fact, brother and sister. She writes, "There is no extrabiblical evidence from the ancient Near East that husbands were killed so that kings could marry their wives."[95]

Who Is Hagar?

When we first encounter Hagar in chapter 16, she is described as a *shifkhah*. The Jewish Publication Society's translation renders *shifkhah* as "maidservant," as do many Hebrew lexicons. In her now classic reading of Hagar's story, Phyllis Trible writes that in chapter 16 Hagar is described as a "virgin, dependent maid who serves the mistress of the house."[96] Similarly, Westermann notes:

The meaning then [of *shifkhah*] is not simply a slave girl, but a personal servant of the wife whose power of disposition over her is restricted to this; the girl stands in a relationship of personal trust to her. . . . In many cases she was the maidservant whom the parents had given their daughter when she was married.[97]

92. Steinsaltz, "Sarah," 27–28.
93. Scherman and Zlotowitz, *Chumash*, 57.
94. Ibid.
95. Schneider, *Sarah*, 32.
96. Trible, "Hagar," 30.
97. Westermann, *Genesis 12–36*, 238.

John W. Waters argues strongly for the meaning of servant in chapter 16. In his essay "Who Was Hagar?" he focuses on both the historical setting of the narrative and the narrative character of Hagar to argue that it would have been unlikely for a wandering farmer to have acquired a slave from Egypt, the most powerful country in the world during the historical setting of the narrative.[98] Similarly, Dora Rudo Mbuwayesango draws a cross-cultural analogy to argue that *shifkhah* should not be translated as "slave," but rather "seems to indicate a woman by whom a man could legitimately have children apart from his first wife (Gen. 12:16) or through whom another woman could have children (Gen. 30:1–24)."[99] In contrast to these readings of *shifkhah*, Robert Alter writes:

> The tradition of English versions that render [*shifkhah*] as "maid" or "handmaiden" imposes a misleading sense of European gentility on the sociology of the story. The point is that Hagar belongs to Sarah as property, and the ensuing complications of their relationship build on that fundamental fact.[100]

Obviously, there is still confusion within the later interpretive tradition over how Hagar is to be imagined in Genesis 16.

Sarah's Treatment of Hagar in 16.6

Sarai's treatment of Hagar is very important for how we understand Sarai as a character. The Hebrew word the NRSV renders as "dealt harshly with her" is *vattanneha*, which is from the root verb *'nh*, which can mean to oppress, humiliate, subdue, violate, or even rape. We can get a better idea of what this verb means from some of the other occasions in which it is used. For example, this verb is used in Gen. 34.2 to denote the rape of Dinah, and in Exod. 1.1–22 to describe the harsh treatment of the Israelites in Egypt.[101] It seems then that Sarai's actions toward Hagar were especially harsh. Jewish interpreters have long found fault with Sarai for this episode. Most famously, Ramban (Rabbi Moshe ben Nahman, or Nachmanides, a famous medieval Spanish commentator) notes, "Sarah our mother sinned in dealing harshly with her handmaid and Abraham too by allowing her to do so."[102] Leibowitz notes that Radak (Rabbi David Kimhi, a famous medieval commentator who flourished in Provence)

> takes a similar attitude and considers that Sarah did not behave in a manner befitting her character. Although Abraham in this matter gave her free rein to "do to her that which is good in thine eyes," she should have desisted and not taken advantage of her power over her handmaid.[103]

98. Waters, "Who Was Hagar?" 187–205.
99. Mbuwayesango, "Childlessness," 30.
100. Alter, *Genesis*, 67.
101. See Darr, "More Than a Possession," 138.
102. Quoted in Leibowitz, *Studies in Bereshit*, 156.
103. Ibid.

In their analysis of Jewish readings of Sarah and Hagar, Adele Reinhartz and Miriam Simma Walfish use the word "torture" to describe Sarah's actions toward Hagar.[104] In his commentary, Sarna writes, "The Hebrew verb here implies that Sarai subjected Hagar to physical and psychological abuse. It carries with it the nuance of critical judgment of her actions."[105] Even Elie Wiesel points out Sarai's less than desirable behavior in chapter 16: "In this story, Hagar is Sarah's victim. Sarah was wrong to impose a role upon her and then resent her for playing it too well."[106] Leibowitz seems to sum up the view of the commentators I have mentioned thus far when she writes, "Our commentators find no excuses to condone Sarah's behaviour, look for no psychological explanations in extenuation of her deeds."[107]

This may be overstating the case, though, for there are many Jewish readers of this story who interpret Sarai's actions as either innocuous or necessary. For example, *Genesis Rabbah* 45.6.2 presents three different explanations of what exactly Sarai did to Hagar, and none of them comes close to the serious violence implied by the verb *'nh*:

> A. [Explaining what the harsh treatment was,] R. Abba said, "She deprived her of sexual relations."
>
> B. R. Berekhiah said, "She slapped her face with a shoe."
>
> C. R. Berekhiah in the name of R. Abba: "Water buckets and towels she gave to her charge for the bath [so humiliating her]."[108]

The meaning of A is that Sarai refused to allow Hagar to pursue any more sexual relations with Abram. Opinion B indicates a single violent act by Sarai, and C infers that Sarai "dealt harshly" with Hagar by returning her status to that of a servant, thereby forcing her to abdicate her newly acquired status of Abram's number one wife. As distasteful as these explanations are, none of them rises to the level of treatment implied by 16.6. Similarly, Sforno (Ovadiah ben Jacob, a sixteenth-century Italian commentator) notes that "Sarai's behavior toward Hagar—whatever form it took— was necessary and justified, in order to restore their servant/ mistress relationship. It was crucial for Hagar to recognize that *she* was the servant, and to cease her denigration of her mistress" [as in 16.4].[109] Finally, Scherman and Zlotowitz paraphrase Rabbi Aryeh Levin (a modern Torah interpreter who lived in Jerusalem) and write, "It is incongruous to believe that a woman as righteous as Sarah would persecute another human being out of personal pique. Rather, Sarah treated Hagar as she always had, but in the light of Hagar's newly inflated self-image, *she* took it as

---

104. Reinhartz and Walfish, "Conflict and Coexistence in Jewish Interpretation," in Trible and Russell, *Hagar, Sarah, and Their Children*, 101–25.

105. Sarna, *Genesis*, 120.

106. Wiesel, "Ishmael and Hagar," 8.

107. Leibowitz, *Studies in Bereshit*, 156.

108. Neusner, *Genesis Rabbah*, 2:152.

109. Quoted in Tuchman and Rapoport, *Passions of the Matriarchs*, 19.

persecution."[110] As such, Jewish interpreters seem divided over exactly how to understand Sarai's actions. Another option is displayed by Steinsaltz. In his reflection on Sarah, he completely omits any mention of Sarai's violent behavior toward Hagar.[111]

Abraham's Laughter in 17.17

Interpreters vary in their reasons for Abraham's laughter, but the majority of them seem not to criticize him for doing so. For example, Tuchman and Rapoport note that Rashi translates the word "and he laughed" as "and he rejoiced."[112] They continue, "Ibn Ezra explains that Abraham's doubt is based not on theological grounds, but on the laws of nature."[113] As such, Abraham does not doubt the Lord, but rather his own frail body. In *Genesis Rabbah* 47.3.2, we see Abraham laughing in surprise over the idea that Sarah's body could possibly conceive: "R. Yudan said, '"Shall a child be born to a man who is a hundred years old?" Why [was Abraham surprised]? Because of Sarah: "Shall Sarah, who is ninety years old, bear a child?" The man does not get old, but the woman gets old!'"[114]

In his work, Alter humanizes Abraham and his experience:

> As incredible as it would be for a hundred-year-old to father a child, it would be even more incredible for a ninety-year-old woman, decades past menopause, to become a mother. The Abraham who has been overpowered by two successive epiphanies in this chapter is now seen as someone living within a human horizon of expectations. In the very moment of prostration, he laughs, wondering whether God is not playing some cruel joke on him in these repeated promises of fertility as time passes and he and his wife approach fabulous old age.[115]

Similarly, Sarna comments that when Abraham throws himself on his face, it is an "expression of awe and submission in the presence of the Lord," and therefore not related to his subsequent laughter, about which Sarna wonders, "Is it the laughter of joy, surprise, doubt—or perhaps a little of each?"[116] Westermann, too, sees Abraham's "falling to the ground" as signifying "reverent acceptance,"[117] but also notes that "Abraham's laughter in 17:17a has something of the bizarre about it in immediate confrontation with God who is making a marvelous promise to him."[118] This reading of Abraham as evincing both praise and doubt

---

110. Scherman and Zlotowitz, *Chumash*, 71.
111. See Steinsaltz, "Sarah," 21–31.
112. Tuchman and Rapoport, *Passions of the Matriarchs*, 25.
113. Ibid., 25.
114. Neusner, *Genesis Rabbah*, 2:171.
115. Alter, *Genesis*, 75.
116. Sarna, *Genesis*, 123 and 126.
117. Westermann, *Genesis 12–36*, 267.
118. Ibid., 268.

is also noted by early twentieth-century commentators, such as John Skinner.[119] In her work, Schneider compares the interpretations of Abraham's behavior in this scene in the standard and widely read commentaries of E. A. Speiser[120] and Gerhard von Rad[121] with their subsequent and more critical readings of Sarah's laughter in 18.12, and concludes:

> The issue motivating translation technique and interpretive methodology appears to be that Abraham is the faithful one who is attentive to the Deity, and the text must be translated and interpreted to uphold that thesis, whether the text supports the interpretation or not.[122]

In other words, these scholars, and the other examples I include, are not as critical of Abraham's laughter as they are of Sarah's because they already have a preconceived idea of Abraham's character and are willing to ignore the evidence of the text if it does not accord with that idea.

Sarah's Laughter and Her "Enjoyment" in 18.12

The issue of Sarah's laughter is an interesting one, especially when compared to interpretations of the laughter of Abraham in 17.17. Several commentators argue that Sarah's laughter has to do with her own body. For example, Rashi notes that Sarah thinks, "Is it possible that this aged uterus will sustain an embryo? That these shriveled breasts will nourish a child with milk?"[123] This preoccupation with her own body's ability to conceive at her advanced age is also related to the position found in several sources that Sarah's body actually began to rejuvenate or grow younger after the promise of a child. Rashi explains that the text does not mention the three visitors eating any of the cakes Sarah had prepared for them in 18.6, and that this must have been due to the fact that "her menses miraculously resumed, signaling her renewal but rendering her ritually impure. Thus, the dough she kneaded was prohibited to her guests."[124] Even the Talmud "describes that her breasts began to firm, her wrinkles to soften" (*Bava Metzi'a* 87a).[125] According to Rabbi Naftali Zvi Yehuda Berlin (also known as the Netziv, an influential nineteenth-century Eastern European commentator), Sarah's laughter is also related to her concern for the biological realities of conception as they relate to Abraham: "Sarah's inner laughter reflects her last doubt. It concerns her aged husband, Abraham. For *he* has exhibited no signs of rejuvenation."[126] That is, Sarah laughs because although she has begun to regain her youth, Abraham has not.

---

119. See John Skinner, *Genesis* (ICC; 2nd ed.; Edinburgh: T & T Clark, 1930), 295.
120. Speiser, *Genesis*, 122–27.
121. Von Rad, *Genesis*, 202–3.
122. Schneider, *Sarah*, 58.
123. Cited in Tuchman and Rapoport, *Passions of the Matriarchs*, 31.
124. Ibid., 28–29.
125. Cited in ibid., 31.
126. Ibid., 31.

In this same verse, Gen. 18.12, Sarah asks herself a question after she laughs. In the Hebrew, or Masoretic Text, Sarah's question to herself reads, "Now that I am withered, am I to have enjoyment—with my husband so old?" Interpreters are divided over what exactly Sarah means here. The United Synagogue of Conservative Judaism's Torah with commentary, the *Etz Hayim*, notes that the word translated here as "enjoyment" (*ednah*) literally means "abundant moisture" and represents the antithesis of the word translated as "withered."[127] In their Orthodox commentary on the Torah, Scherman and Zlotowitz render this noun as "delicate skin" and claim that it represents a simile for the return of youth and fertility.[128] The translators who rendered the Hebrew text into Greek (what we call the Septuagint) in Alexandria sometime after the second century found this talk unbecoming of Sarah, whom they imagined as a proper Hellenistic matriarch, so they altered her speech to read, "It hasn't happened to me yet, and now my husband is old." The Masoretic Text reading, though, shows Sarah as a more human character, as is common in Genesis.[129]

There remains the issue of why Sarah seems to have been reprimanded for laughing here whereas Abraham was not in chapter 17. *Genesis Rabbah* 48.17.1 contains a fascinating account of how early rabbinic interpreters tried to understand the seeming disparity in the responses to Abraham's and Sarah's laughter. The text recounts how when scholars were gathered to create what would eventually become the Greek translation of the Hebrew Bible (which we call the Septuagint), all of the translators had a difficult time explaining why Sarah would have been chided for her laughter when Abraham was not. The resolution to this problem came in an alteration to the Hebrew text during translation. That is, in place of "So Sarah laughed to herself" (18.12), these scholars translated, "Sarah laughed before her relatives." As such, what was a private moment now becomes a public one, and one deserving of a public reprimand.[130] Similarly, in his important commentary titled *Ohr Hachayim*, the eighteenth-century Moroccan interpreter Chaim ibn Attar builds on the idea that God is rejuvenating Sarah's body and explains that "Abraham's joyous laughter was an *immediate* response to God's promise of their fertility; while Sarah's joyous laughter found expression only after she felt the physical changes of rejuvenation."[131] In other words, the immediacy of Abraham's laughter is contrasted with Sarah's delayed laughter, which then leads to the conclusion

---

127. Taken from David L. Lieber, ed., *Etz Hayim: Torah and Commentary* (New York: The Rabbinical Assembly, 2001), 101.

128. Scherman and Zlotowitz, *Chumash*, 81.

129. For a fuller account of the transformation of Sarah in the Septuagint, see Susan Ann Brayford, "The Taming and Shaming of Sarah in the Septuagint of Genesis" (Ph.D. diss., Iliff School of Theology and the University of Denver, 1998); idem, "To Shame or Not to Shame: Sexuality in the Mediterranean Diaspora," *Semeia* 87 (1999): 163–76; and more recently her *Genesis* (Septuagint Commentary Series; Leiden: Brill, 2007), passim.

130. In their work, Tuchman and Rapoport deal with the talmudic version of this story found in Megillah 9a. See *Passions of the Matriarchs*, 32.

131. Summarized in Tuchman and Rapoport, *Passions of the Matriarchs*, 32.

that Sarah's laughter is somehow less genuine, less focused on the promise of Isaac's birth, than Abraham's laughter. However, perhaps the negative attitude toward Sarah here is rooted not in her laughter, but rather in her denial of that laughter in 18.15.

The grammatical structure and ambiguity of this verse raise two important and interrelated questions: (1) Who is speaking to Sarah here? And (2) does Sarah deny her laughter? As I note, most commentators agree that the speaker here in the Lord, even though the text is not specific in terms of the speaker's identity.[132] Even early Jewish interpretations like *Genesis Rabbah* view the speaker here as the Lord (48.20.1).[133] As to the second question, it seems fairly clear that Sarah denied her laughter, as this is what the text implies. However, as both Tuchman and Rapoport[134] and Schneider[135] note, the Hebrew word translated as "But she denied" (*vattkakhesh*) stems from the verb *kakhash*, which usually means "to deny" or "to lie," but can also mean "to cringe." This cringing or cowering could be connected to the description of Sarah as "afraid" in 18.15, as several Jewish readers have done.[136] In her work, though, Schneider contests these readings. Based on the protective nature of the Lord's relationship with Sarah, Schneider argues that "it is hard to imagine that Sarah would fear the Deity."[137] In fact, she continues, of all the characters in this narrative, the most likely object of Sarah's fear would be Abraham, given his actions in chapter 12 as well as his passivity in the face of Hagar's actions in chapter 16. As such, Schneider claims that "it is just as plausible, in fact more likely, that Abraham is the one who says, 'No, you did laugh,' and that Abraham is the one whom Sarah fears."[138] Schneider, then, posits that Abraham is the unidentified speaker in 18.15, and that Sarah's fear in that verse is directed toward him, not the Lord. Sforno agrees with her that Abraham is the speaker, but not that Sarah was afraid of him.[139]

Sarah's Complicity in Abraham's Plan

An important question to consider when examining Genesis 20 is whether or not Sarah agreed to Abraham's plan. She does not speak in this chapter, just as she did not speak in chapter 12. In both chapters there is a strong sense that Abraham is acting out of self-interest and a sense of self-preservation while Sarah serves to ensure his security. In this vein, *Genesis Rabbah* reports very curtly that when Abraham says in 20.2 that Sarah is his sister,

132. See Speiser, *Genesis*, 131; Sarna, *Genesis*, 131; and Alter, *Genesis*, 79. For a contrasting opinion, see Westermann, *Genesis 12–36*, 281–82, who argues that the retort is from one of the Lord's messengers.

133. Neusner, *Genesis Rabbah*, 2:193.

134. Tuchman and Rapoport, *Passions of the Matriarchs*, 34–35.

135. Schneider, *Sarah*, 72–73.

136. See Tuchman and Rapoport, *Passions of the Matriarchs*, 34–35.

137. Schneider, *Sarah*, 73.

138. Ibid.

139. Tuchman and Rapoport, *Passions of the Matriarchs*, 35.

"This was against her will and consent" (52.4.5).[140] This view is also found in a mitigated form in Scherman and Zlotowitz's commentary. They paraphrase the *Gur Aryeh* (a commentary on Rashi composed by the sixteenth-century author Judah Loew Ben Bazalel, also known as the Maharal) and write, "Abraham did not ask Sarah's permission to use this ruse, because she would have refused due to her previous abduction by Pharaoh."[141] It seems they then paraphrase Ramban when they comment:

> On the other hand, he did not expect an abduction to take place in Gerar if the people thought she was his sister. They would have tried to convince her "brother" to give her in marriage, but would not have taken her by force. Consequently he did not feel he was endangering her.[142]

Tuchman and Rapoport compile the comments of several interpreters—including Rashi (his inclusion is not surprising since the *Gur Aryeh* is a commentary on his work) and R. Moshe Alshich (a very popular sixteenth-century speaker who lived in Safed, Israel)—that agree with the *Gur Aryeh* here, namely, that Abraham did not ask Sarah's permission because he knew she would have refused him.[143] As such, there seems to be little confusion among these interpreters that when Abraham formulated and enacted his plan to pass Sarah off as his sister once again, he did so without her knowledge or consent.

Sarah's Beauty or Abimelech's Aspirations?

In her work, Katheryn Pfisterer Darr notes the chronological quandary in chapter 20: Why would Sarah, now almost ninety years old, be so attractive to Abimelech?[144] Sarna presents two options as to why Abimelech might have desired Sarah.[145] First, as we have already seen, various rabbinic commentators opined that Sarah's youth and beauty were physically restored after God's promise to Abraham in chapter 17.[146] Second, as Sarna writes, "In light of the subsequent relations between Abraham and Abimelech (21:22–32), it is quite possible that the king's goal was an alliance with the patriarch for purposes of prestige and economic advantage."[147] That is, Abimelech wanted to ally himself with Abraham's family and attempted to do so by marrying his "sister."[148] With regard to this second option, Schneider raises an interesting alternative:

---

140. Neusner, *Genesis Rabbah*, 2:233.
141. Scherman and Zlotowitz, *Chumash*, 91.
142. Ibid.
143. Tuchman and Rapoport, *Passions of the Matriarchs*, 38.
144. Darr, "More Than the Stars of the Heavens," 104.
145. Sarna, *Genesis*, 141.
146. See *Bava Metzi'a* 87a; Ramban (cited in Scherman and Zlotowitz, *Chumash*, 91); and Tuchman and Rapoport, *Passions of the Matriarchs*, 42.
147. Sarna, *Genesis*, 141.
148. As mentioned in Scherman and Zlotowitz, *Chumash*, 91, this view is also found in the work of the fourteenth-century Spanish commentator R. Nissim.

In this episode, there is no reference to Sarah's beauty, indicating that the issue is not necessarily about Sarah or her looks. What may be at issue is power. Abraham appears with many flocks and people (at least according to Gen 13–15) and there is no indication in the text that he has lost wealth or people. Abimelech may be trying to show Abraham who has power. Rape is not about sex but power and this would be a similar example. Throughout history women have been raped and taken into foreign houses as a show of dominance, not infatuation or love. The Hebrew text does not justify or question why this would happen, nor does it raise the problem of her age or looks.[149]

Abimelech may then have been asserting his primacy in the patriarchal order of society by forcibly taking Abraham's woman as a sign of power. The text's insinuations of physical contact between Sarah and Abimelech (for example, in 20.3–6) would then refer to planned or attempted acts of sexual domination intended to serve as physical markers of social supremacy, not any sort of emotional attraction.

Abraham versus Abimelech

In 20.14, Abimelech gives Abraham an extravagant gift of livestock and slaves as a way of apologizing for taking Sarah. Even though this seems like a very generous gift, rabbinic commentators have looked askance at Abimelech's gesture. In *Genesis Rabbah*, R. Judah bar Ilai comments on the intention behind Abimelech's gift of money to Abraham and imagines Abimelech saying to him, "You went down to Egypt and did business with her, you came here and did business with her. Now if it's money that you want, here's your money" (52.12.1).[150] That is, R. Ilai imagines Abimelech accusing Abraham of using Sarah both in Egypt and in Gerar to obtain money; in other words, Abraham is what we would call a con man. In her work, Schneider makes a comparable note:

> His [Abraham's] quick decision to let Abimelech take her indicates that, in his mind, the benefits of turning his wife over to the leader of a foreign land far outweigh any risks or negative results. The last time he became rich (in Egypt); maybe the same will happen again.[151]

Fewell and Gunn also take a negative view of Abraham's (non)actions here:

> Abraham will give her to any powerful man who might fancy her—and he no longer bothers to explain to her the reason. . . . And, as for Sarah, she allows herself to be sacrificed for the safety of the "chosen one." . . . Her self-worth diminished, she plays the role of traded goods.[152]

---

149. Schneider, *Sarah*, 108 n. 15.
150. Neusner, *Genesis Rabbah*, 2:240.
151. Schneider, *Sarah*, 86.
152. Fewell and Gunn, *Gender, Power, and Promise*, 49.

Similarly, in *Genesis Rabbah* 52.12.4, R. Simeon b. Laqish also imparts a conniving motive to Abimelech and his gifts: "He wanted to make her discontented on account of her husband, so that she might say all those years that she was with him, he [Abraham] had not done a thing for her, and this one [Abimelech], during a single night, has done all this for her."[153] As such, Abimelech was trying to belittle Abraham in Sarah's eyes in order to raise her view of him through his gifts. Both of these comments from *Genesis Rabbah* serve to reverse the characterization we have seen in the biblical text, since therein Abraham is portrayed somewhat negatively and Abimelech is depicted as a righteous, honest leader.

Closing Wombs?

The notice in 20.18 from the narrator that the wombs of all Abimelech's people were closed is intriguing, especially when we recall the issue of Sarah's (in)fertility and the mention of Abimelech being healed as well. What do these verses imply about the afflictions endured by Abimelech and his people? *Genesis Rabbah* 52.13.2 claims that "the 'closing up' applied to the mouth, throat, eye, ear, above and below."[154] As such, it was not just wombs that were closed, but multiple bodily orifices that were blocked. The curious description that these orifices were closed "above and below" probably implies some sort of impediment to normal sexual and reproductive activities. Certainly this would be good news to anyone concerned about the genealogical origin of Isaac; that is, if Abimelech was physically unable to perform sexually, then there is no chance he could be Isaac's father. This is the meaning several Jewish interpreters see in the strange mention of Abimelech being healed. If he was healed, then something must have been wrong with him, namely, some sort of physical malady that we today might call erectile dysfunction. Certainly we see these interests reflected in the comments of Alshich and the *Ohr Hachayim*. The former

> implies that the reason the text enumerates specifically that Avimelech was healed, is so that the reader clearly understands that when Sarah was alone in his presence, he was emphatically "un-healed," and it was therefore physically impossible for him to have impregnated her.[155]

Similarly, the *Ohr Hachayim* "states further that the reason the text uses the double emphatic form of the verb 'closed' [up all the orifices], is to make it absolutely clear to any doubters that Sarah's future pregnancy was not to be credited to Avimelech, but to her husband, Abraham."[156] In his commentary, Alter also mentions the themes of impotence and fertility.[157]

---

153. Neusner, *Genesis Rabbah*, 2:240.
154. Ibid., 242.
155. Tuchman and Rapoport, *Passions of the Matriarchs*, 48.
156. Ibid.
157. See Alter, *Genesis*, 96.

Building on the assumptions that Abimelech was the ruler of Egypt in chapter 12 and that Hagar was his daughter who was given to Abram and Sarai, Wiesel opines that not only was Abimelech punished, but Abraham and Sarah were punished as well for their deceptions:

> Because of their lie, Avimelekh, king of Egypt, is punished: he and his entire royal house become sick. That night, they are all victims of Abraham and Sarah. And what was *their* punishment? The tragedy of Hagar and Ishmael [in chapters 16 and 21]. Had they not lied, the king would not have felt the need to offer his daughter to Sarah. And the history of Jews—and of Islam—might have been different.[158]

Sarah and Abraham: Parents at Their Age?

Evidently, there was skepticism about Abraham's and Sarah's ability to have a child at their advanced age. *Bava Metzi'a* 87a notes that "all the people were skeptical" and accused the couple of trying to pass off "an abandoned child off the street" as their son. In response to this, Abraham held a large banquet to celebrate Isaac's weaning and invited all the people to bring their children, but not their wet nurses. "A great miracle occurred to our mother Sarah. Her breasts opened like two wells, and she nursed all the children." At this, all the people agreed that "Abraham is Isaac's father."[159] Another ambiguity here is the mention of "children" or "sons" and not simply "Isaac" or "her son." That is, since Sarah only had one son, why does the text imply that she is breastfeeding more than one child? *Genesis Rabbah* 53.9.3 links this concern with the theme of Sarah's rejuvenation:

> Sarah was unusually modest. Our father, Abraham, said to her, "This is not a time for modesty, but show your breasts, so that everyone will know that the Holy One, blessed be he, has begun to make miracles." . . . She showed her breasts and they began to spout milk like two fountains. The noble ladies came and suckled their children from her, saying, "We really do not enjoy the merit of having our children suckled by that righteous woman."[160]

As such, Sarah was rejuvenated by God to the point where her breasts contained so much milk they were expressing themselves. Tuchman and Rapoport link up this theme with the theme of general skepticism about Sarah's ability to conceive a child at her age in order to explain the presence of these noble ladies. They argue that these women were doubtful of Sarah's claim to have birthed a son, so they "thrust their hungry infants toward Sarah, demanding that she nurse their sons. Once they saw that mother's milk flowed freely from Sarah's breasts, their wagging tongues were silenced."[161] Thus when the text mentions "children," it is speaking of these children of the noble ladies whom Sarah fed. According to Tuchman

---

158. Wiesel, "Ishmael and Hagar," 19.
159. Quoted in Finkel, *Torah Revealed*, 43.
160. Neusner, *Genesis Rabbah*, 2:251.
161. Tuchman and Rapoport, *Passions of the Matriarchs*, 56.

and Rapoport, Rabbi Samson Raphael Hirsch (the great nineteenth-century German Orthodox commentator) claims that the reason the text reads "children" is that "Isaac and all subsequent generations had their origins at Sarah's breast."[162] As such, according to Hirsch, we are all children of Sarah. In contrast to these readings, Sarna's interpretation seems rather pithy: "The plural ['children'] is merely indicative of species"; that is, it functions as a nonspecific collective.[163]

"Playing" with Ishmael

Most of the interpretations of what exactly Ishmael is doing in 21.9 advocate a negative view, either of him or of his actions. This is most likely an attempt to explain Sarah's reaction in 21.10. The interpretation found in *Genesis Rabbah* 53.11 is central in any discussion of the way in which Jewish readers have interpreted this episode, as it has been very influential.[164] The text begins with a restatement of the biblical text in 21.9, followed by four different readings of the verb "making sport." First, Rabbi Aqiba argues that "making sport" refers to "fornicating," citing Gen. 39.17 as a proof text. From this reading, Aqiba deduces that Sarah observed Ishmael seducing virgins and committing adultery with married women. Second, Rabbi Ishmael—basing his reading on the authority of the Taanaim, Jewish sages and scriptural interpreters who were active from circa 200 B.C.E. to 200 C.E.—argues that "making sport" clearly means idolatry, and he, like Aqiba, offers a proof text to support his reading, namely, Exod. 32.6. As such, Rabbi Ishmael argues that Sarah saw Ishmael constructing altars and making offerings on them. Third, Rabbi Eleazar claims that "making sport" indicates murder, as shown by his proof text, 2 Sam. 2.15. Based on Eleazar's insight, Rabbi Azariah furthers this line of thought by stating Ishmael took a bow and shot arrows at Isaac, all the while pretending to be "making sport," and Azariah bolsters his claim by referencing Prov. 22:18. Finally, Rabbi Simeon brings the discussion back to the biblical text by claiming that the real meaning of "making sport" is bound up with inheritance, which makes sense given Sarah's comment in 21.10. Simeon also includes some fanciful additions to the biblical text, including a note that everyone rejoiced at the birth of Isaac, except Ishmael. Calling all those who rejoiced fools, Ishmael revealed his intention to take a double portion of Isaac's inheritance. As such, Ishmael despised Isaac from the moment of his birth.

These readings of 21.9 are fascinating for their variety and their inventiveness. Each of the four different interpretations provides a possible meaning, which is then supported by a proof text from the Bible in which the same word appears and carries the same meaning. For example, the reading by Aqiba focuses on the possible sexual connotations of the word

---

162. Ibid.
163. Sarna, *Genesis*, 146.
164. For this text, see Neusner, *Genesis Rabbah*, 2:252–53.

"playing" and connects this meaning with the story of Joseph and Potiphar's wife in Genesis 39. At this point in the story, Potiphar's wife is telling her husband her false story about Joseph, and she claims, "The Hebrew slave whom you brought into our house came to me to make sport with me." Since Aqiba detected a grammatical parallel between Gen. 21.9 and 39.17, he extrapolated the meaning of Ishmael's actions in the former based on Potiphar's wife's story in the latter. We find similar interpretive mechanisms present subsequently in *Genesis Rabbah* 53.11, in which other possible meanings, including idolatry and murder, are explored through grammatical connections with other texts in the Bible. Finally, in Simeon's reading the word is connected to the plain meaning of the text, which we are told in 21.10 has to do with inheritance. It is striking, though, that all of these readings cast a pejorative shadow over Ishmael and his behavior.

As I noted above, almost all later Jewish readings base their understanding of this text on the various interpretations found in *Genesis Rabbah*. For example, Sforno, Rabbi Moses Sofer (an influential Hungarian commentator and rabbi who lived in the late eighteenth century and the early nineteenth), and Abarbanel all imagine that "playing" refers to Ishmael's harsh teasing of Isaac.[165] This emphasis on Ishmael's taunting is most likely derived from Simeon's interpretation above. Similarly, the Yalkut Shimoni (an extensive collection of midrashic commentary on the entire Bible, usually attributed to a thirteenth-century German rabbi named Shimon Hadarshan) picks up on Azariah's reading and argues that Ishmael was employing a lethal form of "sport" against Isaac; that is, he was trying to kill him.[166] However, as Speiser correctly notes, "There is nothing in the text to suggest that he [Ishmael] was abusing him [Isaac], a motive deduced by many troubled readers in their effort to account for Sarah's anger."[167] Finally, despite these numerous negative views of Ishmael, the Talmud evidently does not view his actions here as harmful. When discussing 21.17, in which God hears the voice of Ishmael and then acts to save him and Hagar, *Rosh Hashanah* 16b notes:

> A person is only judged based on his actions up to that point in time and not for evil deeds he will commit later in life, as it says, "God has heard the boy's voice where he is," right now, although later he will commit many crimes. God saved Hagar's son Ishmael's life, because at that moment he was still an innocent child.[168]

Thus, even though Ishmael is still viewed in a derogatory fashion because of the crimes he will commit in the future, at this point in the narrative, that is, after he was "playing," he is still considered to be "an innocent child."

---

165. Noted in Tuchman and Rapoport, *Passions of the Matriarchs*, 59.
166. Ibid., 60.
167. Speiser, *Genesis*, 155.
168. Quoted in Finkel, *Torah Revealed*, 43.

Sarah's Death and the Akedah

The abruptness of Sarah's death as well as its proximity to the story of the Akedah have intrigued interpreters for centuries. In their work, Tuchman and Rapoport survey interpretive opinions by focusing on two main questions: Did the Akedah have something to do with Sarah's death, and if so, what? And why did God not act to save Sarah from death? The first question is usually answered in two distinct ways. First, it is often linked with the view of Sarah as a prophetess. On this reading, because of her prophetic and divinatory powers, Sarah foreknew the test of Abraham and "somehow this *knowledge* precipitated her death."[169] Other commentators, such as *Pirqe Rabbi Eliezer*, tell a different story. These readers tell of an encounter Sarah had after the Akedah in which someone (sometimes Satan, sometimes an ordinary person) tells her the truth of what happened on Mount Moriah, and this knowledge causes her to die.[170] As to the second question above, commentators had a difficult time explaining why God, who had saved Sarah's life several times before, would not do so now. Most commentators point out the obvious, that Sarah's age was such that it was simply time for her to die. However, as Rabbi Aharon Yeshaya Rotter notes, perhaps we should not take the proximity of Sarah's death and the Akedah as the starting point for the answer to either of these questions. After all, 22.20–24 separates these two incidents. Therein, we are given a brief genealogy that culminates in Rebecca. Rabbi Rotter unites the two questions by returning to the theme of Sarah's prophetic powers and notes, "Rebecca's birth is narrated *before* Sarah's death in order to inform us that Sarah in fact *knew* of the birth of her grand-niece."[171] As such, he notes "the beautiful symmetry of both Sarah and her sister Milcah, giving birth miles and years apart, to children who are destined to wed and perpetuate God's covenant. This knowledge allowed Sarah to die in peace."[172]

CONCLUSIONS

The preceding pages have surveyed hundreds of years of Jewish thought on the stories of Sarah and Hagar, giving us a clue as to how both of these female characters have been interpreted and kept in the tradition. We have seen readings that laud and criticize, interpretations that extol the beauty of Sarah and those that denigrate Hagar and her son Ishmael. More than this, though, we have seen how readers of Scripture within Judaism immerse themselves in an ongoing conversation with prior interpreters, sometimes agreeing, sometimes arguing, but always engaging the ideas and views that form the basis of the commonly held perceptions about these central ancestresses of the Abrahamic faiths.

---

169. Tuchman and Rapoport, *Passions of the Matriarchs*, 73.
170. See Wiesel, "Sacrifice of Isaac," 92.
171. Tuchman and Rapoport, *Passions of the Matriarchs*, 76.
172. Ibid., 76.

STUDY QUESTIONS

1. In his letter to the Galatians, Paul uses the stories of Sarah and Hagar to illustrate a point he is making about followers of Jesus who also wish to follow the Torah. In 4.21–5.1, Paul distinguishes between Sarah and Hagar as symbols of different attitudes toward the Law: one is free (Sarah) and one is a slave (Hagar). As such, Paul values Sarah more than Hagar, since his point is that gentile followers of Jesus do not have to follow the laws of Judaism. Is his analogy apt? How does Paul use Genesis in this regard? Is his reading harmful to the image of Hagar? If so, why?[173]

2. As I note above, Hagar is an important figure in Islam, yet she is never mentioned by name in the Qur'ān. Luckily, several of the Muslim stories about Hagar are reprinted in Riffat Hassan's article "Islamic Hagar and Her Family."[174] Read through these primary sources and compare them to the sources in Genesis I examine above. How and why does the Islamic understanding of Hagar differ from the Genesis stories? Which one is more sympathetic to Hagar and why? Based on this comparison, how do you understand Hagar?

3. In this chapter I focus on literary sources to examine the afterlives of Sarah and Hagar, but these women also show up in the artistic tradition.[175] Using the websites I mention in study question 6 on page 27, find images of Sarah and Hagar. Try to match the images up with either chapter 16 or chapter 21, and then ask how the women are rendered. Do the artists agree with many of the writers I discuss above that Sarah is more important than Hagar? Or is Hagar portrayed as a sympathetic character? Be sure to examine the images produced by Avi Katz, whose "Alien Corn" series transplants biblical figures into science-fiction settings (see *http://www.avikatz.net/sf/aliencorn/alien-corn.htm*).

4. It may seem odd to us in the twenty-first century that Sarah offers her handmaiden Hagar to her husband in order to continue the family line. Take a few minutes to write out what you imagine Sarah was thinking as she made her decision. What options did she have at that time as a barren wife? Think, too, about what Hagar might have been thinking. What options were open to her for upward mobility? Did she even have a choice? As you write, try to draw parallels to women today who are unable to have children and to surrogate mothers. How might the story of Sarah and Hagar speak to such women?

---

173. For this issue, readers can consult Brigette Kahl, "Hagar between Genesis and Galatians: The Stony Road to Freedom," in *From Prophecy to Testament: The Function of the Old Testament in the New* (ed. Craig A. Evans; Peabody, Mass.: Hendrickson, 2004), 219–32; and Letty M. Russell, "Twists and Turns in Paul's Allegory," in Trible and Russell, *Hagar, Sarah, and Their Children*, 71–97.

174. Found in Trible and Russell, *Hagar, Sarah, and Their Children*, 149–67.

175. See Lynn Huber, Dan W. Clanton Jr., and Jane Webster, "Biblical Subjects in Art," in *Teaching the Bible through Popular Culture and the Arts* (ed. Mark Roncace and Patrick Gray; SBLRBS 53; Atlanta: Society of Biblical Literature, 2007), 188–90 and 193–95.

3

Trollops and Temptresses*

DELILAHS IN JUDGES, CAMILLE SAINT-SAËNS'S *SAMSON ET DALILA*, AND TWENTIETH-CENTURY POPULAR MUSIC

FEW FEMALE CHARACTERS in all of biblical literature are deemed more scandalous than Delilah. She is variously considered to be a harlot, a temptress, and a deceiver. But what are the bases for these assumptions? Does the brief narrative about Delilah's relationship with Samson in Judg. 16:4–22 warrant such vitriolic views? If not, then where do these assumptions about Delilah come from, and why are they so pervasive? I will argue that this negative image of Delilah is found and perpetuated in cultural renderings of Judges 16, as interpreted in literature, film, and, more importantly to this chapter, music. These renderings have a unique power in their ability to alter and adapt biblical narrative for different times in ways with which people can identify. One important contribution to this lecherous legacy is the late-nineteenth-century opera of Camille Saint-Saëns entitled *Samson et Dalila*. This chapter will begin by examining the narrative in Judges 16 and then discuss the ways in which Saint-Saëns's work concretizes ambiguities present in Judges in order to posit a specifically shameful portrait of Delilah. I will then focus on selected interpretations of Delilah in one specific textual repository: twentieth-century popular music. I will argue that although these examples stem from various decades and multiple genres, they all share a similar view of their subject. That is, they all represent Delilah as a deceiver and a "floozy." By discussing these various renderings of Judges 16, I hope to illuminate the harmful repercussions of partial and androcentric interpretations perpetrated through one of the most accessible of all media: music.

---

*Portions of this chapter have been previously published as "*Samson et Dalila*: What French Opera Reveals about the Biblical Duo," *Bible Review* 20, no. 3 (June 2004): 12–19, 44–46; and "Trollops and Temptresses: Delilah(s) in 20th-Century Popular Music," *SBL Forum* 3, no. 3 (2005); online: *http://www.sbl-site.org/Article.aspx?ArticleID=391.*

DELILAH IN THE BOOK OF JUDGES

The story of Samson and Delilah in Judges 16 is relatively compact. Almost all of the action takes place inside a house or a dwelling, usually assumed to belong to Delilah.[1] There seem to be only three main characters in the story: Samson, Delilah, and the lords of the Philistines. The plot is fairly simple as well: Samson falls in love with Delilah, but unlike the case with his previous two women, we are not told exactly why he fell in love with her.[2] After the report of love, the narrator quickly moves to advance the plot; the lords of the Philistines come to Delilah and make an offer: "They said to her, 'Entice him and then see in what lies his great strength, and how we can bind him to subdue him. If you do, we will each give you one thousand and one hundred pieces of silver'" (16.5).[3] Although there is no explicit agreement between the two parties, there does seem to be an implicit one; Delilah embarks on her mission to discover the secret of Samson's power.

Is this implicit agreement the first sign of why Delilah is looked down upon? Should she be disparaged because she agrees to betray the man whom she loves? Even these fairly simple questions betray widespread assumptions imposed on the text that turn and twist the character of Delilah into something she is not. First, does Delilah love Samson? Nowhere in the text does one read that Delilah loved Samson, either by her own admission or by the telling of the implied author.[4] Thus, the issue of Delilah's feelings for Samson is an ambiguous one and as such should not be used as evidence for her deception or betrayal of Samson. Second, why does Delilah agree to the offer from the lords? That is, what are the motivations for her subsequent actions? The importance of this agreement should not be understated.[5] Delilah's acceptance provides ample ammunition for commentators to view her act as a betrayal of Samson.[6] However, we do not seem to have any evidence in the text of Delilah's motivation. Mieke Bal seeks to fill this gap by noting, "In wartime, and it is such a time, no blame is attached to patriotism. Delilah just uses her specific potential for helping her tribe and makes enough money out of it to preserve her financial independence."[7] Danna Nolan Fewell agrees with Bal

1. The vast majority of feminist commentators make this assumption. See, for example, J. Cheryl Exum, "Why, Why, Why, Delilah?" in *Plotted, Shot, and Painted: Cultural Representations of Biblical Women* (JSOTSup 215/GCT 3; Sheffield: Sheffield Academic Press, 1996), 181.
2. See Mieke Bal, *Lethal Love: Feminist Literary Readings of Biblical Love Stories* (Indiana Studies in Biblical Literature; Bloomington: Indiana University Press, 1987), 49–50.
3. All quotes from Judges are my translation.
4. See Exum, *Plotted, Shot, and Painted*, 182.
5. Bal, *Lethal Love*, 50, comments, "Delilah's acceptance of the deal is *the* shocking detail in this episode."
6. In his commentary, *Joshua, Judges, Ruth* (NCBC; Grand Rapids, Mich.: Eerdmans, 1986), 334, John Gray titles the Samson/Delilah story "The Betrayal and Imprisonment of Samson." Also see Robert G. Boling, *Judges* (AB 6A; Garden City, N.Y.: Doubleday, 1975), 249.
7. Bal, *Lethal Love*, 51.

when she notes that Delilah's deal with the Philistine lords is unmediated by any male figures. She continues, "Doubtless, as a woman alone, Delilah finds that the love of a wanted man is no match for the security of wealth."[8] Thus, as with Delilah's assumed love for Samson, her motivations for accepting the deal of the Philistine lords is textually ambiguous. As such, then, Delilah's motivations should not be used to ascribe any extratextual qualities to her.

The main bulk of the story is concerned with the attempts on the part of Delilah to discern the secret of Samson's strength. She makes three attempts to discover his secret, and each time he lies to her. He tells her three different times how to render him powerless, and each time, she follows his instructions to the letter. She then repeats the refrain, "The Philistines are upon you, Samson!" (16.9, 12, 14, 20). After this, Samson breaks free from whatever bonds with which Delilah has bound him. Twice, then, Delilah tells him, "You have mocked me and told me lies. Now, explain how you can be bound" (16.10, 13). Following the third attempt, however, Delilah exclaims to Samson, "How can you say, 'I love you,' when your heart is not with me?" (16.15). She follows this query with another impassioned plea, after which the implied author tells us that "she harassed him with her words all the days and urged him, and his soul was vexed to death" (16.15). Samson then reveals to her the secret of his strength: his status as a Nazirite, metonymically exemplified by his hair. We are then told that when Delilah "recognized that he explained to her with all his heart, she called to the lords of the Philistines" (16.18), whereupon they bring her the silver. In 16.19, the story comes to a climax. The narrator tells us that "she made/let him sleep on her knees, then called to a man, shaved seven locks on his head, and then began to humiliate him. And his strength departed from him" (16.19).

Delilah's actions in this section seem to offer the clearest evidence for her betrayal of Samson, as well as her role in his capture and eventual death. She shaves the hair on his head and then hands him over to the Philistines, who "bored out his eyes" (16.21) and took him away to Gaza. These actions would seem to be fairly damning, but, again, if one scratches the surface, the story becomes a little more ambiguous. First, is Delilah really betraying Samson by asking him how he could be bound? In the story, Samson seems fully aware that Delilah is attempting to discover the secret of his strength; she tells him point-blank, "Explain to me in what lies your great strength and how you could be bound, so as to subdue you" (16.6). Thus, Samson must be aware of her attempts, and he goes along with them. However, it seems as if he is toying with her by giving her incorrect responses to her request, all the while holding on to his secret. Thus, it

---

8. Danna Nolan Fewell, "Judges," in *The Women's Bible Commentary* (ed. Carol A. Newsom and Sharon H. Ringe; expanded ed. with Apocrypha; Louisville, Ky.: Westminster John Knox Press, 1998), 73.

would appear that Samson knows what he is getting into, and if he does, then we cannot hold Delilah guilty of deception.[9] Again we see that "obvious" evidence for Delilah's treachery is not so obvious after all. If Samson knew what was happening to him all along, how can Delilah be the only culpable party?

Even if one accepts the fact that Samson somehow willingly gave his secret to Delilah, it appears that she still acted on it with vicious intent; that is, she is the one who shaved the hair on his head. However, there are problems even with this argument. The Hebrew, or Masoretic Text, tells us that "she made/let him sleep on her knees, then called to a man, shaved seven locks on his head, and then began to humiliate him. And his strength departed from him" (16.19). The question immediately arises: Why would Delilah need to call to a man? The "obvious" explanation would seem to be that of Robert G. Boling: "Apparently the man brought her the razor, and perhaps assisted by holding his head."[10] At first glance, this explanation might make sense. However, Delilah has bound Samson twice already and woven his hair together without the assistance of anyone else, so why would it be necessary to call for assistance in this case? Boling's comment becomes even more absurd if one considers that the previous attempt by Delilah involved manipulating Samson's hair while he slept, exactly what she does in her final attempt, and there she needed no assistance. So why would Delilah "call to a man"? This problem was answered by some ancient translations by specifying exactly what the man's purpose was; in the Septuagint and in the Vulgate—the Greek and Latin translations of the Hebrew Bible, respectively—the man is specifically called a barber, and it is he who performs the shaving. Even modern translations such as the NRSV pick up on this textual tradition and render the verse, "she called a man, and had him shave off the seven locks of his head" (16.19). Since we have at least two versions of who actually cut Samson's hair, it does not (or at least should not) follow that Delilah is solely to blame for Samson's new coiffure. Thus, since we cannot be completely sure that Delilah is to blame, we cannot reasonably hold her culpable, and thus worthy of blame and disregard.

After Delilah hands Samson over to the Philistines, she disappears completely from the narrative. However, the impact of her actions and words remains, albeit ambiguously. We have seen that the four main actions that "obviously" render Delilah treacherous and loathsome, namely, her love for Samson, her acceptance of the Philistine deal, her deceptive questions, and the shaving of Samson's hair, can all be seen as indefinite evidence at best. In each case, there is uncertainty and textual ambiguity. Thus, if these actions are, as I claim, equivocal, then interpreters/readers should not use them to reinscribe the character of Delilah as someone to be reviled.

---

9. On this point, see Exum, "Samson's Women," in *Fragmented Women: Feminist (Sub)Versions of Biblical Narratives* (Valley Forge, Pa.: Trinity Press, 1993), 83; Bal, *Lethal Love*, 52; and Fewell, "Judges," 73.
10. Boling, *Judges*, 250.

CAMILLE SAINT-SAËNS'S *SAMSON ET DALILA*

If the popular image of Delilah as a *femme fatale* is not unambiguously found in biblical literature, then where are we to find it? As I note above, this image has been constructed and maintained in interpretations of Delilah found in aesthetic genres such as literature, film, and music. I have often found in my classes that whereas only some of my students have ever read the book of Exodus, almost all of them can tell the story of Moses from having seen Cecil B. DeMille's *The Ten Commandments* of 1956. In this section of the chapter, I will examine the ways in which one particular cultural rendering of the story of Delilah, namely Camille Saint-Saëns's *Samson et Dalila*, alters and adapts the biblical account.

One of France's greatest yet most underrated composers, Saint-Saëns began working on this topic as an oratorio in 1867. He was inspired by a non-extant libretto written by Voltaire for another great composer, Jean Philippe Rameau. However, due to a lack of musical understanding and a rather low tolerance for biblical subjects in nineteenth-century France, he only scored act 2 before giving it up. Five years later he took it up again, this time as an opera with an original libretto written by Ferdinand Lemaire. Lemaire was a Creole poet from Martinique, as well as the husband of one of Saint-Saëns's cousins. In 1876, Saint-Saëns finally completed the project. Due to the conservative climate in France at this time, the first performance did not take place there. The great pianist Franz Liszt had heard the piece and used his influence to have it premiered in Weimar in December 1877. In fact, France saw no performances of the work until 1892, when it finally played at the Paris Opéra. Since then, *Samson et Dalila* has established itself as the only opera of Saint-Saëns in the common repertoire, and one of his most beloved works.[11]

The three-act work tells the story of Judges 16, but the characters of Samson and Delilah, have been changed dramatically. Samson is no longer pictured as a bumbling oaf or a ladies' man. Instead, he plays the triple role of prophet, military champion, and even priest with great depth and dignity. In act 1, scene 1, Samson speaks with the voice of God to the Hebrews and convinces them not to lose faith in Jehovah. Abimelech, the satrap of Gaza, comes forth and questions the power of the Hebrew God compared with that of Dagon in scene 2. After feeling the Lord enter into him and extolling the consequences in theophanic language, Samson kills Abimelech while defending himself from an attack. It is not until act 1, scene 6, that we meet Dalila, as she and the girls of the Philistines sing an ode to spring. In the midst of this enchanting song, we realize that she and Samson have had a previous relationship. She bemoans the loss of her lover and tells Samson in no uncertain terms that her charms are more enticing than those

---

11. The most comprehensive analysis of this opera remains Henri Collet, *"Samson et Dalila" de C. Saint-Saëns: Étude historique et critique Analyse Musicale* (Les Chefs-d'Œuvre de la Musique Series; Paris: Librarie Delaplane, 1922).

of spring. An old Hebrew tries to warn Samson against the "serpent's poison" contained in the words of this foreign woman, and Samson himself prays to God to still his passion for Dalila.[12] At the end of act 1, though, Samson is completely enraptured by Dalila again, and the stage is set for their infamous rendezvous.

The bulk of the interaction between Samson and Dalila takes place in act 2. The setting is the Valley of Sorek, where Dalila had invited Samson so that she can open her arms to him. In scene 1, Dalila's soliloquy reveals her motivations for enticing Samson. She longs for vengeance, for the satisfaction of her gods, and wants to see Samson in fetters. Noting that her brothers fear him, she claims boldly, "I, alone among all, do dare him and keep him at my knees!" In scene 2, the high priest of Dagon enters to discuss a plan of action with Dalila. After noting that Dagon is within him, much as Samson did regarding Jehovah, he gets to the point. He says to Dalila, "Sell me your slave Samson!" In return, he adds, "[You] can choose from among all my wealth." At this point, Dalila reveals her true feelings for Samson. She tells the high priest, "What matters your gold to Dalila? And what could a whole treasure if I was not dreaming of vengeance . . . for, as much as you, I loathe him!" We then learn that Dalila has already tried to discover the secret of Samson's strength three times and failed. However, after her ode to spring in act 1, scene 6, she is convinced that "he surrendered to [her] power," and that he is coming to meet her "to tighten the bond between" them. Following this, she and the high priest sing together about their hopes for Samson's downfall. They sing of their hate, the need for vengeance against Samson, and exclaim, "Death to the Hebrew leader!" After the high priest leaves Dalila to her mission of revenge, scene 2 ends with Dalila wondering aloud if Samson is coming after all. She does not wonder for long, though, as Samson enters.

In act 2, scene 3, we witness in essence a love triangle between Samson, Dalila, and Jehovah. Samson grudgingly acknowledges his love for Dalila but claims he must submit to the will of his God and "break the sweet bond of [their] love." As she promised to in scene 2, though, Dalila uses her most potent weapon: she begins to cry. Samson cannot resist her tears and loudly declares that he loves her. The two then exchange several verses of amorous exclamations, until Dalila reminds Samson that he has lied to her before, when he misled her as to the secret of his power. He responds that his love means he has forgotten his God, which should be sufficient proof, where-upon Dalila replies that she is jealous of his God because of the vow he and Samson share. She begs him to allay her distrust by revealing the nature of his sacred bond with God. Throughout the scene, distant thunder and lightning have been growing closer, and Samson takes this to be the voice of God telling him to remember his vow. When he tells this to Dalila, she

---

12. All quotes from the libretto are taken from the booklet accompanying *Samson et Dalila* (Chœurs et Orchestre de l'Opéra-Bastille; cond. Myung-Whun Chung; EMI Classics CDS7 55470-2, 1992).

plays her last card and rejects him, saying, "Coward! Loveless heart, I despise you. Farewell!" She turns and enters her house, leaving Samson with his hands in the air. He then hesitatingly follows her in, whereupon Philistine soldiers approach the house. Offstage, Samson has evidently revealed his secret to Dalila, for she calls the soldiers into her house, and we hear Samson scream, "Treachery!" as the curtain closes on act 2.

Act 3 opens with Samson, now shorn and blind, turning a millstone in a Philistine dungeon. Scene 1 consists mainly of Samson admitting his mistake to God and his people. He even asks God to take his life as an atoning sacrifice for Israel so they can be relieved from the suffering he has caused. As we shall see, this noble offer is made manifest in the finale of the opera.

Scene 2 is set in the temple of Dagon and includes the famous "Bacchanale" interlude, in which the frenzied "Oriental" music matches the erotic mood and movements of the worshipping Philistines. Into this milieu, a child leads Samson in scene 3. The Philistines acknowledge Samson with a toast, and Dalila comes forward to taunt him in front of everyone. She tells him, "Love served my purpose; to gratify my vengeance I tore from you your secret . . . Dalila avenges today her god, her people, and her hatred." The high priest takes this opportunity to make a theological point, telling Samson that if Jehovah can give him back his sight, even he will worship him. He continues, "But, since he cannot help you . . . I can afford to scoff at him, to show my hatred, by laughing at his wrath!" This blasphemy is too much for Samson; he offers to avenge the glory of the Lord, if only he could recover his strength for a moment.

The high priest and Dalila then move to the altar of the temple and begin to make offerings to Dagon. They praise their god profusely, while Samson stands to the side, praying. Finally, the high priest asks Samson to move to the center of the temple and make an offering to Dagon on his knees. As he approaches the middle of the temple, between two large columns, all the Philistines begin to rejoice, thinking their victory over Israel is now complete. When he is positioned between the two pillars, Samson again asks God to let him avenge both himself and God. With a loud cry, Samson pushes the pillars down, the temple comes crashing down on everyone, and the opera ends.

At the end, then, Saint-Saëns has turned the story in Judges 16 into a complex tale of competing loyalties and religious/ideological battles. In the operatic version of the story, Dalila emerges as the stronger character. In fact, as Elaine Hoffman Baruch has noted, there is a gender inversion in the opera in that Samson is "passive and vulnerable," while Dalila is "dominant and controlling."[13] In the biblical text, as we saw above, Delilah's motives are uncertain and her role in Samson's downfall is ambiguous. In ascribing to Dalila a vitriolic hatred of Samson as well as a

---

13. Elaine Hoffman Baruch, "Forbidden Words—Enchanting Song: The Treatment of Delilah in Literature and Music," in *To Speak or Be Silent: The Paradox of Disobedience in the Lives of Women* (ed. Lena B. Ross; Wilmette, Ill.: Chiron Publications, 1993), 245–46.

political and religious motive, Saint-Saëns has in effect removed the vagueness of the biblical narrative in exchange for the explicit revenge she takes in the opera.

Along with this confusion of gender roles, there is a religious confusion inherent in the character of Samson. In the opera, Samson is very much the representative of God; that is, he serves not only as a military champion but also as a prophet and priest. However, he gives himself to Dalila, who here is a rival for God in that she has the power to weaken wills and incite wrath. Thus, Dalila is at most a goddess figure and at the least is a champion of Dagon. Samson, in deciding to love Dalila and reveal his divine secret to her, exhibits a spiritual uncertainty that will eventually cause his downfall.[14] Again, this religious confusion is not present in the biblical story, and in adding it to his presentation, Saint-Saëns has rendered the interactions between Samson, Dalila, and their respective deities more complex and more specific.

Subtler than the gender and religious nuances of the opera is its dichotomy between the Hebrews and the Philistines. The former are characterized by their moral monotheism and Western music. The Philistines, in contrast, are presented as the "Other" in this work through characters and the music Saint-Saëns composed to portray them, for example, the "Dance of the Priestesses of Dagon" in act 1 and the "Bacchanale" in act 3.[15] This "Orientalist" distinction between "us" and "them" not only reinforces cultural stereotypes, but also assists the disparagement of Dalila by dint of her Philistine heritage. Thus, Saint-Saëns does not need to show Dalila accepting money for her role in Samson's downfall; her status as a loyal Philistine and worshipper of Dagon more than compensates for this omission.

In sum, Saint-Saëns has both removed certain ambiguities of the biblical text and at the same time complicated the story of Samson and Delilah. He does so through confusions of gender and religiosity, as well as the "Orientalist" subtext of the work itself. In so doing, he not only pays homage to the biblical narrative, but he allows us as readers both to augment and to deepen our interaction with the story based on new questions and insights gained from his complex, brilliant, and sometimes unnerving interpretation of Judges 16.

DELILAH IN TWENTIETH-CENTURY POP MUSIC

Retellings of Judges 13–16

In a project of this scope, it is helpful to organize our examples into categories that will allow us to appreciate the renderings of Delilah in a more

---

14. In her work, Baruch views Samson's love for Delilah as, in part, an Oedipal revolt against God as father. See "Forbidden Words—Enchanting Song," 247–48.

15. See Ralph P. Locke, "Constructing the Oriental 'Other': Saint-Saëns's *Samson et Dalila*," *Cambridge Opera Journal* 3 (1991): 261–302.

accessible way. Therefore, I will discuss four different categories of pop songs in what follows. First, I will examine songs that are retellings of Judges 13–16 in its entirety, that is, songs that tell the story of Samson and therein mention Delilah. In this category we find the most recorded interpretation of Delilah: the traditional folk spiritual "discovered" by Alan Lomax on one of his many recording tours of the South in the 1930s and 1940s, variously titled "Samson," "Samson and Delilah," or, usually, "If I Had My Way." In Lomax's compendium of ballads and folk songs of 1941, this interpretation contains six different verses, and Delilah is mentioned in three of them.[16] Basically, the song implicates Delilah in Samson's downfall by showing her sitting on his knee and speaking "kind" and "fair," so that Samson voluntarily tells her the secret of his strength. Even though this tune has been covered by artists as varied as Blind Willie Johnson (1927); the Grateful Dead; the Blasters; Peter, Paul, and Mary; and Bobby Darin, in my opinion the definitive version was recorded by the Reverend Gary Davis:

> Well Delilah, she was a woman, she was fine and fair.
> She had good looks, God knows, and coal-black hair.
> Delilah she gained old Samson's mind.
> When first he saw this woman, you know he couldn't believe his mind.

> Delilah she sat down on Samson's knee,
> Said tell me where your strength lies if you please.
> She spoke so kind, God knows she talked so fair,
> Well Samson said, Delilah you can cut off my hair.
> You can shave my head, clean as my hand
> And my strength'll come natural as any old man.

> If I had my way, if I had my way, if I had my way,
> I would tear this old building down.

In this song, even though Delilah is clearly the instigator of the events leading to Samson's death and seems to be the one shaving his hair, we get no information regarding her motives or feelings.

This changes when we consider the example of a Yiddish radio program of 1945 entitled "Yiddish Melodies in Swing," which contains a song written by Sam Mendoff called "Samson and Delilah." In the bridge and the chorus of the song, we hear not only that Delilah manipulates Samson through giving him wine, but also that she, not a barber and not the Philistines, both cut, his hair and blinds him. Unlike, "If I Had My Way," Mendoff here portrays Delilah as the one who procures the source of Samson's strength, and the one who acts on this knowledge, thus going above

---

16. John A. Lomax and Alan Lomax, collectors and compilers, *Our Singing Country: A Second Volume of American Ballads and Folksongs* (New York: Macmillan, 1941), 6–9.

and beyond the biblical narrative in Judg. 16.21. Thus, in this category of songs, Delilah is given no motivation for her actions, except for a possible dislike of strong men in general, and as such we as listeners are left with catchy tunes proclaiming Delilah as a woman who takes advantage of Samson in order to enact his downfall.

Songs Focusing on Delilah

The second group of songs I will discuss consists of songs that focus exclusively on the character of Delilah. In these songs, Delilah is portrayed as completely responsible for Samson's demise, and she enjoys it, too. Consider the tune "Sam and Delilah" from the musical *Girl Crazy* (1930), with lyrics by Ira Gershwin and music by his brother, George. This song not only takes pains to paint an unflattering portrait of Delilah, calling her a "floozy" in the first line, but also provides her a motive for her actions. In the third verse, we are told that Samson began to "crave . . . his true wife." Not surprisingly, "Delilah, she got jealous / And she tracked him, and hacked him / And dug for Sam a grave." This motive of jealousy is curious, since it is absent from the biblical account, but it serves to render Delilah as a woman who will not stand for her man to think of other women, thus reinforcing the *femme fatale* aspect of Delilah's character.[17] One of the most curious aspects of this song, though, is not its portrayal of Delilah, but rather the warning it gives to its listeners. The last two verses of the song let us know that Delilah is not the only woman in the world who is capable of deceit and murder in the name of passion, and as such the song's listeners had better beware if they are involved with a woman like Delilah.

This warning about Delilah-like women, as well as the advice to "run away" from them, is also found in the 1960 hit by Neil Sedaka, entitled "Run, Samson, Run" (written by Howard Greenfield). Again, Delilah is portrayed as a woman who cheats on her man, who brings about the downfall of Samson. Here she is also called "a demon, a devil in disguise" who takes in the hero "by the angel in her eyes." In the chorus, Sedaka advises Samson to run because "Delilah's on her way," and tells the listener that he would rather trust the lion that Samson had battled than a cheating woman like Delilah. It is in the last verse, though, that Sedaka gets specific in terms of the "moral" of the song, noting that a little bit of Delilah is in every woman.

By noting the dangers inherent in all women because of their presumptive association with Delilah, Sedaka here is not only repeating warnings regarding female behavior found in texts like Ezek. 23.48, but also implying that Delilah and her actions serve as a discordant model for identity. In doing so, Sedaka is holding up Delilah's character out of its textual confines and twisting it into an androcentric cautionary tale, in which certain

---

17. Curiously, this is also the tactic that drives Delilah to cut Samson's hair in Cecil B. DeMille's film *Samson and Delilah* (1949).

kinds of women are not to be trusted, and you had better watch out if you do.

Along with this trend of rendering Delilah as an anti-model for feminine behavior, certain songs in this category also imagine Delilah as a kind of divine, almost goddess-like figure. The theme song for Cecil B. DeMille's film *Samson and Delilah* (1949), sung by Nat King Cole, characterizes Delilah as a "spirit of love . . . timeless love." This portrayal of Delilah as a timeless spirit of love is concretized in DeMille's film, with its portrayal of Delilah as a schizophrenic woman, both obsessed with Samson and detesting him at the same time. Along these same lines, the Irish band Dagda released a song titled "Delilah" in 2001 that specifically calls Delilah a "Goddess of love." The song, though, adopts a fairly standard view of this goddess's actions, attributing Samson's betrayal to Delilah for monetary gain. The song continues in an almost haiku-like fashion by noting, "Your lover you deceived / Cut off his hair / And weaved / A web of treachery." In sum, the songs that focus exclusively on Delilah are not as restricted as the songs that retell the story of Samson in that by dint of their more limited focus, the former are able to emphasize more the motivations of and potential dangers caused by Delilah, not just in the biblical narrative, but in regard to all men.

"Biblical" Songs with Delilah

The third group of songs I will discuss consists of songs that mention Delilah in a biblical context but are not specifically about her. For example, in the soundtrack album to the film *King Creole* (1958), Elvis Presley includes a song called "Hard-Headed Woman" (words and music by Claude Demetrius), which I mentioned in chapter 1. Elvis makes the song's point (women have been trouble for men since the beginning of the world) by singing about three women from the Hebrew Bible: Eve, Delilah, and Jezebel. Speaking of Delilah, Elvis comments, "Now Samson told Delilah / Loud and Clear / 'Keep your cotton pickin' fingers out my curly hair.'" Here, as in each of the second through fourth verses, the song exaggerates or simply adds to the biblical text to make its point, but the implication is clear nonetheless: Delilah is one of the prime examples of a "hard-headed woman" and as such has been a thorn in the side of man forever.

In his song "Modern Day Delilah" of 1981, Van Stephenson offers no ambiguity toward his female subject. The woman he sings about is compared to Delilah, and in the process Stephenson describes some of her more detrimental character traits. He notes that she always keeps her scissors sharp as a razor, and that when she discovers your weakness, "She'll cut you to the quick, stab you in the heart."

While this song pulls no punches in its negative portrayal of the singer's object of distaste, a song by Eddie Cole and the Three Peppers from the late 1940s called "Delilah (with a Capital D)" presents a much more balanced portrayal of the title character. That is, unlike Stephenson, Cole actually describes some of the appealing qualities of his subject before warning his listener about trying to get close to her. In the bridge and last verse of the song, Cole uses wonderful imagery to describe what will happen to someone who seeks to "make time" with this woman, noting that Delilah will pack up her suitor just like cargo freight and then ship him out to sea. Cole also compares Delilah's lure to that of a flower to a bee, but reminds his listeners that even though the flower is attractive, it is the bee that gets stuck.

What we have essentially in these songs are stories about women who have either wronged the singer or whom the singer knows to represent trouble, either because of presumed personal experience or because that's just the way women are. Either way, the use of Delilah as a comparative trope provides a signal to the audience of the woman's capacity for treachery and deception. It tells us to be wary of these women, because they, too, could be like Delilah, and in that regard their message is similar to the songs we discussed earlier that focused exclusively on Delilah.

Songs about "Delilah"

My last category of songs is made up of songs about women who happen to be named Delilah, but which do not mention anything about the biblical text. Surprisingly, several of these songs actually have neutral or even positive views of their eponymous characters. For example, Major Lance's song "Delilah" of 1962 portrays the title character as a big-city girl whom the speaker is trying to woo so that she will return with him to his country town. Similarly, Marshall Crenshaw's album of 1991, *Life's Too Short*, includes a song called "Delilah," and it is a fairly standard love song, as is the song entitled "Delilah" by the self-described lesbian acoustic folk artist Kaia. However, these songs are often overshadowed by the more popular songs found in this category, the first of which is the song "Beautiful Delilah," first written and performed by Chuck Berry, but popularized by both the Kinks and the Rolling Stones. In this song, Berry paints a picture for us of an attractive girl who is as "sweet as apple pie," but "every time you see her she's with a different guy." This young woman is always fashionably attired and lets everyone know about it, too. Thus here we see a subtle use of the name Delilah in that the woman in Berry's song seems to be a temptress and knowledgeable about love, but still she revels in breaking hearts. A more recent example is the hit song "Hey There, Delilah" by the Plain White T's. The mostly acoustic ballad sounds like a love letter from a songwriter to his girlfriend in New York City, and it is filled with words of longing and promises of better times. However, there are no hints that the girlfriend is anything like the typical image of Delilah in the songs I list above. In fact, she seems almost the exact opposite.

The last example I will discuss from this group of songs is arguably the most famous of them all: Tom Jones's megahit "Delilah" of 1967. It tells the story of a man who sees his woman cheating on him and confronts her. She laughs at him, and so he kills her. The images of treachery and betrayal in the song mesh rather well with the portrayal of Delilah in songs I examine that use the biblical text specifically to tell their story of Delilah. Additionally, the violent response of the male narrator corresponds with the violence done to and later by Samson in Judges 16, but here it is reversed. That is, just like Delilah in many of the songs I discuss, this woman betrays her man; yet unlike in these songs, it is the woman who is the victim of violence in this song, not the wronged man. Thus, this song could be making an intertextual comment on the perceived lack of punishment Delilah receives in the biblical narrative.

CONCLUSIONS

In sum, almost all of the pop songs I discuss in this chapter portray Delilah negatively in comparison with the biblical narrative. In these three-to-four-minute interpretations, she is shown most often to be a harlot, a deceiver, and in some songs a warning to all men. By portraying Delilah negatively, these songs not only ignore the multiple interpretations possible of Judges 16, but they also reinscribe Delilah with the traits patriarchal culture most often associates with the classic *femme fatale*. Thus, these renderings eschew ambiguity and the possibility of more equitable readings of Delilah in favor of stereotypical images of deceiving and dangerous women. The net effect of couching such irresponsible messages in popular music is to make their proliferation all the more probable. However, by noting and exploring these renderings, perhaps we can resist the messages they convey at the same time we are tapping our toes.

STUDY QUESTIONS

1. Aside from musical interpretations of Delilah, there are also many artistic renderings that can be examined. Using the art websites I mention in study question 6 on page 27, gather several images of Delilah from different time periods. Which of these images portray Delilah cutting Samson's hair, and which of them show the barber she calls to in 16.19? How is Delilah dressed in the art you find? Is Samson rendered as a bulky, strong man, or does he appear normally built? How do these images affect your understanding of Judges 16?

2. Along with art, Delilah has enjoyed success in film. The most famous depiction of Delilah in film—and perhaps the most influential interpretation of Delilah in the twentieth century—is Cecil B. DeMille's epic *Samson and Delilah* (1949), with Victor Mature and Hedy Lamarr in the title roles.[18] DeMille transforms Delilah into a conniving and jealous

---

18. For more information on this film, see Exum, "Why, Why, Why, Delilah?", 175–237; and Gerald E. Forshey, *American Religious and Biblical Spectaculars* (Media and Society Series; Westport, Conn.: Praeger, 1992), 59–65.

character, completely obsessed by her love for Samson. She loves him and at the same time despises him. After watching the film, try to determine Delilah's motivations for her actions. That is, why does she do what she does? Is she a stable character? Or is she unbalanced? How does DeMille alter the biblical narrative, and why? What could *his* motivation have been? Finally, return to the biblical narrative and gauge how your perceptions have changed. What new issues do you now see? Is your reading different? If so, why?

3. It should be obvious by now that Delilah is a malleable character. That is, different interpreters can and have interpreted her differently, each according to their own interests and ideologies. In order to understand your own ideology, write a brief character sketch of Delilah in which you describe the characteristics and motivations you find in Judges 16. As you write, try to imagine yourself in Delilah's shoes. What would you do if you were approached with a similar offer by those in power? How far would you go? Finally, how would you feel if people vilified you for your actions?

4

"Gee, Baby, Ain't I Good to You?"

Unreturned and Empty Love in the Book of Ruth

RUTH IS A VERY IMPORTANT biblical character for both Jews and Christians. Jews look on Ruth as the paradigmatic convert due to her moving speech in 1.16–17.[1] Christians focus on the concluding genealogy as confirmation of the pedigree of Jesus as provided in Matt. 1.1–17, especially the mention of Ruth therein, in 1.5.[2] The book that bears her name contains one of the most famous expressions of love in the Hebrew Bible. Most commentators have interpreted the love in this story as an example of *chesed* or loyalty between characters that is mutually expressed.[3] However, in this chapter I will argue that this love is not mutually expressed, even though it is a remarkable form of loyalty in that it is a love expressed by a female character (Ruth) for another female character (Naomi), and it is a love expressed by a Moabite for an Israelite. I will contend that Naomi does not reciprocate Ruth's love, nor does Ruth express any love for Boaz; rather her actions toward him are the result of her love for Naomi. Finally,

---

1. The idea of Ruth as the ideal convert is expressed in numerous rabbinic texts and is presupposed by the commentary of Leonard S. Kravitz and Kerry M. Olitzky. See their *Ruth: A Modern Commentary* (New York: URJ Press, 2005), especially 10–11. See also Yitzhak I. Broch, *Ruth: The Book of Ruth in Hebrew and English with a Talmudic-Midrashic Commentary* (2nd ed.; Jerusalem and New York: Feldheim, 1983), 29–30.
2. For various theories as to why Matthew would have included the women he does in the genealogy he provides for Jesus, see Raymond E. Brown, *The Birth of the Messiah: A Commentary on the Infancy Narratives in the Gospels of Matthew and Luke* (updated ed.; ABRL; New York: Doubleday, 1993), 71–74; Kathleen E. Corley, *Private Women, Public Meals: Social Conflict in the Synoptic Tradition* (Peabody, Mass.: Hendrickson, 1993), 147–52; and Amy-Jill Levine, "Matthew," in *The Women's Bible Commentary* (ed. Carol A. Newsom and Sharon H. Ringe; expanded ed. with Apocrypha; Louisville, Ky.: Westminster John Knox Press, 1998), 340–41.
3. See, for example, Katharine Doob Sakenfeld, *Ruth* (IBC; Atlanta: John Knox Press, 1999), 11–14.

I find little evidence that Boaz loves Ruth, even though he marries her. Following this examination of the biblical text, I will examine the ways in which love in Ruth has been interpreted in literature, with a particular focus on young adult and children's literature and videos, as well as a feature film. In this portion of the chapter, I will seek to demonstrate that not only are the relationships in the narrative simplified, but also love in the story is misconstrued in order to achieve a happy ending for this rather loveless tale.

THE BIBLICAL STORY OF RUTH

In the book of Ruth, we are presented with a story revolving around two widows: one an Israelite named Naomi and one a Moabite named Ruth.[4] Naomi and her husband, Elimelech, leave Bethlehem—which means "city of bread" in Hebrew—during a famine and travel to Moab. This is an odd choice for a refuge, since Moab was traditionally an enemy of Israel.[5] Once

---

4. Providing a date for the story of Ruth is perhaps more important than doing so for the other stories I examine in this book. This is mainly due to the fact that the point of the story is tied so closely to its historical situation. There are two main options with regard to the date of the book of Ruth. On the one hand, some scholars argue for a preexilic date, that is, prior to the exile in Babylon, which lasted from 597 to 539 B.C.E. According to this view, Ruth originated as a tale whose purpose was to justify the reign of David and his family. That is, by providing a genealogical link to David and by alluding to heroic women in Israel's past like Tamar, Rachel, and Leah, the author might be trying to legitimate the rule of David. For this position, see Edward F. Campbell Jr., *Ruth* (AB 7; Garden City, N.Y.: Doubleday, 1975), which dates the composition of Ruth from ca. 950 to 700 (23–28). On the other hand, there are scholars who see Ruth as a postexilic tale, that is, as being composed after the return from exile in 539. Key to this view is the story's acceptance of exogamy and its "universal" theme, which resembles Isaiah 40–55 and Jonah. That is, in Ruth we find an Israelite (Boaz) marrying a Moabite (Ruth). Such marriage outside one's kin group is referred to as exogamy, and it was not the norm for Israel prior to the exile. Also, in several pieces of postexilic literature we see God and God's people show a remarkable concern for other countries and their inhabitants, as well as a general acceptance of foreign cultures. The prime example of this line of thought is the book of Jonah. According to this view of the dating of Ruth, the story was composed as an alternative to the insistence on endogamy and the negative view of foreign wives and women found in Ezra and Nehemiah (see Ezra 9.1–10.6; Neh. 13.23–30). For this view, see John Gray, *Joshua, Judges, Ruth* (NCBC; Grand Rapids, Mich.: Eerdmans, 1986), 369; André LaCocque, "Ruth," in *The Feminine Unconventional: Four Subversive Figures in Israel's Tradition* (OBT; Minneapolis: Fortress, 1990), 84–116; and idem, *Ruth: A Continental Commentary* (trans. K. C. Hanson; Minneapolis: Fortress, 2004), 18–28. Of these two alternatives, a majority agrees with the former, that is, that Ruth was composed in the preexilic period. However, in my opinion, the story could have been composed during the monarchy but then altered to fit a postexilic situation, when it was probably committed to writing. As such, Ruth addresses concerns of marginality and oppression, of immigration and equal rights. In sum, Ruth "is a document for the minorities of every time and every place. . . . The book of Ruth is anti-establishment" (LaCocque, *Ruth*, 27).

5. In fact, enmity between Israel and Moab can be traced back to the story of Lot and his daughters in Gen. 19.30–38. Therein, Lot's daughters, who were under the impression that the world had been destroyed because of the destruction of Sodom and Gomorrah in 19.24–25,

in Moab, Elimelech dies, and Naomi's sons, Mahlon and Chilion, marry Moabite women named Orpah and Ruth. The narrative takes another sad turn, as we are told that both sons die, "so that the woman [Naomi] was left without her two sons and her husband" (1.5).[6] Naomi's situation is quite precarious: she is in a foreign land without the protection of her husband or her adult sons, and from the context of the story we gather that she is also postmenopausal, meaning she is unable to bear any more children. Within the patriarchal ideology of the period, not only would these factors render her in danger because she has no male family to "look after" her, but she would also be considered virtually useless in terms of contributing to the economic well-being of society.[7] In short, Naomi's existence is now in jeopardy.

As such, Naomi makes the decision to return to Israel and tells her two daughters-in-law to remain in Moab. They are still young enough that they can bear children and secure their place within the patriarchal society. Weeping, both daughters object and say they will go with her. Naomi demurs and explains to them that she has nothing more to offer a husband, that life has become "bitter" for her "because the hand of the LORD has turned against me" (1.13). Orpah heeds Naomi's advice and returns home. Ruth in contrast clings to her (1.14) and refuses to leave her. In one of the most moving speeches in the biblical literature, Ruth, the childless Moabite widow, pledges her loyalty to her widowed Israelite mother-in-law and perhaps even her allegiance to Naomi's God:[8]

> Do not press me to leave you
> > or to turn back from following you!
> Where you go, I will go;
> > Where you lodge, I will lodge;
> your people shall be my people,
> > and your God my God.
> Where you die, I will die—
> > there will I be buried.

---

get their father drunk and have intercourse with him in the hopes of repopulating the world. One of the offspring of this intoxicated, incestuous encounter is a boy named Moab—the progenitor of the country that bears his name. The story of Balaam in Numbers 22ff. also evinces tension between the two countries. More specific to our story, Deut. 23.3 specifically states, "No Ammonite or Moabite shall be admitted to the assembly of the Lord. Even to the tenth generation, none of their descendants shall be admitted to the assembly of the Lord."

6. All biblical quotes are taken from the NRSV.

7. The standard introduction to the ideology and historical development of patriarchy remains Gerda Lerner, *The Creation of Patriarchy* (New York and Oxford: Oxford University Press, 1986).

8. As I noted above, these verses are the basis for the view that Ruth converts to Naomi's faith. For this issue, see Campbell, *Ruth*, 80–82.

> May the LORD do thus and so to me,
>> and more as well,
> if even death parts me from you! (1.16–17)[9]

Curiously, Naomi's response to this heartfelt soliloquy is silence. The text tells us that "she said no more to her" (1.18). Dalila Nayap-Pot, in her rumination on biblical women and women's communities in Central America, claims that Naomi's attitude toward Ruth may be a result of her own sense of loss:

> She was so embittered at the loss of her three male loved ones that she forgot to care for the two women in her adopted family! Self-rejection causes us to reject others, even those we love and who love us. While Naomi offered the young women their freedom, perhaps with a sense of guilt at having involved them in her family tragedy (1.13), she did not offer them the possibility of sharing the risk of a new life with her in a new land, *just as she herself had done years before*.[10]

In their work, Danna Nolan Fewell and David M. Gunn express puzzlement over Naomi's response and ask:

> Why should the altruism of Ruth reduce an altruistic Naomi to silent withdrawal? For she speaks not a word to, or about, Ruth from this point to the end of the scene in the arrival in Bethlehem. If Ruth's famous "Where you go, I go; your god, my god" speech can melt the hearts of a myriad preachers and congregations down the centuries, why not Naomi's heart?[11]

In a similar vein, Katharine Doob Sakenfeld writes:

> There is no direct indication that Naomi is inwardly pleased or displeased with Ruth's decision, but *the texture of the larger narrative presses toward displeasure* or, at the very best, ambivalence. Ruth has not accepted the advice of a wiser, older woman, the advice of a woman who in that culture may have held authority over her.[12]

Finally, Kirstin Nielsen notes:

> Naomi's reaction to Ruth's declaration is ambiguous. On the one hand she abandons her attempt to dissuade Ruth and bows to her wishes, on the other hand *there is not a single word in the chapter to show that Ruth's love is returned*, or even that Naomi just accepts her company. Her silence creates a

---

9. The implications of Ruth's decision here are stated nicely by Phyllis Trible in her "A Human Comedy," in *God and the Rhetoric of Sexuality* (OBT; Philadelphia: Fortress, 1978), 173.

10. Nayap-Pot, "Life in the Midst of Death: Naomi, Ruth, and the Plight of Indigenous Women," in *Vernacular Hermeneutics* (ed. R. S. Sugirtharajah; Sheffield: Sheffield Academic Press, 1999), 60.

11. Danna Nolan Fewell and David M. Gunn, "'A Son Is Born to Naomi!' Literary Allusions and Interpretation in the Book of Ruth," in *Women in the Hebrew Bible: A Reader* (ed. Alice Bach; New York and London: Routledge, 1999), 234.

12. Sakenfeld, *Ruth*, 34–35, italics mine.

tension in the story that leads the reader to ask how this unusual relationship can possibly develop.[13]

All of these commentators point to a large gap in the narrative here, as Naomi does not reciprocate the love and loyalty Ruth clearly shows her in 1.16–17. In my opinion, there is no sincere response from Naomi here because Naomi has no sincere feelings for Ruth.[14]

The narrative skips over what must have been an arduous journey for the two women, traveling alone the several days and nights it would have taken them to make the trip. Since Naomi evidently was not speaking to Ruth during this period, the crossing from her country to a strange new land in which she could expect nothing but revulsion must have been especially difficult for Ruth. We can only speculate as to the care Ruth must have provided for Naomi during this journey, but it must have been difficult for Ruth to assist her mother-in-law so loyally and receive silence in return. When the women arrive in Bethlehem, the women of the town engage Naomi in conversation, asking in disbelief, "Is this Naomi?" Naomi's response to the women plays on 1.13, as she says:

> Call me no longer Naomi,
> > call me Mara,
> > for the Almighty has dealt bitterly with me.
> I went away full,
> > but the LORD has brought me back empty;
> why call me Naomi
> > when the LORD has dealt harshly with me,
> > and the Almighty has brought calamity upon me? (1.20–22)

"Mara" is the Hebrew word for "bitter," and as such Naomi is announcing a new attitude and orientation: she is no longer Naomi in that she no longer possesses the relations and possessions she once had. Now she is simply "bitter." Her complaint against God is not without parallel in the Hebrew Bible, as many commentators have noted.[15] More interestingly for our purpose, though, is the claim that she went away full, but now has returned empty. Given Ruth's presence during this speech, as well as her sacrifice and care for Naomi, Naomi's claim that she is now empty seems at

---

13. Kirsten Nielsen, *Ruth* (OTL; Philadelphia: Westminster, 1997), 50, italics mine.
14. For a contrasting opinion, see LaCocque, *Ruth*, 54. LaCocque claims that Naomi's silence "does not betray her bad mood, but a deliberate discretion. Speaking with Ruth now could only encourage her, even indirectly, in her decision to abandon everything. . . . Silence alone is the appropriate attitude in the face of such a sacrifice. Besides, Ruth's words are infused with such emotional importance that they cannot be followed by Naomi's replies, which could only be disappointing." In his commentary, Tod Linafelt claims that we simply do not have enough information to decide on Naomi's internal attitude here. See Tod Linafelt, "Ruth," in *Ruth and Esther* (by Tod Linafelt and Timothy K. Beal; Berit Olam; Collegeville, Minn.: Liturgical Press, 1999), 16–17.
15. See, for example, Linafelt, "Ruth," 20.

the least to overlook Ruth, and at the most to disparage her. Why would Naomi not mention or introduce her loving daughter-in-law once she returns to Bethlehem? Fewell and Gunn argue that Naomi's speech is centered on her own "bitter sense of deprivation." As such, "she sees herself alone. . . . At the heart of Naomi's speech is Naomi."[16] Edward F. Campbell Jr. sees Naomi's speech as an ironic inclusion by the narrator: "Almost playfully, but certainly with delicious irony, the story-teller brings down the curtain on Act I with Naomi complaining about her emptiness while Ruth, the very person who will bring about an end to Naomi's emptiness, stands there, apparently unnoticed."[17] Sakenfeld opines that Naomi might not mention Ruth because of Ruth's status as a foreigner. She writes that when the women arrive in Bethlehem,

> Naomi makes no acknowledgment of Ruth. She subsequently gives Ruth permission to go gleaning (2:2), but with a terseness that is noticeable in a book filled with many longer speech quotations. . . . Naomi's silence may be interpreted as despair, anger, or resignation—in her own word, bitterness. For Naomi, Ruth's presence is as much a reminder of tragedy as it is a potential comfort. Naomi has no idea how she herself will be received upon returning to Bethlehem, and now she has also a foreign companion to be explained. She may have realized that if Ruth had stayed in Moab, perhaps no one in Judah would have learned of her sons' marriages.[18]

In sum, Naomi could be embarrassed by Ruth because she is a foreigner; she could hate Ruth because of the hateful and potential disreputable past she and her family experienced in Moab; or she could simply be registering her dislike of Ruth for both of these reasons. Perhaps Naomi feels that Ruth is a liability to the pursuance of a new life in Bethlehem; that is, what happened in Moab should stay in Moab. Evidently the narrator wishes to emphasize that last point, because at the end of chapter 1, Ruth is again referred to as "the Moabite" who returned with Naomi "from the country of Moab," as if to distinguish her from the rest of the women in Bethlehem.

Chapter 1 ends by noting that it was "the beginning of the barley harvest."[19] At the beginning of chapter 2 this chronological setting is fleshed out, as we learn that Ruth is preparing to glean grain to provide sustenance

16. Fewell and Gunn, "'A Son Is Born to Naomi!'" 234.

17. Campbell, *Ruth*, 84.

18. Sakenfeld, *Ruth*, 35.

19. The mention of the beginning of the harvest leads to the practice in Judaism of reciting the book of Ruth on Shavuot, which is an early summer festival usually held forty-nine days after Pesach (Passover), on 6 Sivan (May–June). Shavuot is also known by its Christian appellation as Pentecost, and it commemorates the Mosaic covenant, since it is considered the day that the Torah was given on Mount Sinai. As such, Shavuot celebrates redemption, as does the book of Ruth. For a more detailed rumination of the relationship between Ruth and Shavuot, see Judith A. Kates, "Women at the Center: Ruth and Shavuot," in *Reading Ruth: Contemporary Women Reclaim a Sacred Story* (ed. Judith A. Kates and Gail Twersky Reimer; New York: Ballantine Books, 1994), 187–98.

for herself and Naomi.[20] As Sakenfeld mentions above, Naomi finally speaks to Ruth in 2.2, when she gives a brief permission for Ruth to glean. Given Ruth's request, one would expect Naomi to be more grateful. By luck, Ruth begins to glean in a field owned by Boaz, whom the narrator describes as "a kinsman on her [Naomi's] husband's side, a prominent rich man" (2.1). In fact, twice in 2.1–3 we are told that Boaz is "of the family of Elimelech." In contrast, between 2.1 and 2.6, the narrator mentions either that Ruth is from Moab or that she is a Moabite three times. Clearly familial and national affiliations play a large role in this story.

Boaz appears on the scene and asks after Ruth. The form of his question is significant; he asks, "To whom does this young woman belong?" (2.5). As such, it is clear that the system of patriarchy in Moab I mentioned above is also in effect in Israel. One of his servants identifies Ruth and tells Boaz of her connection to Naomi. Based on this information as well as her sturdy work habits, Boaz approaches Ruth in 2.8 and proceeds to offer her both advice and protection. The latter would have been especially welcome, since as a foreign widow Ruth could have been the target of abuse and perhaps unwanted sexual advances. That this was the case is verified by the language Boaz uses in 2.9. The NRSV translates a portion of this verse as "I have ordered the young men not to bother you," but the verb rendered here as "bother" is better translated as "molest."[21] When Ruth asks why Boaz is being so kind to her, he tells her:

> All that you have done for your mother-in-law since the death of your husband has been fully told me, and how you left your father and mother and your native land and came to a people that you did not know before. May the LORD reward you for your deeds, and may you have a full reward from the LORD, the God of Israel, under whose wings you have come for refuge! (2.11–12)

Here, perhaps for the first time, Ruth hears an Israelite recognize and praise her for her commitment to Naomi. As Sakenfeld notes, Boaz here is complimenting Ruth on her acts of *chesed*.[22] Boaz's blessing even plays on Naomi's earlier speech, as he wishes Ruth to have "a full reward," whereas Naomi complains of her emptiness.

Based on and perhaps inspired by Ruth's acts of *chesed* toward Naomi, Boaz then goes above and beyond what he is required to do for gleaners according to Mosaic law. He asks Ruth to eat and drink with his reapers

---

20. For the biblical background and laws pertaining to gleaning, see Sakenfeld, *Ruth*, 39. She correctly notes that several texts—including Lev. 19.9–10; 23.22; and Deut. 24.19–22—mandate gleaning as a kind of charity to the poor, but only certain types of gleaning were allowed.

21. See Amy-Jill Levine, "Ruth," in Newsom and Ringer, *Women's Bible Commentary*, 87. Levine also notes that the word "reproach" in 2.15 "might be better translated 'abuse' or 'shame.'" See also Sakenfeld, *Ruth*, 43. For a contrasting view on the meaning of the word translated as "bother," see Jack M. Sasson, *Ruth: A New Translation with a Philological Commentary and a Formalist-Folklorist Interpretation* (2nd ed.; Sheffield: Sheffield Academic Press, 1995), 50.

22. Sakenfeld, *Ruth*, 44.

and then instructs his servants to allow her to glean not only among "the standing sheaves," but also from sheaves that he instructs them to scatter from their own bundles on the ground on her behalf. Throughout all this, Ruth is appropriately humble, and Boaz seems genuinely impressed with her actions.

Ruth gleans all day in Boaz's field and returns home with an abundance of grain, probably enough to "feed two people for about five to seven days."[23] After Ruth provides food for her, Naomi finally speaks to her in 2.19, asking her where she had worked to glean so much. When Ruth replies that she has been in Boaz's field, Naomi excitedly responds, "Blessed be he by the LORD, whose kindness [chesed] has not forsaken the living or the dead! . . . The man is a relative of ours, one of our nearest kin" (2.20). Evidently Naomi is no longer angry with God, as she was in 1.20–21. Neither does Naomi seem displeased with Ruth anymore, as the use of plural pronouns in Naomi's speech shows. That is, whereas Naomi earlier had ignored Ruth, now she includes Ruth by using words like "our."[24] The translation of Naomi's claim regarding Boaz clouds the issue. Instead of "one of our nearest kin," the Hebrew text literally reads, "one with the right to redeem" (gō'ēl). This rather confusing reading (made more so by the plural suffix: "one of our redeemers") could refer to the practice of levirate marriage, as described in Deut. 25.5–10.[25] Put briefly, if a married man dies without siring a son to whom he can leave the patrimony (lands, monies, and other property), then his closest male relative (usually a brother) can marry and have sex with his widow for procreative purposes in the hopes that the act will result in the conception of a male son, who will then legally be considered the dead husband's offspring. In the case of Ruth, it is not clear at this point what responsibilities Boaz bears toward either her or Naomi. As we shall see, this idea of levirate marriage found in Deuteronomy 25 seems very different from the idea of the "one with the right to redeem" presented in Ruth.[26] More specifically, the term used to describe Boaz, gō'ēl, is not the same as the levir in Deuteronomy 25, as the gō'ēl has specific responsibilities that deal primarily with property, but not with marriage.[27] That is, in Leviticus 25 the gō'ēl is said to be someone who can "redeem" hereditary land that has been sold. In other words, the gō'ēl can buy back ancestral lands that have been sold due to financial

---

23. Ibid., 46.

24. See Nielsen, *Ruth*, 63.

25. For this issue generally, see Richard Kamlin, "Levirate Law," in *The Anchor Bible Dictionary* (ed. David Noel Freedman et al.; New York: Doubleday, 1992), 4:296–97. Later rabbinic interpreters also were interested in this issue, and for a summary of their views as expressed in the Mishnah (the collection of rabbinic legal opinions and scriptural interpretations codified by Judah ha-Nasi in approximately the second century C.E.), see Judith Romney Wegner, "The Levirate Widow," in *Chattel or Person? The Status of Women in the Mishnah* (Oxford and New York: Oxford University Press, 1988), 97–113.

26. LaCocque, "Ruth," 93–99.

27. See Linafelt, "Ruth," 56; Nielsen, *Ruth*, 74–76; and Sakenfeld, *Ruth*, 48–49.

hardships so that the land remains in the family. The *gōʾēl* would not keep the land, but rather purchase it for his relative.

The third chapter begins with an extended speech from Naomi outlining her plan for/to Ruth based on the revelation that Ruth has been working in Boaz's field. The motivation given by Naomi is that she desires "security" for Ruth, so that "it may be well with" her (3.1). Security in this context certainly refers to gaining a husband for Ruth so that she can be ensured of the protections such a relationship offers in an androcentric (that is, male-centered) culture.[28] As we shall see, though, Naomi's motivation probably has more to do with her own self-preservation than with any altruistic feelings for Ruth. Naomi's specific instructions deserve to be heard in full. She tells Ruth:

> Now wash and anoint yourself, and put on your best clothes and go down to the threshing floor; but do not make yourself known to the man [Boaz] until he has finished eating and drinking. When he lies down, observe the place where he lies; then, go and uncover his feet and lie down; and he will tell you what to do. (3.3–4)

As many commentators have noted, this plan is "dangerous and deceptive" for reasons I shall mention below.[29] The preparations Naomi outlines have parallels in several ancient Near Eastern texts, including biblical texts, which describe preparations for either sexual encounters or marriage.[30] The location specified by Naomi also has symbolic meaning. As I said earlier, the agricultural setting of the story is the early summer harvest festival of barley. Then, as today, barley was one of the key ingredients of beer, and as such there would have been alcoholic consumption during this festival. Also, there is evidence that ritual sexual activity, most likely associated with agricultural fertility, was enjoyed as a part of this festival.[31] This ritualized sex was known to have been performed on the very threshing floor to which Naomi sends Ruth. It is also important to realize that Naomi specifically tells Ruth to wait until Boaz has "finished eating and drinking," that is, until he is filled, content, possibly intoxicated, and drowsy. In short, until he is likely to be most susceptible to Ruth's feminine advances.[32]

---

28. See the contextually sensitive comments in Sakenfeld, *Ruth*, 55–56.

29. See Danna Nolan Fewell and David M. Gunn, *Compromising Redemption: Relating Characters in the Book of Ruth* (LCBIS; Louisville, Ky.: Westminster John Knox Press, 1990), 99.

30. For these parallels, see Linafelt, "Ruth," 49; Nielsen, *Ruth*, 68; Sakenfeld, *Ruth*, 53–54; and Sasson, *Ruth*, 68. Campbell, *Ruth*, points out that other texts of Ruth—specifically a type of text called the Lucianic texts—mention that Ruth should anoint herself with myrrh, which he then connect to various texts in the Song of Songs (120). Finally, for other postexilic texts dealing with women anointing themselves with cosmetics in preparation for encounters with men (including Susanna 17; Jdt. 10.3; and Esth. 2.3, 9, and 12), see my *The Good, the Bold, and the Beautiful: The Story of Susanna and Its Renaissance Interpretations* (Library of Hebrew Bible/Old Testament Studies 430; New York and London: T & T Clark, 2006), 64–65.

31. See Hosea 9.1 and Nielsen, *Ruth*, 67.

32. For more background on the phrase "he was in a contented mood," see Linafelt, "Ruth," 51.

Ruth is to "uncover his feet and lie down" and then wait for Boaz's instructions. Much ink has been spilled over what Naomi is asking Ruth to do here exactly. Most commentators agree that Naomi asks Ruth not only to place herself in a precarious situation—since this is not normally acceptable behavior for a respectable woman, and if she were rebuffed by Boaz, her reputation would be shattered—but also to place Boaz in a "*test* situation," that is, to gauge his willingness to aid Ruth and Naomi by extreme means.[33] More specifically, what does the text mean by "uncover his feet"? In his commentary, Campbell writes that the word rendered as "feet" in 3.4

> appears elsewhere in the [Hebrew Bible] only at Dan 10:6 where it is paired with "arms" and must mean "legs." This noun is etymologically related to the common noun *regel*, "foot," which can serve as a euphemism for the penis or the vulva, either as sexual organs or as the urinary opening.[34]

So Naomi could be instructing Ruth to wait until Boaz has had a few beers, go to the place where ritual sex is often practiced, uncover his private parts, and then wait for him to tell her what to do next.[35] If this is the case, then Naomi's plan is not simply dangerous; it is scandalous. Is she, to use a modern term, "pimping" Ruth out in order to secure a husband for her? If so, what is her motive? Is she concerned with Ruth's security (3.1) or her own?[36] These questions raise the related question, what options were available to Naomi in seeking this security?[37] Could she have simply gone to

---

33. The phrase is that of LaCocque, *Ruth*, 88. See also Sakenfeld, *Ruth*, 54.

34. Campbell, *Ruth*, 121. The biblical examples he provides include Judg. 3.24; 1 Sam. 24.3; 2 Kgs. 18.27 (and the parallel in Isa. 36.12); Isa. 7.20; Ezek. 16.25; and perhaps also Exod. 4.25; Deut. 28.57; and Isa. 6.2.

35. For a different reading of this section, see Nielsen, *Ruth*, 67–71. Nielsen argues that Ruth uncovers her own genitalia and then asks Boaz to cover her.

36. Sasson answers this question with no reservations: "Naomi was not concerned about resolving her own problem when she sent Ruth on her 'sentimental' journey; her instructions to Ruth were motivated only by her desire to seek a happy future for one who risked all in her behalf" (*Ruth*, 83). Obviously, I disagree with this reading as I find Naomi much more self-centered than Sasson does.

37. This discussion of the options open to women in this story for achieving a measure of security in a patriarchal culture also brings up the analogy between Naomi's plan and the story of Tamar in Genesis 38. Scholars have long noted a relationship between these two stories; for example, see Nielsen, *Ruth*, 12–17; and LaCocque, "Ruth," 105. In both chapters, a woman is seeking security in a patriarchal society by using what would have been considered inappropriate sexual methods. Ruth sneaks to the threshing floor at night and uncovers Boaz's "feet." Tamar dresses in a veil, and her father-in-law, Judah, takes her to be a prostitute. It is uncertain if Tamar dressed as a prostitute or even if she desired to be mistaken for one. In both cases, the women receive the protection for which they long. Ruth marries Boaz and has a son, Obed. Tamar conceives twin boys from her encounter with Judah, one of whom (Perez) becomes an ancestor to David (see Ruth 4.18–21). In both stories, then, these women use subversive means to achieve a place within the patriarchal society that for various reasons had denied them that place; that is, Ruth is a Moabite and Tamar is linked to the deaths of two husbands. Interestingly, though, most commentators do not fault Ruth for her course of action, and most seem to vilify Tamar for hers. For a more balanced view, see Johanna W. H. Bos, "Out of the Shadows: Genesis 38; Judges 4:17–22; Ruth 3," *Semeia* 42 (1988): 37–67.

Boaz and proposed a union between him and Ruth? In her work, Phyllis Trible suggests that perhaps Naomi does not seek out Boaz because she is a woman of her times and as such waits for Boaz to act.[38] Since Naomi and Boaz never meet in this narrative, such an assertion seems reasonable, but the bold initiative taken by Naomi in chapter 3 seems to belie such timidity. Sakenfeld, however, makes a more convincing argument as to why Naomi does not deal directly with Boaz. She notes that

> it is easy to imagine that Naomi would expect to be rebuffed if she approached Boaz herself on Ruth's behalf. . . . His status as a *gō'ēl* ["one with a right to redeem"] does not place him under obligation of custom to marry Ruth, nor is she under such obligation to him. For Naomi to ask Boaz to marry her Moabite daughter-in-law might seem to him the height of foolishness. The occasion at the threshing floor, although fraught with great risk, will provide maximum opportunity for encouraging Boaz toward the desired goal.[39]

Some readers, recalling our discussion of Deuteronomy 25 earlier, might protest Sakenfeld's claim that Boaz is under no obligation to marry Ruth. However, we saw above that Boaz, as one of the ones who can redeem (*gō'ēl*), that is, one of the close male relatives of Elimelech, Naomi's dead husband, is not legally required to marry Naomi or Ruth. As such, the levirate law of marriage in Deuteronomy would apply neither to Ruth nor to Naomi. Such a marriage between Naomi and Boaz would be futile in any case, since Naomi is beyond her childbearing years. So if any security is to be had by Naomi, it must come through Ruth. That is, if Naomi is to again enjoy the safety and rights afforded to women via male protection in a patriarchal society, she must do so through establishing a household for Ruth. In her opinion, the best way to do so is to arrange a nocturnal encounter between Boaz and Ruth.[40] In other words, she knows that Boaz is a *gō'ēl* and that Ruth has gained his admiration by working in his field. She also knows that it is unlikely that any other man would be interested in Ruth because of her ethnicity as a Moabite. As LaCocque argues, Naomi bets everything that Boaz's social conscience will force him to choose not to abide by the prevailing views of the time regarding the value of foreign women, particularly those views voiced in Ezra and Nehemiah.[41] Naomi hopes that Boaz will choose to engage Ruth sexually and thereby either impregnate her or begin a relationship that will result in marriage.[42] Either result would end with Naomi, and Ruth, receiving the protection and benefits of being included in Boaz's household.

---

38. Trible, "Human Comedy," 179.
39. Sakenfeld, *Ruth*, 55.
40. This is precisely why LaCocque argues persuasively that the story of Ruth offers a revitalized interpretation of Deuteronomy 25, in effect updating the concept of the levir to the post-exilic period. See "Ruth," 101–2.
41. LaCocque, *Ruth*, 88.
42. See Fewell and Gunn, "'A Son Is Born to Naomi!'" 238: "entrapment is the goal" of Naomi's plan.

Ruth's terse response to Naomi's plan ("All that you tell me I will do") sets the plan into motion. At first, Ruth does seem to follow Naomi's advice. She goes to the threshing floor, finds Boaz, uncovers his feet, and lies down. Boaz is understandably startled when he awakens, especially if Ruth has indeed uncovered his genitalia, and asks her who she is. Her response marks a significant departure from Naomi's plan. Naomi had instructed Ruth to do whatever Boaz told her to do; most likely she assumed that Boaz would then initiate a sexual encounter with Ruth, and her instructions are specific: Ruth should let him. However, Ruth's reply subverts Naomi's commands. Ruth says, "I am Ruth, your servant; spread your cloak over your servant, for you are next-of-kin" (3.9). Ruth had already referred to herself humbly as Boaz's servant in chapter 2. It is the strange-sounding request to "spread your cloak over your servant" that is key here. Interpreters agree that this is a stylized way of proposing marriage.[43] As such, Ruth has rejected Naomi's advice by not giving Boaz the chance to suggest any sexual activity and has simply skipped to the main thrust of the entire encounter by asking Boaz to marry her. By following this request immediately with the revelation that he is one of the ones with the right to redeem, Ruth is making not only a situational plea but also a legal argument. However, as I note above, the term *gō'ēl* does not imply any marital responsibilities. Rather, as Nielsen writes,

> the duty of the kinsman-redeemer [*go‾'e‾l*] is to intervene in the purchase or sale of property, fields, or houses, as well as in the case of a relative forced to sell himself as a slave; but the redeemer does not appear to be duty-bound to marry a childless widow unless he is at the same time the woman's brother-in-law.[44]

It is precisely at this point that we must make an interpretive choice. Should we claim that Ruth is mistaken in attributing the responsibility of marriage to the traditional duties of the *gō'ēl*? Or should we, as Nielsen and LaCocque do, claim that Ruth (or the story's author) is using this opportunity to argue that the duties of the *gō'ēl* should be expanded to include matrimony?[45] Given the sociocultural context of the narrative, I believe the latter option is to be preferred. That is, the author of the story is using the character of Ruth to make a point about how Israelites should be acting in the postexilic period, namely, in a more compassionate way, especially when it comes to foreign women.

---

43. See Nielsen, *Ruth*, 73; Sakenfeld, *Ruth*, 58–59; and Sasson, *Ruth*, 81. In his commentary, Linafelt argues that the text is ambiguous here and could support another, more risqué meaning. Specifically, the word translated as "cloak" (*kānāp*) can also mean "wing" and "literally means an 'extension' or 'extremity,'" and "may itself, like 'feet,' be a euphemism for male genitalia"; that is, *kānāp* could mean an extended penis ("Ruth," 54–55).
44. Nielsen, *Ruth*, 75.
45. LaCocque, "Ruth," 102; and Nielsen, *Ruth*, 76.

Obviously, a woman, especially a foreign one, proposing marriage was not common practice at this time, but Boaz's response shows no distaste. He praises her *chesed* in approaching him rather than a younger man. He also informs her that there is a *gō'ēl* who is a closer kin relation than he is, but promises that if this unnamed man abdicates his responsibilities as *gō'ēl*, then he will assume them. The logic here is interesting and again seems to belie the oft-held assumption that Ruth loves Boaz and vice versa. First, Boaz praises Ruth's loyalty, her *chesed*, for seeking him out instead of a younger, more suitable man. Why should her proposal to Boaz represent an act of loyalty? Precisely because she

> was not regarded as under legal obligation to marry a relative of her dead husband within the rules of levirate marriage. Her willingness to marry Boaz goes beyond the call of duty; clearly the marriage will ensure Naomi's security, not just her own. Thus it is an act of loyalty, greater because it provides for long-range security beyond the short-term solution of gleaning and greater because it clarifies the depth of Ruth's commitment to the promises she made to Naomi.[46]

As such, the loyalty to which Boaz refers is Ruth's loyalty to Naomi, not him. Therefore, it is not unreasonable to claim that Ruth proposes to Boaz out of her dedication to Naomi, not out of love for Boaz, as both Sasson and LaCocque do.[47] Similarly, and second, Boaz's response betrays no emotional love for Ruth. Certainly there is admiration, but if he was in love with Ruth, why would he proffer the possibility that he might not act as *gō'ēl* to her in 3.13?[48] In other words, his acceptance of her offer reads to me like an enthusiastic response to a business deal rather than an exuberant approval of her proposal.[49] Even his request that Ruth stay until morning does not seem to be a sexual advance or a romantic gesture. He is concerned

---

46. Sakenfeld, *Ruth*, 61–62. Against this reading, see Linafelt, "Ruth," 57–58. Linafelt sees Boaz's response as "flustered" and claims that he "is expressing his gratitude for Ruth's interest in him" (57).

47. Sasson writes, "What may be implied here is that Ruth's identification of Boaz, her choice as husband, as a *gō'ēl* for her mother-in-law, was meant to resolve Naomi's search for a *gō'ēl*. If Ruth was at all anxious to retain bonds with Naomi, it must have occurred to her that the best way to achieve such an end was to have her prospective husband act as Naomi's *gō'ēl*" (*Ruth*, 84). See also LaCocque: "Here again, Ruth shows her [*chesed*], not blind romance. Her choice is motivated by other criteria that will become clearer in the ensuing story, knowing Boaz's noble character, his fidelity toward the Law, his devotedness to the customs of his people, and his compassion for the widow and the poor. Ruth considers these qualities of the man, which she recognizes by intuition and by experience (see chap. 2), as more important than being physically attracted and than being well matched with regard to age" (*Ruth*, 98).

48. Again, Linafelt argues against this reading. Instead, he claims Boaz implies that if the other *gō'ēl* honors his obligations, then he will still marry Ruth. That is, the responsibilities of the *gō'ēl* are focused solely on land, not marriage. See "Ruth," 59.

49. Against this reading, see LaCocque, *Ruth*, 100–101. This reading obviously raises the question of why Boaz would agree to marry Ruth if he did not necessarily love her. In my opinion, his rationale is based on his understanding of both his duties as a *gō'ēl* and his understanding of Torah. For Boaz, then, marrying Ruth is both a legal and a religious obligation, as we shall see below.

with Ruth's reputation, as is clear from 3.14, and he does send her home with even more grain, but again, the entire episode seems to me to be devoid of loving anticipation and passionate expectancy. Rather, it has the tone of a friendly, albeit unusually intimate, contract discussion. Alta C. van Dyk and Peet J. van Dyk claim as much in their work. They posit four different ways of reading chapter 3, and reading from the "male perspective," they find in this chapter "a plot by two women to trap Boaz into something he was reluctant to do. Although Boaz was initially interested in Ruth, and his kindness and gentlemanly disposition caused him to treat Ruth in the kindest possible way, this interest did not necessarily extend to a romantic involvement!"[50] According to this way of reading, Boaz's courtesy, politeness, and high regard for Torah made him the perfect "mark" for Ruth and Naomi. Even though I do not agree with all aspects of this scenario, I do find the van Dyks' suggestion that Boaz was not romantically interested in Ruth quite persuasive.

This platonic tone between Boaz and Ruth is evident when Ruth relates to Naomi what happened. As Sakenfeld writes, "Rhetorically and narratively, what is central to the report about the meeting at the threshing floor is not that Boaz agreed to the plan for Ruth's marriage, but rather what is revealed in v. 17b: Boaz is concerned to provide for Naomi."[51] She continues, "Boaz's explanation of his gift of grain provides a sure clue that he joins Ruth in her concern for Naomi; he is not focused on Ruth alone."[52] As such, the interests of the narrative itself belie the assumption that the encounter on the threshing floor is a romantic one focused solely on Ruth and Boaz. Instead, the concern of the narrative—as well as Ruth's and Boaz's concern—centers on Naomi and providing for her. Naomi's response to Ruth's report is simply, "Wait, my daughter, until you learn how the matter turns out, for the man will not rest, but will settle the matter today" (3.18). Here is no motherly exuberance at the prospect of a daughter's nuptials, but rather a matter-of-fact piece of advice, entirely in keeping with Naomi's overall rather distant and unloving attitude toward Ruth. In fact, Ruth's exchange with Naomi in 3.16–18 is the last quoted speech from either character in the story. When we move into chapter 4, they are consistently treated as objects, never speaking, talked about but not to.

In the last chapter of our story, we move into a world of men and official proceedings. Since women have been so central to the narrative thus far, such an abrupt change is somewhat jarring. The chapter begins with Boaz locating the unnamed gō'ēl, whom he simply calls "so-and-so,"[53] who

---

50. Alta C. van Dyk and Peet J. van Dyk, "HIV/AIDS in Africa: Suffering Women and the Theology of the Book of Ruth," *Old Testament Essays* 15, (2002) no. 1 219.
51. Sakenfeld, *Ruth*, 65.
52. Ibid., 66.
53. Sakenfeld correctly notes that it is impossible that Boaz does not know this man's name, so not naming him in the story must suit the narrative purpose of devaluing him in order to focus more specifically on Boaz. See *Ruth*, 68–69. See also Campbell, *Ruth*, 141–43; and Sasson, *Ruth*, 105–7. Nielsen views the anonymity of the man as pejorative (*Ruth*, 82–83).

is a closer relation to Elimelech than he is, and asking him to sit at the gates of the city, the traditional location of official business.[54] Boaz also asks that a quorum of ten male elders of the city act as witnesses to what is about to transpire. Boaz then informs the anonymous *gō'ēl* that Naomi has returned from Moab and wants to sell the land of Elimelech. This unnamed *gō'ēl*, according to custom, has the opportunity to purchase the land, as Boaz notes. The *gō'ēl* agrees to do so, but Boaz sneakily adds that when he does so, he will also acquire Naomi's daughter-in-law "Ruth the Moabite, the widow of the dead man, to maintain the dead man's name on his inheritance" (4.5).[55] The *gō'ēl* then demurs, noting that if he acquires Ruth, it will damage his own inheritance. This initial meeting ends with the *gō'ēl* abdicating his traditional responsibilities and telling Boaz that if he wishes to perform the duties of a *gō'ēl*, then he is free to do so.

Numerous ambiguities are present in 4.1–6. For example, this is the first mention of Elimelech's land. Why mention it now? There is no indication that Boaz has spoken with Naomi or Ruth about this land, and the possibilities are too numerous for us to survey.[56] Suffice it to say that no one in the narrative seems surprised by the mention of this land, and as such it may have been common knowledge. Second, as we have seen, a traditional and legal distinction is drawn between the duties and responsibilities of the levir and the *gō'ēl*, but here Boaz seems to conflate them. Why is this so? The situation of Naomi is an interesting one in that it combines the traditional duties of the *gō'ēl* and the levir. After all, the *gō'ēl's* duties, as mentioned in Leviticus 25, deal with purchasing land sold by a relative due to financial hardships. This is seemingly a far cry from the duties of the levir, as outlined in Deuteronomy 25, which include marrying a dead male relative's wife in order to produce a male offspring who would then legally be considered the dead relative's offspring, and as such would resolve any issues of inheritance. However, these two sets of responsibilities converge in Naomi's case. LaCocque outlines the issue nicely:

> The "redeemer" redeems property that he himself will not possess, but rather the poor kin that had lost the property. In the case of Naomi, the matter gets complicated. There is no longer any living person in Elimelek's line. For whose profit, therefore, should the "redeemer" redeem the land?[57]

He continues by discussing how these two sets of duties—those of the levir and the *gō'ēl*—merge in the case of Naomi:

---

54. For more information about the type of business that would be conducted here, see Campbell, *Ruth*, 154–55.

55. As Linafelt notes, there is some confusion over whether Boaz says "you will acquire" or "I will acquire" in this verse. For our purposes, though, it is acceptable to prefer the second-person reading. See "Ruth," 68; and Sasson, *Ruth*, 121–36.

56. For a brief examination of the possibilities, see LaCocque, *Ruth*, 111–13; and Campbell, *Ruth*, 157–58.

57. LaCocque, *Ruth*, 109.

Ruth volunteers to extend Elimelek's line by proxy, which would make Boaz the redeemer of the ancestral land (as *gō'ēl*) and the begetter of the one who will eventually inherit it (as *levir*). [That is,] Whoever obtains the field also obtains Naomi/Ruth (Ruth 4:5), precisely because the inalienability of the land is linked to the perpetuation of the family line. Legally, the parcel belongs to Elimelek's descendents. Now Naomi was past the age of childbearing, during which she should have been able, theoretically, to produce a candidate for inheritance (cf. Ruth 1:2 in an ironic fashion). The only resource is Ruth as her substitute. Whoever redeems the land redeems by the same token Elimelek's descent, a forthcoming descent, through the intermediary of Ruth.[58]

As such, Naomi's inability to produce children, Ruth's proposal to Boaz, and the issue of Elimelech's land together force the combination of the duties of *gō'ēl* and levir, for one cannot redeem the land if no one exists to inherit it. This is precisely why Boaz waits to mention Ruth until 4.5; he is in effect putting the other *gō'ēl* on the spot. That is, Boaz is saying to this "so-and-so" that the "so-and-so" had done his duty according to the letter of the Law, but will he now go beyond it to fulfill its spirit?[59] The unnamed *gō'ēl* is unwilling to do so for practical concerns over inheritance, and thus the responsibility passes to Boaz.

Boaz agrees to this proposal, and the other *gō'ēl* and Boaz then engage in what appears to be an ancient custom of exchanging a shoe to signify the sealing of an arrangement.[60] Following this rather odd tradition, Boaz publicly announces that he will redeem Elimelech's land and will also marry Ruth. In his work, Jack M. Sasson raises the simple question of why Boaz would go to all this trouble for Naomi, a woman whom he has never met. He argues that not only is Boaz a loyal friend to Elimelech, but Boaz also wants to please his future bride, whom he will marry "for no other reason but love."[61] However, we have no evidence that Boaz has ever met Elimelech, let alone is a loyal friend, and I have dealt with the lack of love between Boaz and Ruth above. In my view, Boaz accepts his legal and religious responsibilities and takes them seriously, two of which are to marry Ruth and provide for Naomi.

The ten elders bless Boaz in such a way that they connect Ruth with previous matriarchs: "May the LORD make the woman who is coming into your house like Rachel and Leah, who together built up the house of Israel. . . . Through the children that the LORD will give you by this young woman, may your house be like the house of Perez, whom Tamar bore to

---

58. Ibid., 109 and 112–13.
59. Ibid., 115–16.
60. Even though this may remind readers of a similar exchange of footwear in Deuteronomy 25—the chapter dealing with levirate marriage—Sakenfeld rightly notes that the issues here are quite different (*Ruth*, 74–75). See also Campbell, *Ruth*, 149–50; and Linafelt, "Ruth," 71–72.
61. Sasson, *Ruth*, 140.

Judah" (4.11–12). The reference to Rachel and Leah is rather obvious, since they—along with their maids Bilhah and Zilpah—gave birth to Jacob's twelve sons (and one daughter), who would become the eponymous ancestors of Israel. Both Rachel and Leah were also women in strange situations, especially with regard to their marriages and conceptions. The mention of Tamar is a wink to the reader that serves to connect her story with Ruth, as I mentioned above. However, Tamar's son Perez does not have the same pedigree as the sons of Jacob, so his inclusion is somewhat puzzling at this point.[62] The narrative will clear up this reference later in the chapter, though.

Verses 14–17 present an odd conclusion to this narrative. First, Boaz and Ruth get married, but we are told that "the LORD made her conceive" (4.13). This seems an odd inclusion, since we have heard no mention of Ruth's inability to conceive.[63] Second, the women of Bethlehem, acting analogously to a Greek chorus, collectively say to Naomi: "Blessed be the LORD, who has not left you this day without next-of-kin; and may his name be renowned in Israel! He shall be to you a restorer of life and a nourisher of your old age; for your daughter-in-law who loves you, who is more to you than seven sons, has borne him" (4.14–15). Their speech focuses on several key themes in the preceding story. They speak of the Lord's loyalty (or *chesed*) toward Naomi, which she had doubted previously. This loyalty has now produced someone, namely Ruth's son, who will restore and nourish Naomi, actions that will presumably counteract her earlier self-centered feelings of bitterness and emptiness. Tod Linafelt expounds on the idea that Obed serves as both a literal and a symbolic replacement for Naomi's dead sons in his work.[64] That is, as the eventual inheritor of Elimelech's land, Obed will be able to provide for Naomi in her old age, but he also represents new life, as opposed to the death at the beginning of the narrative. In my opinion, the women also chastise or correct Naomi for/in her view of Ruth.[65] Linafelt notes, "In a very striking way, the women also counterbalance Naomi's earlier refusal to recognize Ruth as a significant presence in her life. In 1:19–21, Naomi evaluated her life as empty, even though Ruth had just made her extraordinary statement of solidarity with Naomi."[66] All along, as I have maintained, Naomi has not loved Ruth, but now these women remind Naomi of all that Ruth has done for her, that Ruth loves her

---

62. In her work, Sakenfeld notes that the descendents of Perez are mentioned in two texts usually dated to the postexilic period, namely, 1 Chron. 9.4 and Neh. 11.4 and 6. As such, perhaps the inclusion of Perez here held some meaning for the community hearing Ruth. See *Ruth*, 78.

63. Citing a recurring theme in Ruth, namely, God providing life, neither Sakenfeld (*Ruth*, 80) nor Nielsen (*Ruth*, 92–93) finds this claim curious. See also Linafelt, "Ruth," 76–78.

64. Linafelt, "Ruth," 78.

65. This position is also found in Fewell and Gunn, *Compromising Redemption*, 80–82. For a contrasting view, see Sakenfeld, *Ruth*, 81.

66. Linafelt, "Ruth," 78–79.

and has borne a child for Naomi's benefit. In the eyes of these women, Ruth is, or at least should be, worth "more to you than seven sons." Naomi's response to the claims of the women is, yet again, silence. Naomi never verbally responds to Ruth's actions on her behalf, and indeed, Naomi ignores Ruth now that she no longer needs Ruth. That is, now that Obed has arrived to resolve all of Naomi's anxiety over her future, Ruth is no longer necessary as a legal stand-in for Naomi. As if to symbolize the superfluous nature of Ruth to Naomi, the narrator tells us after the speech of the women that Naomi begins to nurse the boy.[67] The women again enter the story as they name the child Obed and exclaim, "A son has been born to Naomi" (4.17). Against Sakenfeld's view that this claim in 4.17 serves to "highlight the reversal of Naomi's opening lament over her childlessness" in 1.11, I would argue that the women's speech here could be read as ironic; that is, they are expressing Naomi's own inner thoughts.[68] As such, Naomi does not alter her unloving orientation toward Ruth even at the end of the narrative. All along Naomi has regarded Ruth as an embarrassment, a despised reminder of the fate of her family in Moab. At most, she has used Ruth's loyalty and love to further her own need for survival, both physical and ideological. Even her statement in 3.1 carries a self-serving motive; Naomi is not so much seeking security for Ruth as she is placing Ruth in a position with Boaz from which she cannot but benefit. The final image we have of Naomi in the book is a triumphant one, but it is one that excludes Ruth in favor of focusing on Naomi and her reintegration into society.

Finally, in 4.17, we are presented with what I consider to be the "twist" of this entire narrative. In a bit of foreshadowing, the narrator reveals that Obed will have a son named Jesse, who will in turn have a son named David. The genealogical coda in 4.18–22 fleshes out this pedigree and also reveals to us the reason behind the multiple connections between Ruth and Tamar: Boaz, who is the great-grandfather of David, is also genealogically descended from Perez, the son of Tamar. We can legitimately ask, what could be the purpose of the unexpected revelation that Ruth's son is genealogically connected both to Tamar and to David? In the sociohistorical context of the narrative, the purpose here seems obvious enough. The author claims that Ruth's actions and her status as a Moabite are entirely excusable and even laudable in light of the results of her story. That is, the birth of David legitimizes Ruth's identity and her seemingly scandalous actions. The issue of foreign women and their impact on members of the covenant would have been current in the postexilic period, as we know from Ezra 9–10 and Nehemiah 13. The story of Ruth was most likely

---

67. As Campbell notes, this obviously cannot refer to Naomi breastfeeding Obed, since she has made it clear that she is past her childbearing years. He also argues against this referring to adoption. Rather, here is a "grandmother delighted in her grandchild, so much so that the women in verse 17 jocularly participate in her delight" (*Ruth*, 165).
68. Sakenfeld, *Ruth*, 83.

told to counter such narrow views, exemplified in the story by the unnamed *gō'ēl*, who is willing to do his duty according to the Law, but nothing more. In so doing, the author argues for a more inclusive concept of Jewish identity, one that has parallels most obviously with the book of Jonah. This argument marks Ruth as a subversive narrative, one in which its title character saves the day for Naomi and contributes to the line of David, all while remaining profoundly and singularly unloved.[69]

AMBIGUITIES AND QUESTIONS

Many interpreters note the ambiguities created by the author of Ruth, especially concerning what exactly happens in chapter 3 on the threshing floor. Regarding that scene, Campbell writes, "The question is whether the story-teller meant to be ambiguous and hence provocative. It seems to me that he did."[70] He goes on to note the "carefully contrived" and "intentional ambiguity" of this scene.[71] In a similar vein, commenting on chapter 3, Linafelt writes, "The author has created an overriding sense of mystery, secrecy, and ambiguity. . . . The reader often cannot know precisely what is happening, but must instead *negotiate constantly the pervasive ambiguity*."[72] This negotiation is precisely what I will discuss below, but first we must single out the specific issues we will examine in later readings and retellings of Ruth. As should be obvious by now, I believe Naomi does not love Ruth, despite Ruth's feelings or actions because of her *chesed* toward Naomi. I also do not see evidence of love between Boaz and Ruth. This lack of love pervades the entire story, and as such it will serve as the starting point for my examination of aesthetic renderings of Ruth. More specifically, I will survey selected literary and filmed readings to determine how they treat the following ambiguities and questions: (1) What exactly happens on the threshing floor? (2) Does Ruth love Boaz and vice versa? And (3) does Naomi love Ruth? Each of these questions will be treated separately so that the specifics of various renderings will become clear.

---

69. The subversive aspect of Ruth, along with its emphases on relaxing religious norms and strengthening societal norms, could be why so many non-Western female biblical interpreters turn to Ruth as a resource for their own communities of faith. In addition to Nayap-Pot, "Life in the Midst of Death," see also Julie Li-Chuan Chu, "The Inspiration of the Role Dedifferentiation in the Book of Ruth for Taiwanese Women," *Semeia* 78 (1997): 47–54; and Sarojini Nadar, "A South African Indian Womanist Reading of the Character of Ruth," in *Other Ways of Reading: African Women and the Bible* (ed. Musa W. Dube; Atlanta: Society of Biblical Literature, 2001), 159–75. Both Chu and Nadar build upon the important work of Jon L. Berquist, "Role Dedifferentiation in the Book of Ruth," *Journal for the Study of the Old Testament* 57 (1993): 23–37.

70. Campbell, *Ruth*, 121.

71. Ibid., 131.

72. Linafelt, "Ruth," 46 (italics mine).

The Threshing Floor

As I note above, this scene is filled with sexual potential and possible titilla-tion. In general, none of the rewritings of Ruth I surveyed engages this potential and renders the scene as one of a sexual encounter. Most, though, want to stay as true as they can to the biblical narrative, and as such their treatment of the threshing floor becomes somewhat comical due to the question of what to do with Boaz's "feet." This is especially true when examining retellings of Ruth's story in children's literature.

Several children's books have Ruth literally uncovering Boaz's feet and then waiting, presumably for the chilly night air to hit his uncovered feet and wake him. This is the approach taken in Catherine Storr's *Ruth's Story*, as well as Eve B. MacMaster's *God Gives the Land*.[73] In both, Ruth turns back Boaz's blanket and lies down at his feet. He then wakes and finds Ruth next to him. Curiously, Storr does not narrate Ruth's proposal, but MacMaster does. Videos made for children and teens adopt a similar approach. In the 2002 *Ruth* installment of the series Testament: The Bible in Animation, Naomi tells Ruth, "Ruth, if you would only ask him [Boaz], I know he'd honor his duty by marrying you. . . . Go and lie near him. Uncover his feet. He'll wake later with the cold, and when he does, he'll tell you what to do."[74] Ruth follows Naomi's plan and proposes to Boaz subsequently.

The awkwardness of uncovering Boaz's feet is addressed in other retellings in which Ruth not only uncovers his feet, but then covers herself with the blanket. Apparently authors who take this approach are fore-shadowing her request in 3.9 for Boaz to spread his cloak over her. For example, in Francine Rivers's inspirational novella *Unshaken* (2001), this portion of the threshing floor scene is narrated in part as follows:

> When she finally reached him, she hesitated, studying the man in the half-moon light next to the mound of grain. He looked younger, his many responsibilities forgotten in sleep. He lay with one arm flung over his head. Trembling, Ruth knelt as his feet and drew his mantle back carefully so she wouldn't disturb him. He moved restlessly. Her pulse jumped. She curled up quickly at his feet without making a sound and drew his mantle over her so that the cool night air would not awaken him. Then she released her breath slowly, wishing her heart would slow its wild, erratic pace.[75]

Rivers goes on to describe how Boaz smelled to Ruth ("provocative and soothing") before narrating how Boaz awakens to find her. Ruth then reiterates her speech in 3.9, and Boaz agrees out of love. Similarly, in her

---

73. Catherine Storr, *Ruth's Story* (Milwaukee: Raintree Publishers, 1986); and Eve B. Mac-Master, *God Gives the Land: Stories of God and His People; Joshua, Judges, and Ruth* (Scottdale, Pa., and Kitchener, Ont.: Herald Press, 1983).
74. All quotes from this program are taken from *Ruth* (Testament: The Bible in Animation; dir. Galina Beda; Diamond Entertainment, 2002).
75. Francine Rivers, *Unshaken* (Wheaton, Ill.: Tyndale House Publishers, 2001), 101.

young adult novel *Beauty in the Fields: The Diary of Ruth's Fellow Harvester*, Anne Tyra Adams tells the story of Ruth through the eyes of Abi, a young Moabite girl whose family comes with Ruth and Naomi to Bethlehem. When it comes time for Ruth to go to the threshing floor, Abi accompanies her, much like a sidekick. In this way, Adams ensures that nothing risqué will occur in this encounter (even though Abi is asleep most of the night). We see the scene through her eyes: "I watched her move toward Boaz, her red veil catching the breeze and floating around her like wings. She lay down at his feet and lifted up the tail of his cloak to cover herself."[76] When Abi wakes up from her catnap, she hears Ruth propose to Boaz in a literal reproduction of 3.9.

These renderings attempt to reproduce the biblical narrative faithfully and as such encounter problems when it comes to uncovering Boaz's feet. Other literary retellings omit the uncovering of feet in lieu of having Ruth simply cuddle up near Boaz's feet, sometimes on the ground and sometimes not. This is the approach taken in Jean Marzollo's popular picture book *Ruth and Naomi*. She writes, "Quietly, Ruth tiptoed over and knelt down near him. Farmer Boaz immediately awakened."[77] As such, not only does Ruth not uncover Boaz's feet, but also since Boaz wakes up immediately, there is no possibility of any "hanky-panky" occurring. Here, though, it is Boaz who proposes to Ruth, in contrast to the biblical story. Likewise, in her storybook of 2005, Maxine Rose Schur has Ruth lay at Boaz's feet, but when he wakes she is the one who proposes. Even though Schur mentions nothing physical in the encounter between Ruth and Boaz, she provides a rather sensuous physical description of Ruth prior to the encounter: "That evening she smoothed olive oil on her slim, tanned body. She dressed herself in a gown of white linen, and about her head she wound soft scarves dyed with pomegranate and saffron."[78] Following this, Ruth departs to meet Boaz. Given the parallels with women like Esther and Judith who perfume and adorn themselves prior to (potentially) sexual encounters with men, this description in a children's book is a tad disturbing.

Even so, this approach to the difficulty of Boaz's "feet" is the most common one. That is, by having Ruth lie at Boaz's real feet instead of uncovering them, authors nicely sidestep any potential sexual overtones and instead are able to present a rather pious, sanitized version of the events narrated in chapter 3. Indeed, one finds this way of representing the events in other books for children, such as Maud Petersham and Miska Petersham's retelling of 1938.[79] One also finds it in adult retellings of the narrative. In the 1966 verse drama by Charles H. De Lench, Ruth lies at Boaz's feet and proposes as follows when he awakens: "'Tis Ruth! Your

76. Anne Tyra Adams, *Beauty in the Fields: The Diary of Ruth's Fellow Harvester* (Promised Land Diaries Series; Grand Rapids, Mich.: Baker Books, 2005), 129–30.

77. Jean Marzollo, *Ruth and Naomi* (New York: Little, Brown and Company, 2005), n.p.

78. Maxine Rose Schur, *The Story of Ruth* (Minneapolis: Kar-Ben Publishing, 2005), n.p.

79. Maud Petersham and Miska Petersham, *Ruth* (New York: Macmillan, 1938).

own handmaiden, I! / Therefore spread over me your skirt, / For without fear with you I lie / And know you will not do me hurt, / For you are near of kin to me / Because to Mahlon I was wed; / Thus our relationship must be / Upright, in honor of the dead."[80]

In her drama "Ruth the Gleaner" of 1937, Mona Swann adopts a similar approach. Her stage directions indicate that Ruth waits until "Boaz is alone; then she comes and kneels before him" before informing him that he is "a near kinsman, one that hath right to redeem."[81] Ruth does not propose here so much as she reveals information to Boaz, who then takes the hint and agrees to perform his duties.

A compromise between uncovering Boaz's feet and simply lying at them appears in the interpretation of 1839 by the Reverend T. H. Gallaudet. He writes that Ruth was "desirous of placing herself in the attitude of one who had come in the most respectful way to present her request, and in accordance with the customs of the times, she lay down at the feet of Boaz, under the covering of the ample garment which extended quite beyond them."[82] As such, Ruth does not uncover Boaz's feet; she simply lies down under the large covering he is using and waits for him to wake up. As if to further protect Ruth's actions from any possible misinterpretations, Gallaudet continues:

> Men of corrupt minds, and disposed to scoff at the sacred Scriptures, have sometimes endeavored to pervert it [this scene], in connection with what follows, to suit their own depraved taste and unworthy purposes. But it defied their contaminating touch. We have already seen . . . that these transactions in which Naomi, Ruth, and Boaz took a part, were alike marked by the strictest purity and delicacy of deportment towards each other, and by a reverential regard to the divine commands.[83]

Here, he leaves no doubt in his readers' minds that nothing risqué occurred because all three characters are paragons of virtue. This is not the last time we will see readers overdetermine the love and piety of these characters to suit their own exegetical presuppositions.

Finally, some interpreters of Ruth omit the scene altogether, perhaps due to concerns over presenting the scene to their target audience. In her *Bible Stories for Jewish Children*, Ruth Samuels skips from Ruth's gleaning in Boaz's field to his proposing marriage.[84] Catherine F. Vos's popular book

---

80. Charles H. De Lench, *The Love Story of Ruth and Boaz: A Dramatic Verse Version of the Biblical Story* (New York: Exposition Press, 1966), 53.
81. Mona Swann, "Ruth the Gleaner," in *At the Well of Bethlehem: A Narrative Drama in Three Parts* (Boston: Baker's Plays, 1937), 23.
82. T. H. Gallaudet, *Scripture Biography for the Young, with Critical Illustrations and Practical Remarks: Ruth* (New York: American Tract Society, 1839), 34.
83. Ibid., 36.
84. Ruth Samuels, *Bible Stories for Jewish Children* (Jersey City, N.J.: KTAV Publishing House, 1973), 24.

The Child's Story Bible adopts the exact same tactic: Ruth gleans so well in Boaz's field that he eventually proposes to her.[85] Ruth L. Sprague and Margaret Nixon adopt a medial interpretation of this section in their *People of the Old Testament*. They have Naomi narrate her plan, but then they skip over the implementation of the plan. Ruth returns and confirms that she lay at his feet, but we are not shown the threshing floor.[86]

We find a similar approach in film as well, in which all sexual ambiguity is removed from the threshing floor, and negotiation takes its place. Vision Video has released a scripturally didactic series titled *Jacob's Ladder*, in which a group of six teens "magically" travel to and within biblical stories a la the popular Magic Tree House series of children's books. In episode 4, "Ruth and Boaz," Ruth goes to the threshing floor, but there is no uncovering of feet. Instead, she simply says, "I need your protection. So does Naomi."[87] Likewise, in the 1960 feature film *The Story of Ruth*, Naomi instructs Ruth to go to the threshing floor, not to secure a husband, but rather to secure the *right* husband.[88] That is, the other gō'ēl (here named Tob) is forcing Ruth to marry him via the levirate law I discussed above. Naomi sends Ruth to Boaz in order to ensure that he will marry her. Again, there is no uncovering of feet, but in this case it is Boaz who proposes.

While this survey is obviously limited to nineteenth- and twentieth-century literary and filmic renderings, mostly targeted to children, I would venture to say that other readers in different genres experience the same difficulties we have seen here in terms of deciding how to render the scene at the threshing floor. We have seen, then, three main options: (1) Ruth uncovers Boaz's real feet; (2) Ruth simply lies at Boaz's feet; (3) the scene at the threshing floor is omitted entirely, not shown to the reader, or altered to focus on the dialogue of Boaz and Ruth. All of these share in the common desire to lessen the sexual ambiguity we saw in chapter 3. In so doing, they render Naomi, Ruth, and Boaz as more pious and ethical, while also strengthening the emotional ties between them. After all, these readers seem to be asking their audiences, if every hint of sexuality is excised from chapter 3, what is left but love and devotion?

Ruth and Boaz Sittin' in a Tree?

If the events that occur on the threshing floor are shrouded in ambiguity, the emotional content of the relationship between Ruth and Boaz is perhaps

85. Catherine F. Vos, *The Child's Story Bible* (5th ed.; revised by Marianne Catherine Vos Radius; Grand Rapids, Mich.: Eerdmans, 1983 [1934]), 129.

86. Ruth L. Sprague and Margaret Nixon, *People of the Old Testament* (Boston: United Church Press, 1964), 81.

87. All quotes from this program are taken from *Jacob's Ladder*, episodes 3 and 4 (dir. Billy Engel; Vision Video, 2003).

88. For an examination of this film, see J. Cheryl Exum, "Is This Naomi?," in *Plotted, Shot, and Painted: Cultural Representations of Biblical Women* (JSOTSup 215/GCT 3; Sheffield: Sheffield Academic Press, 1996), 129–74, especially 161–68.

more so. That is, I argue above for admiration and respect between the two characters based on texts like 2.11–12 and 3.10–13, but not emotional love. However, many of the sources I examine here characterize the relationship between the two as one of mutual love. Ruth loves Boaz because of the way he treated her and the food and protection he provided; Boaz loves Ruth because she chose him above all other men and for her loyalty (*chesed*) to Naomi. Some of the retellings leave the ambiguity I find in Ruth intact. Whether intentionally or not, some do not claim Ruth and Boaz love each other.

In her retelling for children, Vos simply states, "When Boaz saw the beautiful Ruth gleaning day after day in his fields, he fell in love with her. He asked her to become his wife."[89] Similarly, Samuels writes, "Boaz came every day to the field where Ruth gathered grain, for he could not forget her lovely, sweet face. Then one day Boaz asked Ruth to become his wife, for he had fallen deeply in love with her."[90] Schur expands on Boaz's reply to Ruth in 3.10–13, adding the following to Boaz's dialogue: "If you will have me, I will cherish you forever . . . on the soil of Earth and in the sky of Heaven." She then comments, "Ruth had never felt happier."[91] In her rendering, Marzollo invents a new dialogue for Ruth and Boaz, sparked by Ruth's "true feelings" for Boaz:

> **Ruth:** Remember when you first met me? You said that you hoped God would reward me. Well, God did reward me by sending you to care for me.
>
> **Boaz:** Dear Ruth, I do care for you, and I believe God sent you to me! You are a wonderful woman, Ruth. Will you marry me?[92]

In all of these examples, the love of Boaz for Ruth is obvious, whereas in the biblical narrative it can only be inferred from indefinite dialogue like that in 3.10–13. Likewise, Ruth's feelings for Boaz are intensified, because in the book of Ruth we have no overt evidence that Ruth loves him.

These processes are at work in adult literature as well. In De Lench's poetic rendering, Ruth spies on the proceedings at the city gates, and once Boaz agrees to fulfill his duties, she exclaims:

> O happy, happy day that makes our marriage sure / With the enactment sealed, our future is secure; / No longer is there need to quench the fires we know. / From this day forth, we feel, the flames will brighter glow. / All worry, doubt and fear have now been set at rest / As we in truth foresee our lives by Heaven blest / With such delight and rapture as we never felt / Within our hearts, and know a surfeit will be dealt / Our outstretched hands, for truly, every loving deed / Will be fulfillment of our everpresent need.[93]

---

89. Vos, *Child's Story Bible*, 129.
90. Samuels, *Bible Stories for Jewish Children*, 24.
91. Schur, *Story of Ruth*, n.p.
92. Marzollo, *Ruth and Naomi*, n.p.
93. De Lench, *Love Story of Ruth and Boaz*, 70.

Similarly, in Rivers's treatment of Ruth, she provides us an interior view of Boaz's feelings for his nocturnal Moabite visitor: "Lord, Lord, how do I ever dare hope for a girl like this? There are obstacles. Is this a test? I must do what's right rather than do what I want. And You've known since the first time I heard about this girl that my heart was softened toward her. Such a woman . . ."[94] Rivers continues, "It was beyond reason that she might love him, but his heart had been fixed upon her firmly from the beginning." When Ruth accidentally brushes his leg in the dark, "his body had caught fire. He wasn't such an old man after all. The power of his feelings for her shook him."[95] Just as Rivers uses Boaz's perspective to reveal the depth of his feelings for Ruth, so Adams uses the perspective of Abi, Ruth's companion from Moab, as a lens for the reader into the feelings Ruth and Boaz have for each other. In one section, Abi is pestering Ruth with questions about marriage and asks her what she would like in a husband. Ruth responds:

> "All right, then . . . Let's see . . ." She stared into the fields where Boaz was talking to one of his workers. I watched her eyes follow him as he walked, and she was quiet for several minutes. "I would like for him to be kind and generous and loving," she said after several minutes. Her eyes never left him as she spoke.[96]

Later, as Abi observes the proceedings at the city gate, she is shocked to hear that someone else could possibly marry Ruth. She exclaims to her friend Ahmed, "If he redeems the land, he has to marry Ruth! . . . He can't marry her, he just can't. She's in love with Boaz, and Boaz is in love with her."[97] By putting this information in the mouth of Abi, the reliable narrator of the novel, Adams ensures that the audience will believe the report.

In several of the filmic retellings of Ruth, this loving resolution to the ambiguity I find in the story is present. In the *Jacob's Ladder* series, one of the time-traveling teenagers approaches Ruth to try to persuade her to talk to Boaz about marriage. She asks Ruth if she loves Boaz, and Ruth responds, "I don't know." The teen then asks if Ruth wants to marry Boaz, to which Ruth replies, "I think so. Naomi and I both need protection. We both need to belong to a family." Following this, their dialogue becomes more specific and flowery, with the teen reassuring Ruth that Boaz really does love her, and as such she will not have to be with him out of obligation, but rather out of love.

After Ruth proceeds to Boaz and tells him she and Naomi need protection, he advises her to consider his foreman, who is younger and more attractive than he is. Ruth caresses his cheek and says, "I'm not in love with him." Boaz replies, "Ruth, I'd love to marry you. Will you marry me?" They then kiss.

---

94. Rivers, *Unshaken*, 103.
95. Ibid., 104.
96. Adams, *Beauty in the Fields*, 117.
97. Ibid., 136.

In the film *The Story of Ruth*, things get even more complicated because of the more active role of Tob, the other *gō'ēl*. He wants to marry Ruth even though Ruth and Boaz obviously have feelings for each other. As I note above, Naomi sends Ruth to the threshing floor in order to prevent her from marrying Tob. Once Boaz wakes up, he says, "I love you, Ruth. I've loved you from the day we met in my field." Ruth then muses, "It must have been God's goodness that brought me to your field that day. Perhaps he's been directing me to you all my life." They then kiss, after which Boaz says, "Ruth, I want you for my wife." Right before leaving the threshing floor, Ruth tells Boaz she loves him.

As I note above, though, some interpretations retain the emotional ambiguity I find in the biblical narrative. That is, some retellings leave open the possibility that Boaz does not love Ruth and vice versa. This is true in all of the retellings that copy Boaz's speech in 3.10–13 verbatim. One finds instances of this in the works of Selina Hastings, Sprague and Nixon, Storr, and Swann.[98] There are also sources that treat this issue in the same way I do above. For example, in Gallaudet's young adult biography of Ruth, he writes:

> The reply of Boaz to the request of Ruth was truly characteristic of his piety, delicacy, and frankness. He spoke as a father to his child, endeavoring to relieve her from any perturbation or embarrassment of feeling that the urging of her claim in the manner which she did might produce. . . . Her reverence for the divine law, he perceived, had led Ruth to wish that, in her own case, its requisitions might be strictly fulfilled by the kinsman of her deceased husband becoming her husband.[99]

In essence, Boaz recognizes that Ruth does not love him; rather, she is only adhering to the customs of the *gō'ēl*, as I discussed them above. This is why he speaks to her in a paternal fashion, in contrast to the anxious and fumbling speech Rivers composes for him. Likewise, in the stop-motion animation production of Ruth from the series Testament: The Bible in Animation, after Boaz awakens on the threshing floor, he says, "May God reward you. Such a sacrifice for Naomi's sake is great indeed. . . . You could have married for love. . . . Whatever the outcome you will have a husband today." By including the phrase "You could have married for love," the writers make it clear that Ruth does not love Boaz, and he shows no signs of loving her either.

In contrast to the lessening of ambiguity we saw when rendering the threshing floor, later retellings of Ruth treat the relationship between Boaz and Ruth in various ways. Some emphasize a loving, emotional relationship

---

98. See Selena Hastings, *The Illustrated Jewish Bible for Children* (New York: DK Publishing, 1994), 107; Sprague and Nixon, *People of the Old Testament*, 81; Storr, *Ruth's Story*, 22; and Swann, "Ruth the Gleaner," 23–24.
99. Gallaudet, *Scripture Biography*, 38.

between them, while others prefer to retain the ambiguity found in the biblical narrative. Others adopt an approach analogous to mine, that is, that Boaz and Ruth do not love each other. The first approach most likely portrays a loving relationship because it fits our cultural desire for a romantic twist on this tale. That is, if these characters will live "happily every after" in the sense of getting married and having a child, then they must be in love. The sources that retain the ambiguity found in Ruth probably do so out of an attempt to "faithfully" reproduce or retell the biblical narrative; that is, most of these sources stem from communities of faith and therefore would want to minimize any hint of risqué behavior between Ruth and Boaz, as we saw above. As such, they portray Boaz as a man of duty, not one of errant passion.[100] Finally, sources that view the relationship between Ruth and Boaz as "strictly business" may be attempting to remove any and all hints of sexuality, as Gallaudet does.

Does Naomi Love Ruth?

I argue in my reading of Ruth above that the answer to this question is no. That is, Naomi does not love Ruth, for a variety of possible reasons. She could associate Ruth with the tragedy that befell her family in Moab. She could dislike Ruth simply because she is from Moab, which was not exactly on friendly terms with the descendents of Abraham and Sarah. She could even dislike Ruth because, as she herself says, she is bitter and does not like anyone. However, unlike the previous two ambiguities, all of our retellings and interpretations leave no doubt whatsoever in their views that Naomi loves Ruth. Why is this the case? I will try to answer this question, but only after I mention how these renderings alter the biblical story to infuse Naomi's character with love for Ruth.

The logical starting point for determining Naomi's feelings for Ruth would be her response to Ruth's moving speech in 1.16–17. Some retellings, though, provide a more comprehensive backstory for Ruth, such as the film *The Story of Ruth* (1960). In this version of the story, Ruth is a priestess of Chemosh, the god of the Moabites, when she meets Mahlon, an artisan hired to provide jewelry for the children who are sacrificed to Chemosh. Ruth begins to question her devotion to Chemosh as Mahlon tells her more and more about God. As a result, she disrupts one of the child sacrifice, and Mahlon, along with his father and brother, is arrested. After serving six months in solitary confinement, Ruth is released and is determined to help Mahlon escape from his punishment in the stone quarries. He is mortally wounded in the escape, but he and Ruth are married

---

100. This is not to imply that sources that employ the first approach do not stem from communities of faith or religious publishers. Many do, and the work of Rivers is especially conspicuous in this regard, since it is a Christian romance novel. For an examination of this genre, see Rebecca Kaye Barrett, "Higher Love: What Women Gain from Christian Romance Novels," *Journal of Religion and Popular Culture* 4 (2003); online: *http://www.usask.ca/relst/jrpc/art4-higherlove.html*.

moments before he dies. Interestingly, it is not Naomi who is bitter after Mahlon's death, but Ruth. She questions the blessings of Mahlon's God, and Naomi responds by telling Ruth that she (Ruth) is one of God's blessings for her behavior toward Boaz. Instead of "my lady," Ruth asks Naomi to call her Ruth, to which Naomi agrees and adds that she will recall Ruth tenderly and lovingly. Ruth then delivers her famous speech, and even though Naomi does not respond, the film shows us their perilous journey to Judea. Right before they cross into Judean territory, Naomi confides to Ruth her feelings and memories of her first journey to Moab. Clearly, these two women share an emotional bond even before they arrive at Naomi's old home. Adams also provides a backstory for Ruth in Moab and notes Naomi's kind and maternal manner toward Ruth. At one point, Ruth tells Abi that even though she is a Moabite, Naomi welcomed and loved her as a daughter, and now it is Ruth's turn to return that love. She then asks Abi if she knows that honoring one's mother is one of God's laws. In so doing, Adams shows not only Ruth's love for Naomi and vice versa, but also the religious underpinnings of that love. In other words, Ruth is an observant Jew already in Moab.

In other retellings, too, authors recast Naomi's feelings toward Ruth in the early portion of the narrative. After Ruth's speech in 1.16–17, Samuels writes, "At these words, Naomi's eyes filled with tears and she kissed Ruth tenderly." Samuels then has Naomi respond, "My own daughter could not love me more."[101] Rivers paints an emotional scene around Ruth's speech in her novella. Naomi tries desperately to convince Ruth to stay in Moab, but Ruth rebuffs every argument. "Weeping now, Naomi placed her hands on Ruth's head and stroked her hair. Naomi looked up at the heavens. She had never hoped for this, never expected that this young Moabitess would be willing to give up everything in order to go with her."[102] After Ruth proclaims that Naomi's God will be her God, Rivers writes:

> How could Naomi say no to such words? Hadn't she prayed that Ruth's heart would be softened toward the God of Israel? One prayer had been answered, one prayer among thousands. "Be at ease," she said gently and loosened Ruth's arms from around her waist. Cupping Ruth's face, she smiled down at her. She smoothed away Ruth's tears. "As God wills. Whatever comes, we'll face together."[103]

Here, Naomi's acceptance of Ruth's plea seems tied to Ruth's willingness to convert. That is, her love for Ruth is tied to her love for God. Finally, De Lench augments the biblical narrative by including a lengthy reply from Naomi to Ruth's speech. Naomi says:

> Demean yourself you should not do, / For never in these ten long year / Has anything 'twixt me and you / Led me to think you insincere. / What you have

101. Samuels, *Bible Stories for Jewish Children*, 22.
102. Rivers, *Unshaken*, 27.
103. Ibid.

pledged will cherished be / And sealed forever in my heart. / Nothing must sunder you and me / Hereafter until death us part. / Now, having made our fervent vows, / We must proceed upon our way / With faith our enterprise allows / The strength to meet each toilsome day / Until in Bethl'em we appear, / That little town where I was born, / Where friendships that my heart holds dear / Should mean for us a bright new morn.[104]

Naomi's words to Ruth in this speech are obviously filled with emotion and perhaps even allude to matrimonial vows. It is little wonder that Ruth's words in 1.16–17 have been used for centuries in wedding ceremonies for both heterosexual and homosexual couples.

Even though some authors expand the biblical story with extra dialogue, some do not and simply replicate Naomi's silence both after Ruth's speech and along the journey to Bethlehem. Even though these sources do not augment the biblical narrative here, Naomi is still shown to have loving and even maternal feelings for Ruth. For example, in the children's animated video *Ruth*, upon returning to Bethlehem, Naomi introduces Ruth to the women of the town, saying, "She is all I have. Ruth, wife of my eldest son. She is my only family now." Marzollo also records a conversation between Ruth and Naomi after the return to Bethlehem. Therein, Ruth tells Naomi that she will not call her Mara, because she will be happy someday. In response, Naomi says, "I doubt it, but I will say this. Ruth means 'friend,' and you surely are a friend to me, Ruth."[105] In the same way as Rivers does, Gallaudet connects the love of Ruth and Naomi with their love for God. More specifically, Ruth refuses to let Naomi depart without her because of her love for Naomi's God.[106]

In both episode 4 of *Jacob's Ladder* and *The Story of Ruth*, the filmmakers adopt a similar approach to the issue of Naomi's feelings toward Ruth. They place the two women within a family dynamic so that the audience perceives them as being simply mother and daughter. Both episode 4 and the film have the women refer to each other as mother and daughter, and they almost always act in perfect accord. In *The Story of Ruth*, Naomi even utters a heartfelt prayer to God, entreating God to help Ruth so that she will not have to marry Tob instead of Boaz. A stranger named Jehoam appears and speaks a prophecy about the importance of the future child of Ruth and Boaz, so Naomi now has divine assurance that all will turn out well.

In sum, all of the retellings examined here are unanimous in their view that Naomi loves Ruth. Some trace that love back to Moab, and some locate the origins of that love in the women's religious devotion. They all seem to agree with De Lench's Naomi when she says, "I would do anything for you, / My daughter, for I wish you well. / You toiled relentlessly for me

104. De Lench, *Love Story of Ruth and Boaz*, 32–33.
105. Marzollo, *Ruth and Naomi*, n.p.
106. See Gallaudet, *Scripture Biography*, 13–16.

/ And nothing could your ardor quell."[107] None of them, though, adopts the reading of the biblical narrative I argue for, namely, that Naomi does not love Ruth but instead only uses her to achieve her goal of reincorporation into Judean society.

CONCLUSIONS

As we have seen, almost all of the secondary retellings and interpretations of Ruth seek to resolve the ambiguities and uncertainties I find in the biblical narrative through supplying a positive emotional content to the relationships between the characters. That is, the vast majority of these—and I would venture to say, other—renderings of Ruth downplay the sexual nature of the threshing floor and inscribe loving feelings between Ruth and Boaz and between Naomi and Ruth. The question now is, why do they do so? The easiest explanation has to do with audience. The retellings I survey above are mostly aimed at a young audience, and most of them stem from a religious perspective. As such, authors most likely assume that it is not appropriate for a children's book to show Ruth disrobing Boaz in an attempt to curry his favor. So these authors must find other ways to deal with the text in an age-sensitive fashion while still staying as close as possible to the narrative. This approach leads to some of the awkward scenes I describe above, with Ruth uncovering Boaz's literal feet in an attempt to wake him using the cold night air. Why Ruth does not simply wake Boaz up by poking him or shaking his shoulder is an unresolved issue simply because the biblical text mentions feet, and as such the retelling must use Boaz's feet somehow.

The reasons behind the inscribing of love into the relational dynamics of the narrative are similarly concerned with audience. It would be difficult, I imagine, for young readers or viewers in our cultural context to imagine Ruth following Naomi if the two women did not love each other. Even the decidedly adult film *The Story of Ruth* places Ruth and Naomi into a family dynamic so that no question of their love is even possible within the context of the film. Likewise, a younger audience today might be hard pressed to understand why Boaz and Ruth would marry if they did not love one another. All of these assumptions reflect our modern understanding of relationships and our own somewhat confusing concept of love. I do not think I am on shaky ground when I claim that a postexilic audience (after the sixth century B.C.E.) would not share our modern understandings and concepts regarding relationships and love. Anytime one attempts to retell a story, one's own cultural conditioning and social perceptions play a role in how one tells the story. It is most likely the case that the authors of the examples I examine above cannot conceive of the story of Ruth as being as loveless as I find it, so they augment the narrative with our modern notions

---

107. De Lench, *Love Story of Ruth and Boaz*, 50.

of love and companionship. In the process, though, they sweeten the story and their retellings lose something of the character and flavor of the narrative. Or, as many of these authors might claim, they are simply trying to find the "happily ever after" in a story that is bereft of love.

STUDY QUESTIONS

1. Since almost all of the interpretations I discuss in this chapter are literary, use the websites I mention in study question 6 on page 27 to gather images of Ruth from the history of art that depict the scenes I examine. After you have collected several of these images, try to assess how they approach the ambiguities I discuss. Do any of the images show Naomi's love for Ruth, or Ruth's for Boaz? Do any of them depict Ruth's actions on the threshing floor? If so, where would you place them along the spectrum of responses that I mention earlier in the chapter? And how does viewing art dealing with Ruth change the way you reencounter the biblical text, if at all?

2. In this chapter, I discuss Henry Koster's film *The Story of Ruth* (1960). Curiously, Ruth has not enjoyed much life on film, and Koster's interpretation is certainly not a literal rendering of the biblical story. An even stranger adaptation is the Israeli filmmaker Amos Gitai's *Golem, the Spirit of Exile* (1992), which merges the story of Ruth with that of the Golem—the mythical creature constructed by Jews in Prague to defend them against their enemies. Gitai sets the film in modern-day Paris and centers it on a mother and her two daughters who are forced into exile after the deaths of their husbands. After watching the film, compare and contrast it with both the biblical narrative and Koster's film. What similarities do you see? Are there themes that pervade all three stories? If so, what are they? How does the combination of visual images and audio affect your understanding of the story of Ruth? That is, does film impact your reading of Ruth more than art or music? If so, why?

3. Biblical scholars have long noted the parallels between the stories of Tamar (Genesis 38) and Ruth. Read these two narratives and compare the characters of Tamar and Ruth. How are they and their situations similar or different? What options are available to them in their society? Pay attention to the desires, actions, and speech of these female characters, as well as the ways in which the other male and female characters

---

108. For a comparison between Ruth and Tamar, readers can consult Bos, "Out of the Shadows"; and Nielsen, *Ruth,* passim. Readers interested in Tamar can consult Esther Marie Menn, *Judah and Tamar (Genesis 38) in Ancient Jewish Exegesis: Studies in Literary Form and Hermeneutics* (Supplements to the *Journal for the Study of Judaism* 51; Leiden: Brill, 1997); and John Petersen, "Redeeming a Patriarch: Plotting in the Tale of Judah and Tamar," in his *Reading Women's Stories: Female Characters in the Hebrew Bible* (Minneapolis: Fortress, 2004), 119–64.

relate or respond to them. Be sure to pay attention to issues of sexuality and to how the narrator and other characters view female sexuality.[108]

4. As I note above, Ruth is an important character for Christians due to her inclusion in Matthew's genealogy of Jesus. Why does Matthew include her? That is, are there qualities Matthew prizes in Ruth that make her a worthy ancestress of Jesus beyond her contribution to the lineage of David? How do Ruth and her actions compare to the other women listed in the genealogy? In his work on Abraham, Rabbi Joseph B. Soloveitchik addresses the issue of Ruth's connection with the Messiah, as understood in Jewish thought.[109] How do his comments compare with your observations, and how does his description of the Messiah compare with how Matthew understands Jesus?

5. Take a few moments to write a personal response to the book of Ruth. Imagine yourself in Ruth's position. How much loyalty (*chesed*) would you be willing to show your mother-in-law? How far would you go to save your family? Many women today find themselves in Ruth's position in the sense that they are foreigners in a land that may not welcome them. They may be illegal immigrants or simply women who have wound up in unfamiliar territory due to chance.[110] How would you behave in that case if presented with Ruth's dilemma? Think especially about chapter 3; would you be willing to go along with Naomi's plan? What would you think of God if you were in Naomi's place?

---

109. See his *Abraham's Journey: Reflections on the Life of the Founding Patriarch* (ed. David Shatz, Joel B. Wolowelsky, and Reuven Ziegler; *MeOtzar HoRav* Series: Selected Writings of Rabbi Joseph B. Soloveitchik 9; Jersey City, N.J.: Toras HoRav Foundation/KTAV Publishing House, 2008), 176–82.

110. For this issue, readers should see Nayap-Pot, "Life in the Midst of Death."

5

"If I Perish, I Perish"

ESTHERS IN FILM

THE STORY OF ESTHER is well known in Judaism because of its connection to the holiday of Purim, for which children dress up in costumes as characters from the narrative in a carnival-like atmosphere. Candy is consumed as the *megillah*, or scroll, of Esther is read publicly, and every time Haman's name is mentioned, everyone present screams "Boo" as they shake noisemakers known as graggers. Adults are even commanded by the Talmud to drink so much alcohol that they cannot distinguish between Haman and Mordecai (*BT Megillah* 7b).[1] At times, Purim can seem like a Jewish Halloween, with the costumes and candy, but beneath the happiness lies a rather gruesome and sexy story about a young Jewish virgin who saves all the Jews in Persia from complete genocide at the hands of an ancient enemy. No wonder Rabbi Irving Greenberg calls Purim perhaps "the darkest, most depressing holiday of the Jewish calendar."[2]

However, Purim does not represent the totality of Esther. Before the holiday is mentioned in the narrative, we are presented with a story of a heroic young woman who risks her own life to save those of her people. There is sexual intrigue, an assassination plot, ancient rivalries, and this young woman named Hadassah who will become Queen Esther. The story is so thematically rich that interpreters have long been drawn to it, and some of the most interesting examples of these interpretations in the twentieth century are cinematic ones. This chapter will (a) examine the story of Esther as told in the Hebrew Bible; (b) raise three main questions arising from the narrative; and (c) discuss how five different cinematic renderings

---

1. See Elie Wiesel, "Esther," in *Sages and Dreamers: Biblical, Talmudic, and Hasidic Portraits and Legends* (New York: Summit Books, 1991), 133–34.
2. Rabbi Irving Greenberg in his "Confronting Jewish Destiny: Purim," in *The Jewish Way: Living the Holidays* (New York: Simon & Schuster, 1988), 224.

of Esther treat the questions. In chronological order, I will survey how Rauol Walsh's *Esther and the King* (1960); Amos Gitai's *Esther* (1985); Raffaele Mertes's *Esther* (1998); *VeggieTales—Esther: The Girl Who Became Queen* (2001); and Michael O. Sajbel's *One Night with the King* (2006) deal with certain issues of the narrative. My discussion will focus on issues of gender, sexuality, and religious identity as they pertain to the character of Esther. Specifically, I will address the ways in which these renderings alter and adapt these aspects of Esther's character in the Hebrew Bible in an attempt to sanitize this often sexy and gruesome story.

THE BIBLICAL STORY OF ESTHER

Because the book of Esther is lengthy and complex, and because many interpreters view it as two separate stories edited into one,[3] I will focus on three specific scenes within the narrative.[4] By doing so, I will focus my examination on the characters of Vashti and Esther so that we are able to see more clearly the way in which the biblical story imagines women.

---

3. For this position, see Elias Bickerman, "The Scroll of Esther, or Esther and Mordecai," in *Four Strange Books of the Bible: Jonah, Daniel, Koheleth, Esther* (New York: Schocken Books, 1967), 171–240.

4. Esther has been well served by secondary literature. For a more inclusive examination of the text in commentaries, see Carol M. Bechtel, *Esther* (IBC; Louisville, Ky.: John Knox Press, 2002); Adele Berlin, *Esther* (Jewish Publication Society Bible Commentary Series; Philadelphia: Jewish Publication Society, 2001); Jo Carruthers, *Esther through the Centuries* (Blackwell Bible Commentaries; Oxford: Blackwell, 2008); Linda Day, *Esther* (AOTCS; Nashville: Abingdon Press, 2005); Jon D. Levenson, *Esther* (OTL; Philadelphia: Westminster, 1997); and Carey A. Moore, *Esther* (AB 7B; Garden City, N.Y.: Doubleday, 1971). Several helpful books also exist, including Timothy K. Beal, *The Book of Hiding: Gender, Ethnicity, Annihilation, and Esther* (London and New York: Routledge, 1997); Michael V. Fox, *Character and Ideology in the Book of Esther* (2nd ed.; Grand Rapids, Mich.: Eerdmans, 1991); and Timothy S. Laniak, *Shame and Honor in the Book of Esther* (SBLDS 165; Atlanta: Scholars Press, 1998). Finally, there are numerous shorter studies of Esther, the best of which include Katheryn Pfisterer Darr, "More Than Just a Pretty Face: Critical, Rabbinical, and Feminist Perspectives on Esther," in *Far More Precious Than Jewels: Perspectives on Biblical Women* (Gender and the Biblical Tradition Series; Louisville, Ky.: Westminster John Knox Press, 1991), 164–202; Lillian R. Klein, "Honor and Shame in Esther," in *A Feminist Companion to Esther, Judith, and Susanna* (ed. Athalya Brenner; Sheffield: Sheffield Academic Press, 1995), 149–75; André LaCocque, "Esther," in *The Feminine Unconventional: Four Subversive Figures in Israel's Tradition* (OBT; Minneapolis: Fortress, 1990), 49–83; Sidnie Ann White, "Esther: A Feminine Model for Jewish Diaspora," in *Gender and Difference in Ancient Israel* (ed. Peggy L. Day; Minneapolis: Fortress, 1989), 161–77; Wiesel, "Esther"; and Lawrence M. Wills, "Esther and Greek Esther," in *The Jewish Novel in the Ancient World* (Myth and Poetics Series; Ithaca, N.Y., and London: Cornell University Press, 1995), 93–131. Finally, for a modern graphic rendering of the text, readers should engage J. T. Waldman's exquisite *Megillat Esther* (Philadelphia: Jewish Publication Society, 2005). More information on Waldman's work can be found in my "The Bible and Graphic Novels: A Review and Interview with the Authors of *Marked* and *Megillat Esther*," *SBL Forum* 4, no. 1 (2006); online: http://www.sbl=site.org/Article.aspx?ArticleID=477.

Vashti and Her Refusal

The initial story recounted in 1.10–2.4 details the actions behind the removal of Vashti as queen and how that removal is carried out.[5] From the start, Ahasuerus's authority and power are expressed by characterizing him as a king and by providing a list of his seven named servants. We are told in 1.11 that he has ordered Vashti, his queen, to appear before all the peoples and officials in her royal garb, presumably to reinforce his status as both a powerful king and, because of her beauty, a potent man. However, Vashti refuses to come when summoned. Her reason(s) for this act are not given to us in the text, but we could posit that this act is one of resistance; that is, Vashti resists the king's attempt to define her as a passive object of admiration and beauty by refusing his command. That is, the royal discourse is trying to shape her as a passive/docile body. It could also be that she is attempting to reduce the status he seems to be seeking by undermining his authority to summon her. In either case, this act of resistance causes the royal discourse, embodied in Ahasuerus and his various minions, to alter the way in which it seeks to demonstrate its power. That is, if the king cannot increase his status or power through his use of Vashti, then he must fall back, regroup, and try to do so through other means.

In 1.13, the king consults the "sages who knew the laws." Even before we hear what he asks them, we get a list of the sages, who we are told are seven Persian and Median officials. This list, composed as it is of named characters called officials from important geopolitical entities, serves once more to confer additional prestige and power to the royal discourse. Only one of the officials, Memucan, replies to the king's question of what should be done with Vashti in 1.16–20.

> Not only has Queen Vashti done wrong to the king, but also to all the officials and all the peoples who are in all the provinces of King Ahasuerus. For this deed of the queen will be made known to all women, causing them to look with contempt on their husbands, since they will say, "King Ahasuerus commanded Queen Vashti to be brought before him, and she did not come." This very day the noble ladies of Persia and Media who have heard of the queen's behavior will rebel against the king's officials, and there will be no end of contempt and wrath! If it pleases the king, let a royal order go out from him, and

---

5. Power, knowledge, and resistance seem to be key themes in this section, and so my examination of Vashti's story will use some ideas from the work of the French historian-philosopher Michel Foucault, whose writings have done so much to illuminate these themes in history. Foucault's work on power and resistance can be confusing for the novice, and the best places for the newcomer to Foucault to begin are his chapter titled "Method," in *The History of Sexuality*, vol. 1, *An Introduction* (trans. R. Hurley; New York: Random House, 1978), 92–102; the six hypotheses on power listed in "Power and Strategies," in *Power/Knowledge: Selected Interviews and Other Writings, 1972–1977*, (ed. and trans. Colin Gordon; New York: Pantheon Books, 1980), 142; and finally his "Power and Sex," in *Politics, Philosophy, Culture: Interviews and Other Writings, 1977–1984* (ed. Lawrence D. Kritzman; trans. A. Sheridan et al.; New York and London: Routledge, 1988), 110–24.

let it be written among the laws of the Persians and the Medes so that it may not be altered, that Vashti is never again to come before King Ahasuerus; and let the king give her royal position to another who is better than she. So when the decree made by the king is proclaimed throughout all his kingdom, vast as it is, all women will give honor to their husbands, high and low alike.

There are two important things to note about Memucan's response. First, he seems to imply that the royal discourse encompasses not only the officials, but also "all the peoples who are in all the provinces of King Ahasuerus." This expansion of the royal discourse serves again to bestow added prestige upon the king and his power. Second, he notes the implications of Vashti's refusal for the royal discourse as well as the patriarchal discourse operating at the time. The latter discourse is implied by Memucan's concern over the rebellion, contempt, and wrath that will ensue as a result of women's responses to Vashti's action. Memucan's advice is to send out a royal order, which will be added to existing Persian and Median laws, banning Vashti from the king's court and ordering that "another who is better than she" be appointed queen. Here we can see clearly a reshaping of the royal discourse intended to alter the knowledge it disseminates. That is, if Vashti will not play the game according to the rules set down and implied by the royal discourse, then she will be removed as queen, thus allowing someone else to be appointed to that position who will hopefully do what Vashti was unwilling to do: play the passive role of queen so as to confer and/or reproduce power upon/for the royal discourse. Also, Memucan implies that by treating Vashti in this way, that is, by propagating this knowledge about her in this way, other women will also be made more passive and docile with regard to the implied patriarchal discourse, as seems clear from 1.20.

The king is pleased by this suggestion, and an order is sent out. Again, the text details the extent and power of the royal discourse by noting that the king "sent letters to all the royal provinces, to every province in its own script and to every people in its own language, declaring that every man should be master in his own house" (1.22). Here, not only do we have a reinforcement of the royal discourse, but also a more overt reference to the patriarchal discourse through the last phrase in 1.22.

This act concludes the pericope. The question now becomes, what conclusions can we draw based on the above observations? First, it seems obvious that the text is striving to confer power upon the royal discourse. Almost at every turn some device is used to reinforce the preconceived notion that a king has power, for example, the detailing of named servants and officials in the king's entourage as well as the mention of the reach of the royal discourse in 1.16 and 1.22. In this way, we are able to see that the royal discourse seems to be dominant in the control of power mechanisms and the distribution of knowledge. Second, even though Vashti has no reported speech and is the subject of only one verb, her act of resistance has far-reaching effects. As I note above, one could postulate that her act of refusal was also one of resistance to the dominant power structure, namely, the royal discourse and its attempts to define her as a passive object within the knowledge produced by the apparatuses of power at work within that discourse. Her sole act in the pericope, then, forces the royal discourse to reformulate its structure and its knowledge by altering its makeup. It does this by linking itself with the patriarchal discourse lurking behind the text and playing on that discourse's concern with female control. The royal discourse redefines itself by ousting Vashti as queen and putting forth propagandistic knowledge about her intended both to reinforce its own power and to bolster the control of women in the discourse of patriarchy. At the end of the pericope, we're not sure if the royal discourse has succeeded in its efforts, and we're not sure what happened to Vashti. It is ironic, however, that as a result of Vashti's act, Esther eventually gets appointed as queen, and she proves to be much more resistant and subversive than Vashti was. In conclusion, in this text there is a complex operation of power and its accompanying knowledge emerging as a response to an act of resistance.

The Gathering of Virgins and the Competition

Chapter 2 begins with Ahasuerus recalling all the events that had taken place in the first chapter, so presumably some time had elapsed between the two chapters.[6] Once he recalls Vashti and the events surrounding her dismissal, his servants are quick to propose a solution.

> Let beautiful young virgins be sought out for the king. And let the king appoint commissioners in all the provinces of his kingdom to gather all the beautiful young virgins to the harem in the citadel of Susa under the custody of Hegai, the king's eunuch, who is in charge of the women; let their cosmetic treatments be given them. And let the girl who pleases the king be queen instead of Vashti. (2.2–4)

This plan is of course not the accepted way a queen would have been chosen at this point in the Persian Empire.[7] Rather, it highlights the way in which the king is at the mercy of his bureaucracy, his royal discourse. As Jon D. Levenson notes, "*Everything* in Ahasuerus' realm is absurdly bureaucratized; even the king's sex life requires commissioners."[8] As such, the king is shown to be a rather ineffectual character, unable to perform tasks without help and suggestions from his entourage.

This plan also highlights again the patriarchal interests of the narrative. We saw in chapter 1 how Vashti's refusal to appear before the king alarmed

---

6. Levenson, *Esther*, 54, notes that Esther is taken before the king four years after the dismissal of Vashti. Since the virgins all underwent at least a year's worth of treatments in preparation for their meeting with the king, the time elapsed between chapters 1 and 2 is around two and a half years or so.

7. See Berlin, *Esther*, 23.

8. Levenson, *Esther*, 54.

his advisors to the point where they distributed an empire-wide admonition that "every man should be master in his own house" (1.22). Now that Vashti—the very symbol of resistance against patriarchal and royal authority—has been removed, more representatives of the royal discourse want to replace her with a new queen, one whose only requirements are "virginity and beauty."[9] Presumably they imagine that the new queen will be more docile and easier to control than Vashti, since royal lineage, education, and courtly knowledge do not factor into the king's decision. Docility was, of course, the quality that was lacking in Vashti, and by encouraging the king to make his decision solely on the basis of physical delight, the representatives of the crown hope to secure their own status within the royal discourse.

The narrator gives no indication that these virgins acquiesced to this plan, or that they had the freedom to do so. In fact, it appears that these women were simply taken to serve the interests of the king and his entourage. After they are taken, the narrative is specific as to what they can expect.

> The turn came for each girl to go in to King Ahasuerus, after being twelve months under the regulations for the women, since this was the regular period of their cosmetic treatment, six months with oil of myrrh and six months with perfumes and cosmetics for women. When the girl went in to the king she was given whatever she asked for to take with her from the harem to the king's palace. In the evening she went in; then in the morning she came back to the second harem in the custody of Shaashgaz, the king's eunuch, who was in charge of the concubines; she did not go in to the king again, unless the king delighted in her and she was summoned by name. (2.12–14)

We see clearly now the nature of this contest and its repercussions for the virgins. First, they spent an entire year preparing their bodies for an encounter with the king, which lasted only one night. They could take anything they wished with them for that encounter, but after their one night, they were consigned to a second harem, the place of the concubines, unless the king asked for them by name. Although the emphasis on beauty preparations has led many readers of Esther to assume that this is some sort of beauty contest, Michael V. Fox is probably correct when he writes, "The actual competition . . . is a sex contest, with the winner being whoever can most please the king during her night with him. Nothing but attractiveness to the king and sexual skills will, in this legendary account, determine who will become queen of Persia."[10] The implications of this claim are staggering. The king has sex with all of the attractive virgins from his kingdom, and then they are sent to his harem to remain as his concubines. As Adele

---

9. Fox, *Character and Ideology in the Book of Esther*, 27.
10. Ibid., 28. For a more skeptical view of the sexual nature of the contest, see Day, *Esther*, 51–52.

Berlin notes, "It is clear that none of the women returns home."[11] Since during this time virginity would have been a prerequisite to honorable marriage according to the societal mores of patriarchy, none of these former virgins would have been suitable for marriage after their royal encounter. In essence, the king is eradicating an entire generation of fertile women from his empire for his pleasure. In a startling comparison, the king's sexual genocide parallels Haman's desired genocide of the Jews. This act only reinforces the less than desirable characterization of the king that was initiated in chapter 1. As we shall see, though, one of these attractive virgins redeems the character of the king and in the process manages to save her people from genocide.

We first meet Esther in 2.7 in the context of the introduction of Mordecai. The latter is her cousin and has raised her as his own daughter, since she has no parents. As all good biblical heroines, she is "fair and beautiful" (2.7). Evidently she is also a virgin, because she too is taken away as part of the royal plan to find a new queen. She is put in the control of Hegai, the king's eunuch charged with preparing the virgins, and in 2.9 we are told, "The girl pleased him and won his favor, and he quickly provided her with her cosmetic treatments and her portion of food, and with seven chosen maids from the king's palace, and advanced her and her maids to the best place in the harem." The narrative is not specific as to how Esther pleased Hegai, but the results are impressive. As we saw above, each virgin was free to choose whatever she wished to take with her for her sexual romp with the king, but it seems only Esther relied on Hegai's advice (2.15). After the narrator makes sure we know that "Esther was admired by all who saw her" (2.15), she is taken to the king for her sexual encounter. Although the narrator provides us with no details as to what she took with her or what transpired between Esther and the king, evidently the encounter was memorable. Verse 17 relates the aftermath of Esther's night with the king in no uncertain terms: "The king loved Esther more than all the other women; of all the virgins she won his favor and devotion, so that he set the royal crown on her head and made her queen instead of Vashti."

An important yet puzzling component of Esther's rendezvous with the king is her cousin Mordecai's warning in 2.10 not to "reveal her people or kindred." That is, he cautions her not to tell anyone at the court that she is a Jew. Curiously, Mordecai's pedigree as a Benjaminite descendent of survivors from the exile is provided in 2.5–6, but no explanation of Esther's background is given. As such, the audience would be unsure at this point as to why Mordecai would ask Esther to do such a thing, since no emphasis seems to be placed on her identity as a Jew and no obvious threat to Jews is yet apparent. The narrative, though, is insistent on keeping this issue alive, as it mentions it again after Esther is crowned queen in 2.20.

---

11. Berlin, *Esther*, 28.

Of course, once Haman the Agagite is introduced in 3.1, the purpose of
Mordecai's warning and the inclusion of his Benjaminite ancestry becomes
clear.[12] At this point, though, it is satisfactory for us to note that Esther
has become queen, and the introduction of Haman in 3.1 sets the narrative
on a new course, one that will lead to potential annihilation for Esther and
her people.

Esther's Revelation

Haman hatches his genocidal plan to exterminate all the Jews in Persia in
chapter 3 after Mordecai refuses to bow before him. Once Haman convinces the king to dispatch a royal order "to destroy, to kill, and to annihilate all Jews, young and old, women and children, in one day, the thirteenth
day of the twelfth month, which is the month of Adar, and to plunder their
goods," the fate of the Persian Jews seems sealed (3.13). However,
Mordecai sends word to Esther, alerting her to the situation. Esther
demurs, noting that she cannot appear without being summoned before the
king. Mordecai's response is direct, but also loving. In 4.13–14, he says:

> Do not think that in the king's palace you will escape any more than all the
> other Jews. For if you keep silence at such a time as this, relief and deliverance
> will rise for the Jews from another quarter, but you and your father's family
> will perish. Who knows? Perhaps you have come to royal dignity for just such
> a time as this.

Esther's secret identity, it turns out, has guaranteed that she will not be
grouped with the other Persian Jews, destined for execution and plundering.
It is at this point that Esther is faced with a terrible decision. She can continue to hide her identity as a Jew, hope that no one will discover her secret,
and live; or she can "out" herself in an attempt to save her people. Of
course, she opts for the latter course and instructs Mordecai to ask all the
Jews to fast on her behalf, and she will also. On the third day of the fast,
she will go before her king, presumably to expose Haman's plot and beg for
the lives of the Jews. Esther makes this decision with a full appreciation of
the consequences, as she notes in 4.16: "I will go to the king, though it is
against the law; and if I perish, I perish."

The story's emphasis on Esther's actions and heroism is perhaps due to
one of the most noticeable qualities of the narrative: God is never mentioned. Instead, the story focuses entirely on the human realm, and yet

---

12. The animosity between Haman and Mordecai stems from an ancient feud between their
kin groups—Amalekite and Benjaminite, respectively. The Amalekites have been a hereditary
enemy of Israel ever since they attacked the Hebrews as they escaped from Israel (see Exodus
17 and Deuteronomy 25). In 1 Samuel 15, Saul (a member of the tribe of Benjamin) was
ordered to put the Amalekites to the *cherem*, that is, to completely destroy their civilization.
Saul's reluctance to do so leads to his rejection as king over Israel in favor of David. Evidently,
our author imagines the feud not only to have lasted into the postexilic period, but also to be
present in Persia.

things work out well for our protagonists and the "bad guys" get what is coming to them. In his work on Esther, André LaCocque notes that since the book does not present the reader with a sustained view of God, or theology, the "principle of peripety, the Aristotelian *peripeteia* (sudden change of fortune), is in Esther a veritable although implicit theology."[13] He continues, "Put in a nutshell, the 'theology' of Esther is Judeo-centered. Human action—*Jewish* action—either assists or resists the ultimate causality beneath the surface of events. When there is conformity between the two, history appears as a serendipitous sequence of cause and effect."[14] That is, when Esther and other Jewish characters engage in appropriately Jewish behavior, things turn out well for them. God, then, is working behind the scenes in the book of Esther, watching out for those Jews who follow Torah and protecting them. As we shall see, Esther and Mordecai will need all the protection they can get.

Esther approaches the king in 5.1, and he allows her to come forward without imposing any penalty. Apparently Esther still holds the king's favor, as he asks her, "What is it, Queen Esther? What is your request? It shall be given you, even to the half of my kingdom" (5.3). This is the moment when we expect Esther to reveal all to her king, to expose Haman's plot against her people, and to save the day. Instead, she invites the king and Haman to a banquet she will prepare for them. At the banquet, the king repeats his earlier question (5.6), and again we expect Esther to divulge her secret, but instead she asks them both to come to yet another banquet. They agree, and it is at this point that the narrative shifts focus to reveal Haman's deepening hatred for Mordecai (5.9–14). Once again, Mordecai refuses to bow before Haman, and Haman, still reveling in his status after dining with the royal couple, "was infuriated" (5.9). On the advice of his wife and friends, he has a gallows constructed for Mordecai that is "fifty cubits high," or a little over seventy feet high (5.14). Given that the preferred method of execution during the narrative setting in Persia was impalement, one can only speculate as to the deeper meaning of Haman's large phallic gallows as a remedy for his symbolic emasculation at the hands of Mordecai.

Furthermore, the narrator also raises the audience's anticipation by including the ironic and humorous story of Mordecai's royal lauding by Haman, no less, in chapter 6. Here, reference is made to Mordecai's uncovering and reporting of an assassination attempt against the king, which then was prevented in 2.21–23. In 6.1, we hear that the king is having trouble sleeping and wants the royal annals read to him to assist him in dozing off. As luck would have it, the portion read recorded Mordecai's act in chapter 2. The king discovers that Mordecai has yet to be honored for his service, and at this exact moment Haman enters, hoping

---

13. LaCocque, "Esther," 55.
14. Ibid., 62–63.

to persuade the king to allow him to impale Mordecai. Instead, the king asks Haman what should be done for the man the king wishes to honor. The irony is that Haman assumes the king is speaking of him, and as such he suggests a number of royal treatments. The king then orders Haman to do all these things for Mordecai. Having to honor Mordecai in public only inflames Haman's hatred for him and, by extension, all Jews. By the end of this chapter, the stage is set for Haman's downfall and Esther's triumph.

The scene in chapter 7 opens with the king, Esther, and Haman all eating amicably. For a third time, the king repeats his question to Esther in 7.2 (cf. 5.3, 6). This time, though, Esther finally answers, and in so doing reveals not only her secret, but also the plot against her people.

> If I have won your favor, O king, and if it pleases the king, let my life be given me—that is my petition—and the lives of my people—that is my request. For we have been sold, I and my people, to be destroyed, to be killed, and to be annihilated. If we had been sold merely as slaves, men and women, I would have held my peace; but no enemy can compensate for this damage to the king. (7.3–4)

The king asks for the identity of the plot's author, and Esther responds, "A foe and enemy, this wicked Haman!" The king becomes so upset that he leaves the feast, whereupon Haman begins to beg Esther to intercede for him. The king returns and believes that Haman is attacking Esther, and thus he orders that Haman be impaled on the very gallows he had constructed for Mordecai.

However, our story does not end with the execution of Haman. The royal edict has already gone out permitting Persians to attack, kill, and plunder Jews. Once the king appoints Mordecai to Haman's old position, Esther again petitions the king to rescind the edict. Once a royal edict is sent, though, it cannot be revoked, so Esther and Mordecai settle for the next best thing: they send another edict allowing Jews to defend themselves and to take revenge on their attackers. They were also given permission to plunder their attackers, but none of them did so (9.10, 15, 16). The days that the Jews successfully defended themselves are designated an official holiday in 9.20–32, called Purim after the lots thrown by Haman to determine the days on which he would exterminate the Jews. The story ends with a description of Mordecai's power and position in the Persian Empire.

CINEMATIC INTERPRETATIONS OF ESTHER

In the following section, I will examine the ways in which each of the five films I list above interprets and retells the above three scenes. My goal is to illuminate how the films retain or alter the characterizations I discussed above, and how these cinematic choices affect how we encounter the scroll of Esther.

"They Try to Make Me Come to Banquet, and I Say No, No, No"

As we saw above, the biblical narrative offers no indication as to why Vashti would refuse the king's invitation to join him at his banquet. The most common answer within Jewish interpretation is taken from *Esther Rabbah* and *Megillah* 12b. That is, when the king issues an order in 1.11 "to bring Queen Vashti before the king, wearing the royal crown, in order to show the peoples and the officials her beauty; for she was fair to behold," he means that she should come wearing nothing but the royal crown.[15] One can approach this reading charitably, in which case one could argue that Vashti refused the king's command out of pragmatic necessity; that is, she was smart enough not to subject herself to a roomful of drunk men wearing only a crown. In contrast, Jewish readers who are most unsympathetic to Vashti claim that it was not some fear or moral outrage that kept her from appearing; rather, the angel Gabriel appeared and afflicted her with leprosy. As such, she could not show herself to the king and his entourage in this state.[16]

In his film *Esther and the King* (1960), producer and director Raoul Walsh takes a decidedly different path. It seems clear that Walsh was trying to produce a lavish "biblical spectacular" along the lines of films like Cecil B. DeMille's *Samson and Delilah* (1949) and *The Ten Commandments* (1956), as well as Henry King's *David and Bathsheba* (1951), but it seems equally obvious that he failed.[17] His Vashti, played by the sultry Daniela Rocca, is not only having an affair with Haman; she has also had other lovers while the king has been away at war. By making Vashti an adulteress and involving her sexually with Haman, Walsh turns the biblical Vashti into a slutty schemer. In the film, when the king returns from war, he asks Mordecai—called by the king "the eye of the king, the keeper of the accounts, my all-knowing minister"—about Vashti's behavior in his absence. Mordecai remains silent, upon which the king confronts her and privately condemns her as dead to him. As such, the king does not send for Vashti to appear at his banquet at all. Nevertheless, she shows up and performs a striptease, winding up topless before the king sends her away. In response, she spits on him in front of all his guests, and the king orders her to be banished. At this, Haman sees an opportunity. Walsh depicts Haman as a drug user, an embezzler, and a seller of military secrets to the Greeks. Since Haman is obviously power hungry, he offers to find the king a new queen, presumably one who will work with him to overthrow the king. As we shall see, Haman even plants his own contestant among the other

---

15. See Darr, "More Than Just a Pretty Face," 169; and Louis Ginzberg, *Legends of the Jews*, vol. 2, *Bible Times and Characters from Moses in the Wilderness to Esther* (JPS Classic Reissues Series; Philadelphia: Jewish Publication Society, 2003), 1135.

16. Again, see Darr, "More Than Just a Pretty Face," 169; and Ginzberg, *Legends of the Jews*, 2:1135.

17. This term is taken from Gerald E. Forshey, *American Religious and Biblical Spectaculars* (Media and Society Series; Westport, Conn.: Praeger, 1992).

virgins. Haman then orders Vashti to be killed so that she will not be able to reveal any of his illegal enterprises. As such, Walsh significantly alters the biblical narrative in order to highlight the immorality of Vashti and to further the palace intrigue that lies at the heart of the character of Haman.

In the film *Esther* (1986), writer and director Amos Gitai presents the viewer with a starkly different understanding of the biblical story. He is quite literal to the narrative, and yet he intersperses scenes set in ancient Persia with sounds and scenery from the time of filming in the Arab village of Wadi Salib, near Haifa in Israel.[18] This chronological confusion serves to highlight the thematic parallels between the scroll of Esther and the way Gitai interprets Israeli actions and policies in the mid-1980s.[19] This overlap is especially evident in the powerful ending, where actors in the film all break character and begin to talk about their relationship to Israel, and in some cases, what they think of their characters. However, Gitai seems unconcerned with the story of Vashti and treats her textual existence in less than two minutes. This is a very short period, considering that the first four minutes of the film have no dialogue and only show a steady shot of the king's feast. When the king finally summons Vashti, the scene shifts to her tent, and her only response to his command is to shake her head vigorously. She then utters her only line in the film: "No." Gitai does not show the king's royal decree in response to Vashti's refusal, nor does he show her banishment. In sum, Gitai nearly negates Vashti's role in the narrative entirely, while preparing for Esther's entrance.

Raffaele Mertes's film *Esther* (1998), which is part of Five Mile River Films' The Bible Series, takes a decidedly more literal approach to the character of Vashti. The king—here played by Thomas Kretschmann and depicted as an unbalanced, immature ruler—holds a rather dour banquet at which Haman is challenged by another official to name the king's jewel he would most desire himself. After some equivocating, and a critique from the king himself for not answering the question directly, Haman diplomatically responds that the most precious jewel of the king's is Vashti. The scene then shifts to Vashti's quarters, where she is watching a play that ridicules Mesopotamian deities. When her guests object to the contents of the play, Vashti rebukes them strongly, noting, "I am the queen, and I do as I please in my chambers." At this point, the king's eunuch Harbona arrives with his order summoning her to his banquet. Vashti's refusal is based on her understanding of her status as a lady and a queen; to wit, she tells Harbona that it is unbefitting of someone of her stature to appear before a drunk, even if it is the king.

---

18. For more information on the setting of the film, see the recollections of Richard Ingersoll, the art director for the film, found in Paul Willemen, ed., *The Films of Amos Gitai: A Montage* (London: British Film Institute, 1993), 56–60.

19. Tamar Meroz notes that "this duality remains throughout the film as a counterpoint: the stylised Biblical plot and its metaphoric value for the here and now" (quoted in Willemen, *Films of Amos Gitai*, 62).

The king, being both inebriated and childish, responds with disbelief and acquiesces to his minister's suggestion that Vashti be banished. The film portrays this event very sympathetically, with mournful music and a close-up of Vashti's disconcerted face as she is carried out of the palace. After the banquet the king asks for her, and when he is told that he banished her, he blames it on the wine and asks in a pouting voice to rescind his order. His chief minister tells him that a royal edict cannot be overturned, and so the king asks his court for advice on the legal niceties of procuring a new queen. At this point, Haman proposes the collection of virgins, which I will discuss below. Mertes's film, then, depicts Vashti as a strong, independent character who refuses the king's demand out of her own feminine and royal dignity.

In 2000, Big Idea, Inc.—a leading Christian producer and marketer of children's books, videos, and music—released *VeggieTales—Esther: The Girl Who Became Queen*, a nonthreatening, nonsexual, nonviolent retelling of the book of Esther complete with musical numbers. The purpose of the film, as stated on Big Idea's website, is to teach the value of courage; more specifically, "The story of Queen Esther teaches kids that *you never need to be afraid to do what's right!*"[20] In keeping with this goal, the film certainly does not show the king having a lavish, boisterous drinking party. Rather, the filmmakers alter the biblical tale so that Vashti's removal as queen stems from something much more age-appropriate. The king wants Vashti to make him a sandwich at 3:00 a.m., and she refuses. As the queen is kicked out of the palace (in her curlers, no less), the king seems very upset. His advisor and confidant, Haman—who for some reason is depicted as a pseudo-mobster, with his pin-striped suit and gold tooth—tells him, "If she got away with that, no one would listen to you." The film, as such, provides no character traits for Vashti aside from her annoyance at being woken at such an early hour for such a silly task. Therefore, Vashti could still possibly be seen as a symbol of feminine resistance since she refused to be treated as a servant in her own house; but with no context to frame her refusal—as well as the pragmatic fact that the film's target audience is so young—it is more likely that this scene will simply be seen as a humorous one that paves the way for Haman's call for all "eligible young ladies" to see who will be the next queen.

A very different view of Vashti is found in the recent film *One Night with the King*, directed by Michael O. Sajbel and released in 2006. The film provides a lengthy historical introduction that begins with the events in 1 Samuel 15 in order to explain the enmity between the descendents of Benjamin and Agag. It also inserts the story of Agag's queen, who escaped Samuel's wrath while pregnant. The film also introduces Esther, Mordecai, and Haman before turning its attention to Vashti a full twelve minutes after

---

20. See Big Idea, Inc., product information for *Esther: The Girl Who Became Queen*; online: *http://bigidea.com/products/shows/shows_content.aspx?pid=43* (emphasis theirs).

its opening. We first encounter Vashti as a visitor in the king's chambers. It is clear that she loves the king and vice versa, and she tries to persuade him to resist all the calls for war with Greece to avenge the death of his father, Darius. Instead, she encourages him to stay in Persia and build up the kingdom's culture and education. To wit, she reminds him that he is not a warrior, but more of an artist. As such, Vashti is a more rounded character here and is obviously opposed to the brewing war.

The king's banquet is huge, raucous, and loud. By the time we are shown the drinking festival, we are aware that one of the king's princes, Admantha (played by John Noble, and looking identical to his character Denethor in *The Lord of the Rings: Return of the King*), is plotting to usurp the king. He is informed that Vashti is holding her own banquet in protest of the king's plans to go to war and manages to trap the king by issuing a public compliment to Vashti. Immediately following his compliment, he signals one of his men in the crowd, who begins calling for Vashti to come forth. The king, knowing of Vashti's views on the war, knows she will not come, but his princes put him on the spot by saying if she does not, the people may riot at the hint of a divided kingdom. So the king acquiesces and summons her. Her response, while similar to Mertes's Vashti, makes it clear that pacifism, as well as dignity, underlies her refusal. When the report is brought to the king, Admantha shrewdly tells him that when the Greeks hear about Vashti's refusal, they will assume that the king is weak and the kingdom divided. The king then proclaims that the kingdom is now without a queen, and we are shown a sad king watching Vashti led out of the palace. Sajbel thus shows us a Vashti who is far more rounded than we have seen, except perhaps in Mertes's film, and in so doing he lays the groundwork for the recurring theme of the king's remorse over sending her away.

In sum, our films present Vashti as a slut, a dignified queen, a pacifist, and a fairly ordinary housewife. Almost all of these characterizations are found in other renderings, as we have seen above. What all of the portrayals share, though, is the sense that Vashti is a prologue, a stepping-stone, for the coming of Esther, whose presence will allow the king to become a more just and compassionate ruler. Before she can accomplish that feat, though, she must enter the royal household. For that, we must examine how our films render the gathering of the virgins.

Hunting for Virgins and Esther's Success in the Competition

We saw above how Vashti's refusal to appear before the king constitutes a challenge to the power structure of the royal discourse and necessitates a restructuring of that discourse in order to ensure a consolidation of power. That restructuring requires removing Vashti and finding a replacement queen who would be more docile, more malleable than Vashti. As such, an empire-wide hunt is initiated for attractive virgins to take Vashti's place. These virgins are to undergo a year-long beautification treatment in preparation for a one-night sexual encounter with the king. After this, if the king does not summon the former virgin by name, she is sent to live in the second harem. If the king favors one of the virgins and calls for her by name, then she will become queen. The biblical narrative presents a fairly bleak picture of the competition, as it implies that every woman who has sex with the king will be trapped in the second harem, unsuitable for marriage. Some of our films retain this dreary image, but we also see glimpses of enjoyment, merriment, and riches.

Esther and the King presents the gathering of the virgins as a frightening kidnapping, complete with ominous music. Curiously, the film's use of kidnappers on horseback chasing their prey through fields tall with stalks is reminiscent of another kidnapping scene, although in the film *Planet of the Apes* of 1968, the prey are human slaves and the kidnappers are gorillas. Both the virgins and the human slaves, though, seem destined for lives of forgotten servitude. In our film, Esther is engaged to a young soldier of the king's named Simon, and the hunt for virgins coincides with her wedding. She is actually snatched at the altar in her wedding gown. Simon tries to fight for her and attacks a Persian soldier, causing a pogrom against the Jews. Mordecai even comments, "From that one spark, a holocaust!" After Esther is taken to the royal compound, Mordecai goes to see her. He tells her that she can save their people from further persecution by becoming queen and swaying the king. She objects that she wants to go home to Simon, but Mordecai tells her, "This is your war, Esther." It is at this point that he encourages her to hide her Jewishness.

Once Esther is in Hegai's charge, the film narrows its focus to Esther's plight, and the eunuch becomes impressed with Esther's modesty. She is not happy to be in his charge, though, and tries to escape. Along with two other candidates, she is assaulted by several palace guards before the king intervenes and saves the women. Neither the women nor the guards know that he is the king, though, as he is not wearing any royal garments. In spite of his chivalrous defense of the women, the king seems totally disinterested in choosing a new queen, and his reticence, along with Esther's modesty, precludes the film from portraying the competition as a sex contest. Rather, it is a beauty contest based on first impressions. To add intrigue to the plot, Haman is backing a specific contender, so that if she becomes queen he can consolidate his political power. Because of this, Haman orders Esther to be killed so that his candidate for queen can have a better chance. Esther's modesty saves her life from this plot, as Hegai presents Esther with a lovely gold cloak to take with her for her catwalk in front of the king. Observing this, Haman orders his assassin to kill the girl in the gold cloak. However, just before her turn arrives, Haman's candidate for queen steals Esther's cloak and is thereby murdered. Esther is not upset at the loss of her cloak, for Hegai reveals to her that those virgins not chosen will be allowed to go home, and the prospect of reuniting with Simon fills her with joy. As such, when she does her strut before the king, she tries to be done with it as quickly as possible. Once she sees that the king is the man who saved her, though, her interest piques, as does his. Even though she tells him she was about to be married, he explains that he is bound by the law, disgruntled with it though he may be. As such, he does not command, but rather he asks Esther to stay with him for a while so she can decide if she wishes to be queen. She agrees, and Hegai leads her away.

In this film, then, the hunt for virgins is just that, a hunt that is frightening for the young women who are captured and devastating for the families they leave behind. Once in the castle, though, it is clear that the women are treated well. They are subject to massages and oiled and primped and preened. Most significantly, though, they are not made to have sex with the king. Rather, they are told to dress in their finery, walk before the king, bow, and then leave. If he does not stop them, they are free to return to their homes, unmolested. As Hegai tells Esther, "You are children of the kingdom, not captive concubines." The morphing of the biblical contest into a beauty contest allows Esther to remain pure and modest, but more importantly for this film, it allows the king to be portrayed in a kind and compassionate light, a characterization that is dominant throughout the film.

As with the previous issue, Gitai's film presents us with a very different rendering of these scenes. In contrast to Walsh's film, we are not shown any virginal abductions. Instead, we see nine virgins arriving at the palace before the scene shifts to the harem. Gitai spends a good deal of time showing us the harem, which he sets in a steam bath. The virgins are being attended to in towels by female attendants while a man sings "an Arab wedding song."[21] The lyrics focus on the transition between girlhood and womanhood with multiple references to the loss of virginity.

The repeated refrain, "O little girl, tomorrow you will be a woman," serves to highlight the situation of the virgins in the harem, as well as the fact that Gitai represents the competition as a sex contest. Prior to their encounter with the king, most of the virgins would have been pubescent girls, around the age of thirteen or so. As such, they would have been very much "little girls." After having sex with the king, though, they would no longer be girls but would be seen as women. Had they had sex with their spouses, they would have been ready for childbearing and other duties of wives in the ancient world. In this narrative, though, they would simply be sent to the second harem to live out their days as concubines.

After the beauty treatments, Esther is brought before the king during the daytime, and he extends his royal scepter to her. Since Gitai does not include any love scene between the two, there is some confusion over the meaning of this scene. Does the extension of the scepter imply that the king chooses Esther to be his queen without having sex with her? Or are we simply not shown the sex scene? This confusion is magnified by the inclusion of a long close-up of Esther's face after the encounter with the king, in

---

21. Rachel Neeman, "Esther," in Willemen, *Films of Amos Gitai*, 60.

which a female voice recites Song 2.16–3.4. This poetry of longing for a lost loved one is followed in the film by a nocturnal scene between the king and Esther in which he places a crown on her head. Gitai then shows us the wedding of Esther and the king, with a long processional of guests bearing gifts.

Gitai's interpretation of the biblical narrative is quite interesting. First, he flouts what I will show to be the common cinematic rendering by following the biblical narrative closely and excluding any kidnapping scene. Second, his harem and the song sung therein highlight the condition of the virgins in the narrative in a stark way, something none of our other films will attempt. Third, in omitting the near obligatory movie love scene between the king and Esther, Gitai allows viewers to draw their own conclusions as to how exactly Esther is chosen queen. Finally, he includes a wedding, which is not found in the biblical text, but the wedding scene seems more focused on showing the vast number of guests than on revealing anything of the nature of the relationship between the king and Esther. By continually flouting the methods and emphases of our other films, Gitai forces viewers to find their own meaning(s) in the images he presents.

In *Esther*, Mertes, like Walsh, shows the abductions of the virgins. Here, doors are kicked in, houses are searched, and the virgins—some of whom are obviously young teens—are dragged kicking and screaming from their homes. Once Mordecai realizes what is happening, he rushes home to try to hide Esther.[22] His attempt fails, and she and numerous other young women are taken into the palace. There, she meets Hegai as he tells all the girls they will be prepared to encounter the king in the royal bedchamber. As such, the contest here is based on sex, not just good looks. We are shown the candidates' beauty treatments only briefly, and during this scene Esther asks the servant massaging her about sex. This is a curious inclusion, as it marks Esther as interested in sex, when usually she is portrayed as piously disinterested.

For his part, the king is definitely disinterested. When Esther enters his bedchamber, he can hardly be bothered to look up from his work to acknowledge her. They engage in small talk, but once he sees her face, the background music swells and he rises from his desk. As I note above, though, Thomas Kretschmann plays the king as an emotionally unhinged fool, so he immediately accuses Esther of being just like the other candidates, lying in order to obtain his favor. Resigned to making love to her, he utters, "Well, let us do what has to be done." At this point, a rose falls from Esther's veil as the king removes it. As he questions her about the flower, his demeanor changes as she admits she did not bring it as a gift for him, but rather picked it for herself. She asks his forgiveness, and he tells her that

---

22. This idea that Mordecai tries to prevent Esther from being taken is an ancient one that originates among Jewish interpreters of Scripture. See Darr, "More Than Just a Pretty Face," 172–73; and Waldman, *Megillat Esther*, 38–39.

she is in fact not like the others because of her courage. Esther responds, "Perhaps. The truth is that I've always been afraid of the unknown. And I've never known a man." The king tenderly replies, "Esther, no one will hurt you," as he unties her dress. The ensuing love scene is very gentle, but also very "PG." Afterward, there is no deliberation, no insight from the king. Esther is simply crowned queen. By highlighting Esther's sexual inexperience, as well as portraying several of the virgins as young teenagers, the film (most likely unintentionally) emphasizes the sexually abusive nature of the contest for those forced to participate. Furthermore, by showing the king's tenderness, Mertes makes his character appear all the more unstable, as this tenderness does not last in the film.

As one might imagine, the gathering of queenly candidates in the *VeggieTales* Esther film is depicted somewhat differently than in our other films. Here, Haman drives through town in a long black sedan with a trailer attached and simply orders all "eligible young ladies" to come with him. When he approaches Esther and orders her to get in, he has a comical run-in with Mordecai during which we learn that Mordecai will not bow to Haman. This conflict lays the foundation for Mordecai's instruction to Esther not to tell anyone she is related to him or their family, because then Haman would hate her, too. Tellingly, the film never mentions the word "Jew," and by turning the ancient feud between Mordecai and Haman into a family squabble, the story is robbed of its religious nature. That is, by negating any and all Jewish identity from the story of Esther, *VeggieTales* explicitly vanquishes any religious specificity from the story, and in so doing turns the near genocide of Jews into a possible familial banishment to the Island of Perpetual Tickling (no, seriously). Given our situation in a post-Holocaust world, this denigration of anti-Jewish persecution is irresponsible, to say the least.

Esther obviously does not want to be in the palace, and she even sings about it in a Disney-esque tune. More singing is to come, because in this film the contest is obviously not a sexual one. Rather, the competition resembles a school talent show or a Broadway audition, as it is set in an auditorium with the king and Haman the only members of the audience. After contestant number 37—who played the accordion and sang about puppies—Esther has her turn. She sings a song her grandmother used to sing to her about trusting in God, and we see the king's face light up in awe. After she finishes, both he and Haman give her a thumbs-up sign, and the announcer introduces her as Queen Esther. By altering the biblical narrative in such a way, the film is obviously trying to appeal to its audience through humor and song along with an obviously religiously didactic message, but lost is the objectification of women, the sexual abuse, the hopelessness of the contestants, and the absence of God in the biblical narrative. After viewing these scenes, one wonders if more discretion in choosing appropriate biblical stories for a *VeggieTale* adaptation would have been in order. That is, the scroll of Esther has been so changed by the producers and so little of the original story is left that I wonder what the point of rendering Esther for young children could be.

One Night with the King also includes some interesting interpretive alterations to the biblical text in its portrayal of the gathering of virgins and the competition. First, the film makes it clear that the search for a new queen is a political necessity. As the king prepares to wage war on Greece, a queen is needed in order to unify the people in his absence. Second, as if to temper the gathering of virgins, the film shows us a kidnapping of young men to become servant-eunuchs for the captured virgins, a fate that befalls Esther's love interest, Jesse. Third, the film betrays its religiously didactic purpose by having Esther worry about keeping the commandments if she is chosen for the harem. Mordecai tries to reassure her by telling her that God will notice her internal adherence to the commandments, yet even this modest claim exceeds the biblical narrative's interest in God. Fourth, Sajbel stays close to some of our other films by depicting the capture of the virgins as a terrifying event, during which Esther's special necklace is ripped from her neck. This necklace was a gift from her parents, who received it from Israel, and when held to a flame, stars of David are refracted through the crystal pendant. Once they arrive in the palace, Esther begins to pray aloud to ease her discomfort and that of her friends. She also prances around, whimsically adorning her friends with silks in an attempt to cheer them up. Esther's peppiness here bears more than a passing resemblance to Disney princesses, a characterization that recurs more than once in the film, as Donna Bowman has recently noted.[23]

Fifth, once all the virgins are asleep, the film shows Esther having a flashback to her parents' murder in an Agagite pogrom. By connecting her capture and her parents' deaths, the film seems to imply that the anti-Jewish nature of the pogrom and the sexually abusive nature of the virgin hunt are compatible. The scene that immediately follows this flashback shows Esther dancing in a palace field, imagining that she is in a storm of snow (or possibly manna). Hegai interrupts her and she sees that she is standing in the field with nothing falling on her. In the exchange that follows, Sajbel again highlights Esther's childlike demeanor as well as shows how it affects others in the harem, especially Hegai, who watches her smiling as she continues to dance in the field. The film, then, seems interested in portraying Esther as a fanciful girl with a creative imagination and a plucky courage, as a dreamer who is both kind and smart—again, all traits that are associated with Disney princesses.[24] Sixth, we are shown some of the beauty

---

23. See Donna Bowman, "The Bible-Shaped Mirror: Biblical Women and Contemporary Culture in Recent Film," *SBL Forum* (summer 2008; online: *http://www.sbl-site.org/Article.aspx?ArticleID=778*), par. 3.

24. See Jennifer Liberts Weinberg's preschool-level book *What Is a Princess?* (New York: Random House, 2004) for these and other traits of Disney princesses. In her work, Bowman describes the film's characterization of Esther as a "Manic Pixie Dream Girl" ("Bible-Shaped Mirror," par. 4).

treatments in the harem, but unlike in Gitai's film these images are fleeting, mere accompaniments to Hegai's description of harem life as potentially idyllic: Esther clearly does not embrace life in the harem, as she takes some pork under the watchful eye of Hegai but then gives it the to roaming monkeys in the palace gardens. She then expresses to Hegai her discomfort with the beauty treatments and lessons she and the other candidates have been receiving, saying that none of them will help with actually being queen. This involves, Esther claims, "the thought well thought, the word well spoken, and the deed well done." Amused by this, as well as her claim to be literate and multilingual, Hegai brings her some stories to read, specifically Gilgamesh. As Esther reads aloud, more and more of the candidates, as well as Hegai himself, come to listen. Thus, we see Hegai's fondness and admiration of Esther growing as she demonstrates her intelligence and independence of thought. Seventh, the biblical narrative states that the candidates may take with them whatever they choose for their encounter with the king. Here, Sajbel tweaks this to mean that each candidate may take—and keep—whatever they wish from the royal treasury. As the other virgins gleefully run into the treasury, Esther demurs. After she requests his help, Hegai gives her a necklace, the very necklace that had been taken from her when she was captured. This necklace—with its beautiful crystal and stars of David only visible when light is refracted through it—serves as a symbol for Esther, with her beauty and hidden Jewishness, and it will resurface later.

Eighth, Hegai invites Esther to read the official chronicles for the king at night prior to the official selection of the queen. The king does not see her at first, but as she deviates from the royal chronicle and begins to tell him the story of Jacob, Rachel, and Leah (found in Genesis 29–30), he becomes intrigued and invites her to see the figures he is sculpting. As the king queries Esther about the story, they talk of love, and it is clear that they are interested in each other. The king tells Esther that she will read for him again, and Esther, for her part, dreams that the king comes to her bed and kisses her. Esther's interest in the king is seen even more clearly when Jesse, now a eunuch, tries to get her to escape and she refuses. By this inclusion, the film lays the groundwork for an emotional connection between Esther and the king that reiterates her intelligence as well.[25] Ninth, Sajbel shows us humorous scenes with other candidates. One evidently has taken so much jewelry from the royal treasury that she cannot mount a horse without aid. The second is so nervous that when her night comes she vomits from her anxiety, unable to remain in the king's presence. By including these scenes as well as Hegai's pronouncement to each virgin that even though she enters as a peasant she will emerge as a princess, the

---

25. Bowman argues that the story of "Jacob working seven years for Rachel and Laban's trickery in substituting Leah, becomes a thematic framework on which the filmmakers hang the whole tale" ("Bible-Shaped Mirror," par. 8).

film tempers the sexual nature of the royal encounters. Tenth and finally, this absence of sex is also seen in Esther's rendezvous with the king. There is no sex here, but quite a bit of verbal sparring. The king accuses Esther of equating him with Rachel, and berates her for wearing only her simple necklace as an adornment for their encounter. When Esther offers her necklace to the king as a gift, he accepts it grudgingly, and they proceed to converse on love. During this emotional conversation, the king offers Esther his heart as a gift and asks her to marry him.

Immediately following this is no sex scene, but a wedding complete with a Disney-esque song interspersed with scenes of the royal couple following the wedding. As if to reinforce the love between the king and Esther, the king tells her after the wedding that he greatly desired to return to Esther after his first night with her, and that he even invented excuses not to entertain other contestants. The scene then closes with the two fully clothed, kissing on the edge of the royal bed.

These ten alterations serve to imbue Esther with traits extraneous to her characterization at this point in the biblical narrative, traits such as intelligence, literacy, free thinking, and courage. They also render the relationship between the king and Esther as a loving one. Both of these interpretive moves decrease the abusive nature of the virgin hunt and increase the religiousness of the story. By doing so, Esther becomes something of a Jewish Disney princess, and the king is reshaped into a caring and complicated character, quite unlike his biblical counterpart. In sum, Sajbel alters the contest so it becomes more sanitary, a wonderland of free treasures, and a series of amusing encounters that lead up to the finding of true love.

All of our films insert significant alterations into their retellings of the scroll of Esther. Most portray the gathering of virgins for the king as a frightful kidnapping with families being torn apart and young teenage girls being dragged from their homes. The nature of the contest is also changed; in three of our films the contest is certainly a sexual one, but only one of those films actually shows the viewer the king and Esther having sex. Another film portrays the contest as a beauty show, and *VeggieTales* interprets it as a high-school talent show, complete with sashes and a house band. By retelling the story in a way that downplays the violence and sexual abuse of the abducted virgins, these films diminish the harsh reality portrayed in the biblical narrative. Similarly, Esther's encounter with the king proves fertile ground due to the biblical narrative's reticence. Several films imagine Esther as being an unwilling participant, but Walsh, Mertes, and Sajbel all show Esther as being interested, infatuated, or in love with the king, respectively. Another key addition found in all of the films except Gitai's and Walsh's is the superimposing of a religiously didactic moral onto Esther's story. That is, the three remaining films all interpret the story in explicitly religious terms by having Esther pray or worry about keeping the commandments or tell stories from Torah or even sing about God. This is part and parcel of a common fleshing out of Esther's character, taken to new and rather strange heights in Sajbel's film, as we have seen. The net effect of all these additions and alterations is to expand the characterization of both Esther and the king, as well as to deemphasize the sexual nature of the contest.

Esther as Heroine: The Revelation in Chapter 7

As I note above, Esther's "coming out" occurs after Mordecai informs her of Haman's genocidal plot to exterminate all Persian Jews. She could have remained quiet; after all, no one save Mordecai knows she is a Jew. However, during the second of two banquets, she reveals her religious affiliation before the king and Haman. The king then sentences Haman to death on the very gallows Haman had prepared for Mordecai. Almost all of our films use the report in the biblical text to make Esther look even more heroic than she does therein, and in so doing they turn her into a champion of human rights and religious freedom.

After the competition in *Esther and the King*, Esther still has not decided if she wishes to be queen. Her mind is made up after her former fiancé, Simon, breaks into the palace in a rescue attempt. She refuses to come with him, and after the guards engage him in a high-speed pursuit, she and the king have an exchange in which Esther tells Ahasuerus that she wants to be his wife. He responds that she should don the crown, and then anything she desires will be hers. All that she wants, Esther retorts, is his heart, filled as it is with love and mercy. Nobly, the king says that his heart is already hers, that she rules both his heart and his life. Here, the film reiterates its emphasis on the king's compassion and mercy and links these qualities specifically with Esther's love. Additionally, the film explicitly shows Esther and the king in love, which is not clear at all in the biblical text.

Following this scene, we are shown Haman's plot to exterminate all the Jews taking shape in response to the king's plan to withdraw money from the royal treasury at Persepolis. The viewer knows that Haman has been looting money from the treasury for some time, and now it appears he will be discovered. Haman quickly devises a plan to divert attention from his embezzling as well as increase the royal revenue in the hopes that the money will not be missed. He proposes a law that anyone who does not bow down to the Persian gods should be executed and their properties seized by the throne, and specifically mentions Judeans as a tremendous source of wealth if the law is passed. Both Mordecai and Esther speak out against the law. The king sides with Esther, decrees religious toleration for the Jews, and announces that Haman will be relocated to a post in the Syrian Desert. Haman then decides to persuade the king to reverse his decision by framing Mordecai as a traitor, a seller of military secrets—something that Haman has been doing all along. He even publicly accuses Esther of conspiring with Mordecai after observing the two of them meeting privately.

The king orders the execution of Mordecai and the death of all the Jews based on Haman's fabricated evidence. It is at this point that Esther speaks up and accuses the king of deceiving her with his earlier gift of mercy. She then announces that she is a Jew, at which the king pauses and asks her to abandon her faith. In one of the most moving lines in the film, Esther refuses, noting that she and her people will still be practicing their faith when the Persian kingdom is nothing but rubble. She concludes by saying she does not blame the king, because she knows that Haman is silently manipulating him.

Based on her suspicions of Haman, she advises the king not to enact his order until he visits the treasury at Persepolis for himself. He decides to go, and Haman's men attempt to kill him on the way there. Esther's former love, Simon, even shows up to try to kill the king for taking her from him, but the king and he reconcile. Once the king learns of Haman's plot from one of his men, he sends Simon back to arm the Judeans. Simon manages to save Mordecai from the gallows but is mortally wounded in the battle. The king returns to the city just in time to thwart Haman's escape and to order his execution. The film ends with Simon's death and Esther uncertain about her relationship with the king. As the Persians return from a defeat at the hands of the Greeks, Esther runs to the king and embraces him. The two ride off together into the sunset in his chariot.

The convoluted plot Walsh hatches in this film omits Esther's banquets as well as her grim preparations before speaking to the king. Instead, her revelation seems more a spur-of-the-moment decision here, even if her speech is rather eloquent. The king's response also differs from the biblical narrative. Here, he is deeply wounded by Esther's dishonesty and even tells her that he no longer believes she loves him. Haman's plan for the Jews is more political expediency than religious hatred, and, as played by Sergio Fantoni, Haman comes across more as a crooked politician looking for a scapegoat than as a genocidal anti-Semite. The most important change is to remove Esther and her revelation from center stage. Indeed, Esther seems overshadowed by the intrigues and attempted murders with which Walsh populates his film. By diminishing Esther's role, emphasizing the king's mercy and compassion, and rendering Haman as a rabid politico, Walsh effectively morphs the story from one concerning religious identity, piety, and survival to a soap opera drama that focuses more on style than substance.

Gitai's *Esther* is far more interested in exploring the nature of Haman's plan than it is in examining Esther's revelation. Haman and the king discuss Haman's plan, and the king gives his permission to enact the plan. Gitai then spends a full eight minutes of the film having the narrator recite the decree over and over again in different settings. Curiously, the narrator includes a speech in the decree that warns listeners about an evil people who isolate themselves from the rest of the world through their unique practices and worship, and as such this people should be destroyed for the peace and security of the kingdom.

This speech is very close to one of the Greek additions to the book of Esther, most likely composed in the first century B.C.E.[26] In Addition B, inserted between 3.13 and 3.14, the text of Ahasuerus's decree is recorded, and 13.3–7 is very similar to the narrator's speech. Mordecai's reaction is similar to the biblical text; he is shocked and despondent. Word is sent to Esther, and she offers no resistance to Mordecai's plan. In fact, her attitude is one of quiet resignation and acquiescence. As we shall see, this is not the case with our other films, nor is the lack of concern over violating protocol by coming before the king unsummoned.

Gitai does include a scene in which Esther prepares to go before the king. Like the scene in the harem, Gitai includes an Arab song here. The song focuses on the anguish that the speaker feels as they face death, and notes that if they die they shall return to their homeland, in which they will use their blood to plant flowers.

The meaning here more than makes up for any lack of dramatic engagement on the part of Esther. She goes to the king and requests that he and Haman attend a banquet. At that banquet, she asks that they come to another banquet. Gitai follows the biblical text rather slavishly at this point, having the actors repeat the text almost verbatim. In fact, Esther's revelation is played as a rather bland, unemotional scene by Simone Benyamini. As such, Gitai shows that he is less interested in Esther's character than in using her story as a springboard for provoking a wider discussion about the ramifications of religiously based violence, and perhaps the situation of Palestinians under Israeli rule.[27]

In the film *Esther*, Mertes too lavishes attention on Haman's plan in a rather thinly veiled series of allusions to the Holocaust. First, Haman delivers a vitriolic speech in which he charges the Jews with cheating everyone and flaunting their wealth before declaring that all the Jews should be destroyed. Since the king in this film is an unbalanced and paranoid figure, he believes Haman's anti-Jewish vitriol and gives him royal power to issue his decree. Mordecai's response to the edict offers another parallel to the Holocaust, as he expresses disbelief that their neighbors, their friends,

---

26. For a brief summary of the dating of the Greek additions to Esther, see Elias J. Bickerman, "The Colophon of the Greek Book of Esther," *Journal of Biblical Literature* 63 (1944): 339–62; Sidnie White Crawford, "The Additions to Esther," in *The New Interpreter's Bible* (ed. Leander Keck et al.; Nashville: Abingdon Press, 1994–2002), 3:970–72; and my "(Re)Dating the Story of Susanna: A Proposal," *Journal for the Study of Judaism in the Persian, Hellenistic, and Roman Periods* 34 (2003) 2:132–34.

27. Neeman writes, "At one level, the film is a statement against the historical lesson learnt by the Jews, who were once a repressed minority and are today a repressive military presence. 'They are persecuting an innocent people,' cries Mordecai in Wadi Salib. But the casting of an Arab actor in the role of Mordecai the Jew introduces a new dimension, and with it an even more original comment: when the oppressed Palestinian refugees become independent, they too will go through a similar process and discover for themselves an object for oppression. The transition from oppressed to oppressor will not spare them and Mordecai, in Gitai's film, is not only the present day Jew but also the future Palestinian" ("Esther," 61).

would let anything like this happen. Once the reality sets in, Mordecai mourns and wails publicly in sackcloth and ashes. He also manages to send word to Esther, who is despondent and confused upon hearing the news. Once she finishes weeping, she arranges a meeting with Mordecai in which she recounts her plan in 4.16.

Esther is portrayed as very nervous to go before the king due to her impending violation of court protocol, as well as the punishment for such a violation: death. Prior to her entering the court, the films intersperses scenes of prayer from Ezra, Mordecai, and Esther. Like Gitai, Mertes draws upon the Greek additions to Esther, but here Addition C is used, in which we find a prayer from Esther to God (14.3–19). The inclusion of this panoply of prayer highlights the religious nature of the tale, and specifically Esther's faith. When she enters the court, the film uses a combination of music and slow motion to show her fear along with the shocked looks of court officials that demonstrate the extent of her violation. The king's forgiveness of Esther as well as Esther's subsequent invitation and banquets all follow the biblical story closely. Even Esther's plea for her people in 7.3–5 is repeated nearly word for word. The king is outraged at Haman's plot, crying out to Esther, "You cannot be sold! You're mine!" Haman is condemned to be hung, and the rest of the narrative again parrots the narrative of Esther, with two important exceptions. First, the king comes to Esther after the violence recounted in chapter 9 and makes a request of her. He asks her to be his queen and in uncharacteristically flowery language assures Esther that he loves her as he has never loved any other woman. Esther very simply agrees to be his queen. This inclusion serves to further the underdeveloped love story between Esther and the king, and it rather confusingly renders the king as a tender man, wholly committed to Esther, a characterization that is far from apparent in the rest of the film. Second, the film ends not with Purim, but with the journey of Ezra to Jerusalem. In fact, the last dialogue in the film consists of a recitation of the opening of Genesis 1 by Ezra. By connecting the story of Esther with the continuation of the Jewish community in what will become Israel, Mertes evidently wants to put a positive spin on the violent end of Esther. Given what we know of Ezra and his and Nehemiah's attitudes toward cultural assimilation, though, it is doubtful that he and the family of Mordecai would have been so chummy.[28] In sum, then, Mertes shows us more of the internal workings of Esther's dilemma through the concern over court protocol as well as the scenes of prayer, but the inclusion of Haman's hatred allows the film to be seen as a precursor to modern violence against Jews.

As I note above, *VeggieTales* does not include any mention of anti-Jewish hatred, or anything about Jews at all, for that matter. As such, Haman's plot does not center on the genocide of all the Persian Jews, but rather consists of a plan to send Mordecai and all his family to the Island of Perpetual

---

28. See Ezra 2; 9.1–10.17; Neh. 2.20; 7.5–69.

Tickling. He convinces the king to sign off on his plan by singing a song about a family that cannot be trusted, and once Mordecai discovers Haman's plot, he goes to Esther for help. Esther flatly refuses, telling Mordecai that she never wanted to be queen in the first place, along with the fact that she fears for her life since she cannot go before the king without being called. After trying to convince her, Mordecai leaves and Esther is left alone to search out her conscience. This she does through singing again her two songs, and this scene nicely parallels both Gitai's and Mertes's films in that we are given a glance inside Esther's decision to go before the king. Whereas those films include both a mournful song about sacrificing one's life and a prayer adapted from the Greek additions to Esther, *VeggieTales* again injects a hefty dose of generic religiosity into its story.

After her songs, Esther decides to go see the king uninvited. Not surprisingly, there is no fasting here, presumably because fasting is too complicated a concept for the film's target audience. The scene in which Esther enters the royal court is tense, and she is obviously nervous. The tension is finally broken when the king says, "Come on over here, queenie-poo!" Esther then begins to speak, but falters as all she can think of is to invite the king and Haman to a banquet. At the banquet—where Chinese food is served and Trivial Pursuit is played—the queen musters up all her courage, but again demurs and invites them to another banquet. Of course, it is at the second banquet that she finally reveals Haman's plot to the king and announces, "Mordecai is my cousin. His family is my family." The king is very upset with Haman and banishes him to the Island of Perpetual Tickling, saying that anyone who plots against Esther's family will be banished, too. Obviously, there is no retribution, no violence, and no Purim here. There is, however, a moral to the tale. In the context of summarizing the story, the narrator tells us that even though Esther may not have been born great, she believed in God, so she accomplished her goals. And as if to punctuate the point, the narrator reminds the audience that Esther was an ordinary kid, "just like you."

I asked above what the point might be in adapting a story like Esther for children since it seems so emphatically inappropriate. The producers of *VeggieTales* show here what their point is in rendering this story, namely, to hold Esther up as a paragon of faithful courage. However, since the danger to her "family" is effectively negated, it is difficult to see Esther's courage in this context. As such, I remain confused as to why the story of Esther was chosen for inclusion by a company that markets videos to children.

Our final film, Sajbel's *One Night with the King*, increases the danger for Esther and the Jews by creating the most evil and nefarious Haman yet (played to the hilt by James Callis, better known for his portrayal of Dr. Gaius Baltar in *Battlestar Galactica*). As I note above, the film takes pains to establish the antiquity of Haman's hatred of the Jews and even gives him his own symbol. Just as Esther has her special, secret Jewish necklace, Haman has a talisman made by his mother that oddly resembles a swastika.

If we add this symbol to Haman's anti-Jewish pep rally following the marriage of Esther and the king—at which he claims to have proof of a Jewish conspiracy with the Greeks to take over the world (obvious shades of the *Protocols of the Elders of Zion*)—then it is obvious that Sajbel, like Mertes, is making full use of history's anti-Jewish repertoire, especially in the shadow of the Shoah.[29] However, this is a major motion picture, not a history lesson, so Sajbel intertwines Haman's plots with a romantic twist for our lovers. The king returns from battle to surprise Esther but sees her exiting the "Lovers' Gate" of the palace after speaking with Mordecai. Since the king is unaware of her relationship with Mordecai, he assumes that she is having an affair. Later, when she approaches his bedchamber, she hears giggling coming from inside, and she assumes that he is having an affair, when in fact it is merely the servants making his bed. The king attempts to reconcile with Esther, even telling her, "I believed I was your Rachel, but it appears I am only Leah and you serve time with me for another."[30] Esther cannot reveal her relationship with Mordecai, though, without revealing her Jewishness. Thus, the couple becomes estranged, paving the way for Esther's consternation later over not being summoned by the king.

Haman's ambitions are furthered when he presents his plan to annihilate the Jews to the king as a political solution to the problem of military funding. The king's general, Memucan, resigns in protest and convinces Esther to talk to the king about Haman's plan. When she approaches him, the king exclaims that Esther cares more for the Jews than for him, and sends her away with the warning that she should come before him no more or else her punishment will be more severe than Vashti's. Again, Sajbel is highlighting the alienation between the king and Esther while at the same time showing Esther's increasing concern over the fate of her people. This encounter is followed by the sending of Haman's orders regarding the slaying of the Jews. After the edict is made public, Mordecai sends word to Esther, pleading with her to go before the king, but because of their estrangement as well as the royal protocol, Esther refuses. However, Sajbel shows us

---

29. The document we now refer to as the *Protocols of the Elders of Zion* was a forgery produced in Russia in the first decade of the twentieth century. Its appearance closely followed the First Zionist Congress in 1897, and its purpose seems to have been to convince its readers that Jewish leaders were intent on subtly taking over the world. This theory found many subscribers, and in 1920 the automobile magnate Henry Ford even sponsored a series of articles based on the *Protocols*. For more information, see Naomi Pasachoff and Robert J. Littman, "The Protocols of the Elders of Zion," in *Jewish History in 100 Nutshells* (Lanham, Md.: Jason Aronson, 1995), 265–68; and Will Eisner, *The Plot: The Secret Story of "The Protocols of the Elders of Zion"* (New York and London: W. W. Norton, 2005).

30. Bowman examines this gender-bending in the film and posits a plausible reason for its presence: "The weirdness can be traced back to the attempt to inscribe several contemporary, and mutually-exclusive, gender relationships on this ancient story: the Disney fairy tale of the independent girl who nevertheless craves the fulfillment of a man, the romance novel plot of the powerful man captivated by the bewitching and bewildering maiden, and the feminist fable of a powerful woman exerting political influence to change history" ("Bible-Shaped Mirror," par. 17).

interspersed scenes of Mordecai tearing his clothes and putting sackcloth on his head while Esther prays to God. Her prayer is not taken from the Greek additions to Esther, which Mertes uses, but it has the same effects of heightening the religiosity of Esther and making the struggle of the Jews all the more rooted in scriptural history. To that end, Mordecai is shown reading an excerpt from Isa. 40.28–31, and the encounter between Haman and Mordecai only occurs after the issuing of the edict. As such, Haman's hatred for the Jews is based not on his dislike for Mordecai, but rather on his Agagite genealogy.

Haman's hatred and determination grow after he is forced to parade Mordecai around, and we learn that when the king leaves to attack Greece, Haman will be appointed as regent in his absence. As such, Mordecai again sends word to Esther, saying that she must go before the king before he leaves for Greece if they are to have any chance for survival. As Mordecai's messenger gives Esther the necklace her parents gave her, she instructs him to have all the Jews fast and pray for her. She then repeats 4.16 ("If I perish, I perish") to ominous music and loud thunderclaps.

Sajbel does his best to present Esther's decision to go before the king as the key dramatic moment in the film. It is raining, and Hegai refuses to summon a litter for her out of concern for her safety. Their exchange heightens the tension and again reveals the scriptural underpinnings of Esther's story, as Hegai seeks to persuade Esther not to go by reminding her that she is not simply going before a man but before a king in his royal hall. As such, the ensuing challenge will not be between Esther and the king, but rather between Esther and royal protocol. Esther responds by comparing herself to David going out to meet Goliath. Hegai's response is that David is just a story, and as such should not influence Esther's actions. Esther counters that David was successful not because of his military prowess, but rather because of his faith.

After this, Esther runs out into the rain barefoot, as we hear the king appoint Haman as his regent. It is obvious that Sajbel has been building to the moment Esther throws open the doors of the royal hall, and the music swells as we are shown Esther pushing the doors open four times from different angles. Everyone present is appropriately shocked as she makes her way down the aisle, soaking wet with no crown. It takes her a full minute to walk to the steps before the king, and amid the calls that protocol has been broken, soft music suddenly breaks over the audio as she ascends the steps. We are shown flashbacks of her parents for the first three steps she climbs, and the audio returns as a guard draws his sword. Esther looks at the king and smiles as the guard's sword falls. At the last moment, the king stops the blade and holds out his scepter as Esther falls to the ground in a faint, the screen fading to black.

As the film comes back into focus, we see the face of the king, and he is holding Esther on the steps in the royal hall. The scene then shifts to Esther walking back to her quarters, telling her friend Jesse that she could not make her petition to the king in front of everyone. Instead, she has invited him and Haman to a banquet. Unlike in Mertes's film, the banquet takes place at night, and the scoring alerts us to the impending danger at the meal. At the banquet, the king asks Esther for her petition, and her request is that he allow her to finish telling him the story of Jacob. She begins relating how Jacob had twelve sons who became the ancestors of a people, but the king interrupts her, annoyed with the delay to his departure for Greece. In response, she recites 7.3–4 and admits to the king that she is a Jew. Unlike in our other films, here Esther rather proudly tells the king and Haman her Hebrew name and lineage, at which the king expresses disbelief. Haman calls her story pathetic and tells the king that Esther is merely another Vashti. What Haman means to do is connect Vashti's protest against the war with Greece and Esther's sudden revelation; that is, he is implying that Esther's claim to be a Jew is a tactic designed to weaken the Persian war effort. In response to Haman's protestations, Esther removes her special necklace and holds it above a candle. Stars of David begin to dance around the room, but as Haman claims he cannot see anything, they disappear. The king stands and leaves the room, leaving Haman and Esther alone. Haman's speech to her is threatening, sinister in tone, and represents by far the most treacherous Haman we have encountered thus far. He asks her if she thought he would beg, like Agag did before Saul. As he circles Esther, he begins to feign distress and begs her for his life in a mocking tone.

Upon uttering his last mocking plea, Haman grasps Esther by the throat as he mutters "Jew" under his breath. Of course, the king reappears and rescues Esther, ordering Haman to be hung on the gallows he erected for Mordecai. The king embraces Esther, and she asks, "What made you come back?" Choking back tears, he says, "I saw them. I saw the stars." They then kiss as their wedding song begins again.[31] The film does mention Purim, but it is more of an afterthought, and no violence is actually shown.

Sajbel has effectively heightened the dramatic tension by including the romantic subplot between the king and Esther, as well as by creating the most villainous Haman yet on film. The speech that Esther delivers at the banquet shows a stronger identification with her Jewish heritage than we have seen in our other films, and the danger posed to her personally is also greater. Through not only the elevated danger posed to her and her people through the viciousness of Haman, but also the numerous ways in which the religious nature of the story is accentuated, Sajbel has crafted a tale that stresses religious identity even as it celebrates acculturation and nostalgic romanticism.

---

31. Bowman correctly observes the very standard romantic pattern at work here in the relationship between Esther and the king. She writes that the film follows "the standard model found in romance novels and the basic Disney princess storyline: girl captivates boy, girl gets boy, girl loses boy through entirely avoidable misunderstanding, girl gets boy back" ("Bible-Shaped Mirror," par. 14).

In all of the films surveyed here, pains are taken to render Esther as a heroine and, more often than not, her revelation of her Jewishness as an act of immense bravery. Mertes and Sajbel do so through their insistence on the danger of both Haman's plot and the violation of court protocol. Walsh's film opts for a revelation that seems more tangential than necessary, and Gitai's retelling of chapter 7 seems as if he is merely putting his actors through the motions. However, he does include an indication of her struggle through the song her attendant sings, and *VeggieTales* includes a similar musical peek into Esther's decision-making process. What *VeggieTales* and Gitai fail to do, though, is to portray Esther and the king as lovers, something in which all of our other films are interested. As we saw with Sajbel, this romantic plot can add to the drama of Esther's decision or, as with Walsh, it can simply be seen as a necessary component in a Hollywood recipe. Many of our films also take pains to portray Esther as more explicitly religious and, in the case of Mertes's and Sajbel's films, more Jewish. Esther's revelation, then, becomes based not on personal survival but on a religious mission. Whatever the basis of her actions, our films (save perhaps Gitai's) interpret Esther's actions as heroic, and she is justly rewarded for her bravery with security for her and her people, as well as the love of the king.

CONCLUSIONS

In this chapter we have surveyed three key scenes in the story of Esther and examined how five films render these scenes. Along the way, we have seen strikingly literal readings as well as highly imaginative, almost fairy-tale interpretations of our story. In all of this, though, it is clear that the story of Esther remains at its core a story about a young woman faced with a horrible decision: either to admit her identity and most likely die for doing so, or to remain quiet and bear witness to the annihilation of her people. Instead of taking the easy way out, the way that would assure her safety, she shoves herself in the way of forces larger than her. She admits her Jewishness to her husband and Haman, and in so doing averts the genocide of all the Jews in Persia. Whether later filmmakers spice up her story with love or songs or even God, the central point of this tale is Esther's rescuing of her fellow Jews. And every Purim, Jews around the world are instructed to listen to her story aloud amid revelry and children as a reminder of our continued existence.

STUDY QUESTIONS

1. I have focused exclusively on film in this chapter, but Vashti and Esther have enjoyed a long and interesting existence in art as well. Using the websites I list in study question 6 on page 27, gather a good cross-section of images depicting Vashti and Esther. Try to determine how the artists imagined them and how their portrayals compare both

to the biblical narrative and to the films I examined above. Is Vashti rendered sympathetically or harshly? How is Esther depicted? What scenes do you find rendered more than others, and why might this be? Finally, how does your excursion into art affect the way(s) you understand the biblical story?

2. One aspect of the book of Esther I did not examine above is the ending. Replete with violence and bloodshed, and supported by Esther and Mordecai, the ending seems to strike an odd note given both what comes before and the celebration of Purim. In his work on Esther, the Nobel Peace Prize winner Elie Wiesel connects this ending with the absence of God in the narrative. Wiesel writes, "He refused to be associated with the denouement—with the bloodshed. It was His way of saying, Don't ascribe this to me; I had nothing to do with it; you wanted revenge, all right—but don't make me responsible for it."[32] How does the story of Esther view and/or endorse violence, both against Jews and perpetrated by Jews? What attitude does Esther herself take toward violence? Does the book's treatment of violence change the way in which you view Esther? Various commentators have used Esther to support acts of violence throughout the centuries.[33] Does this legacy change your view of Esther? At the same time, some interpreters look to Esther for inspiration in liberation movements.[34] How is it that one story can contain so many different meanings? Is there one meaning you find dominant or meaningful? If so, which one, and why?

3. One way to read the story of Esther is to focus on the tensions and motivations within the character of Esther. Try to make a list of all the character traits you can find in the narrative. Next, think about the main conflicts Esther encounters, for example, whether to conceal or reveal her identity and whether or not to risk her own life to save her people. Ask yourself what you would do if faced with these problems. Would you be willing to admit that you are a minority, especially if you knew you might be persecuted? What would you sacrifice for your nation, your people, your religion, or your family? What groups or individuals today are facing these same choices, and how could Esther serve as a paradigm of action for them?

---

32. Wiesel, "Esther," 150.
33. For example, the Reverend Paul Hill—who was the first person executed in the United States for the murder of an abortion provider—used Esther to support his actions in a personal recollection entitled "I Shot an Abortionist" (online: *http://www.armyofgod.com/PHill_ShortShot.html*). More generally, see Elliot Horowitz, *Reckless Rites: Purim and the Legacy of Jewish Violence* (Princeton, N.J., and Oxford: Princeton University Press, 2006).
34. See Itumeleng J. Mosala, "The Implications of the Text of Esther for African Women's Struggle for Liberation in South Africa," *Semeia* 59 (1992): 129–37; and Sarojini Nadar, "Gender, Power, Sexuality, and Suffering Bodies in the Book of Esther: Reading the Characters of Esther and Vashti for the Purpose of Social Transformation," *Old Testament Essays* 15, no. 1 (2002): 113–30.

6

"Judy in Disguise"*

D. W. GRIFFITH'S *JUDITH OF BETHULIA*

THE APOCRYPHAL STORY of Judith is one of the most reinterpreted
and retold tales in all of biblical literature. Several works have appeared
that analyze many of these interpretations, yet strangely, almost no work
has been done on one of the most notable retellings of this narrative: D. W.
Griffith's film of 1913, *Judith of Bethulia*.[1] This film, partially based on
Thomas Aldrich's play, is significant not only because of the unique place it
occupies in Griffith's cinematic output, but also because of its transformation of the story of Judith. Before addressing the film, though, it would be
prudent to summarize the story of Judith briefly. Following this, I will discuss Aldrich's and the film's interpretation of that story, as well as comment
on how the film—like all significant artistic interpretations—allows us to
reencounter the original narrative with new questions and perceptions.

SUMMARY AND ANALYSIS OF THE BOOK OF JUDITH

The first seven chapters of the story of Judith recount the military buildup
of the Assyrians prior to the introduction of Judith in chapter 8. The narrative tells of the increasing presence of the Assyrian army in Palestine, and of
the rising tensions between the Assyrians and the citizens of Bethulia, a

---

*This chapter is an expanded version of my article "Judy in Disguise: D. W. Griffith's *Judith of
Bethulia*," in *Studies in Jewish Civilization*, vol. 14, *Women and Judaism* (ed. Leonard J.
Greenspoon, Ronald A. Simkins, and Jean Axelrad Cahan; Omaha, Neb.: Creighton University Press, 2003), 119–30.
1. One of the most thorough treatments of Judith and its artistic and cultural recyclings, Margarita Stocker, *Judith, Sexual Warrior: Women and Power in Western Culture* (New Haven,
Conn., and London: Yale University Press, 1998), 146, 184, and 200, only mentions Griffith's
film in passing.

small town in Judea. Things begin to get serious when the Assyrians cut off the water supply to the town, after which the Bethulians begin to urge their leaders to surrender.

In 8.4–6, we hear about the social status of Judith: she is a widow. Implied in the narrative is that she is exceedingly pious; she dresses herself as a widow in sackcloth and fasts "all the days of her widowhood," except the day before the Sabbath and during the Sabbath itself. Following this report of her social status and her great piety, we hear of Judith's great beauty in 8.7: "She was beautiful in appearance, and was very lovely to behold." In 8.8, we hear again of her "great devotion" to God, and that because of this devotion she had acquired somewhat of a reputation. Thus, from the information we receive at the outset of Judith's textual existence, we know that she is both exceedingly pious and exceedingly beautiful. We also know that she is a widow and apparently is content to remain a widow. That is, she is content to remain in her socially assigned role until she hears of Uzziah's plan to surrender to the Assyrians.

When Judith hears of this plan, she sends her maid to summon not only Uzziah, but also the elders of her town. Her reputation must have preceded her for these men to actually come in such a time of conflict! The ensuing monologue of Judith is both a reprimand and an exhortation. She chides them for putting God to the test and encourages them to set an example for the people. Uzziah counters that even though she is very wise (8.28–29), the people are dying of thirst because Nebuchadnezzar has cut off the water supply to the town. Judith admonishes him not to worry because she is "about to do something that will go down through all generations of our descendants" (8.32). However, she keeps Uzziah and the elders in the dark as to what exactly her plan is; they meekly give her a blessing and return to their posts.

Following this exchange, Judith prays a long prayer to God (chap. 9) and asks for his help to defeat their enemies through her "deceitful words." After this prayer, Judith does something extraordinary: she takes off her widow's garb, removes the sackcloth she has been wearing for over three years, and dresses herself in fine clothing. We are even told explicitly her purpose in changing her appearance: "Thus she made herself very beautiful, to entice the eyes of all the men who might see her" (10.4). She then packs food and drink from her own, presumably kosher/clean stock and heads for the city gates, along with her maid. At the gates, she again encounters Uzziah and the elders, who again seem not to understand Judith's purpose, so they offer yet another routine blessing. We even get a hint in the text that Judith is not impressed with their blessing, because after the blessing we are told that "she bowed down to God," not to the men. Also, after this, Judith commands them, "Order the gate of the town to be opened for me so that I may go out and accomplish the things you have just said to me." In my opinion, this is obvious sarcasm; Judith has already formulated her plan and made all the necessary arrangements. Surely she need not pay heed to the ineffective male leaders when they attempt to co-opt her plan by uttering a noncommittal blessing. Thus, her response seems to be to dripping with sarcasm and is the first in a series of ironic statements by Judith.

After leaving her city, Judith and her maid progress alone to the Assyrian camp. On the way, they are met by a patrol, whose members question her as to why she is here and who she is. Her response is that she is a "daughter of the Hebrews" and that she is fleeing from them because they are about to be defeated. The text specifically tells us that "when the men heard her words, and observed her face—she was in their eyes marvelously beautiful," they took her to meet their leader, Holofernes. As they lead her through the camp, many Assyrians come out of their tents to look at her: "They marveled at her beauty and admired the Israelites, judging them by her" (10.19). Again, when she is brought into Holofernes's tent, everyone there "marveled at the beauty of her face."

In the exchange between Holofernes and Judith that follows, Judith explains in more detail why she has run away from her city. She tells Holofernes that the people have sinned against God by eating the firstfruits. Because of this sin, Judith asserts, she was sent to Holofernes to aid him in destroying the Jews so that, presumably, all will know the fury and righteousness of God. In fact, Judith even goes so far as to tell Holofernes that she will lead him to Jerusalem, where she will personally set him upon the throne. Of course, this speech pleases Holofernes and his minions immensely, so much so that Holofernes asserts, "If you do as you have said, your God shall be my God, and you shall live in the palace of King Nebuchadnezzar and be renowned throughout the whole world" (11.23). As we will see, Judith does not do as she said she would.

Holofernes orders food to be brought, but Judith declines, saying that she must eat the presumably clean food she has brought with her. Holofernes then asks her what she will do when her supply runs out. Her reply is yet another case of irony; she replies, "As surely as you live, my lord, your servant will not use up the supplies I have with me before the Lord carries out by my hand what he has determined" (12.4). Of course, the reader suspects what she really means, but Holofernes assumes she is referring to her part in the destruction of the town. In the morning, after the feast, she goes out of the camp to pray and continues to go out every morning for three days. On the fourth day of her stay in the camp, Judith gets invited to a special banquet in the presence of Holofernes, whose intentions have to do with more than culinary desires. In preparing for this banquet, Holofernes tells his servant Bagoas, "It would be a disgrace if we let such a woman go without having intercourse with her. If we do not seduce her, she will laugh at us" (12.12). When Bagoas approaches Judith to invite her to this banquet, she replies with yet another ironic comment: "Who am I to refuse my lord? Whatever pleases him I will do at once, and it will be a joy to me until the day of my death" (12.14).

When Judith enters the tent of Holofernes and lies down before him, we are told that his "heart was ravished with her and his passion was aroused, for he had been waiting for an opportunity to seduce her from the day he first saw her" (12.16). He immediately suggests that she have a drink with him. Again, her response is ironic; she says, "I will gladly drink, my lord, because today is the greatest day in my whole life" (12.18). Holofernes then proceeds to get exceedingly drunk, and, after evening comes, all his servants depart from the tent, presumably to allow him and Judith to get to know each other. After everyone has gone, Judith prays to God in her heart to give her strength, claiming, "Now indeed is the time to help your heritage and to carry out my design to destroy the enemies who have risen up against us" (13.5). She goes up to the bedpost, takes down Holofernes's sword, and with two strokes cuts off his head. She then rolls his body off the bed and gives the head to her maid, who places it in their food bag.

After this assassination, Judith and her maid go out of the camp like they have done for the past three days, and of course no one stops them. The two continue on until they reach the gates of her city. Upon entering the city, Judith exclaims, "Praise God, O praise him! Praise God, who has not withdrawn his mercy from the house of Israel, but has destroyed our enemies by my hand this very night!" She then pulls the head of Holofernes out of her bag and displays it for the people. Even though she killed him, she still affirms that "the Lord has struck him down by the hand of a woman." Following this display, Uzziah, who seems finally to understand exactly what Judith has done, praises her with the highest regard:

> O daughter, you are blessed by the Most High God above all other women on earth; and blessed be the Lord God, who created the heavens and the earth, who has guided you to cut off the head of the leader of our enemies. Your praise will never depart from the hearts of those who remember the power of God. May God grant this to be a perpetual honor to you, and may he reward you with blessings, because you risked your own life when our nation was brought low, and you averted our ruin, walking in the straight path before our God. (13.18–20)

All the people agree with this statement of praise.

After this, Judith instructs the people what to do with the head. They are to place it on the wall of the city and then attack the Assyrians. When the Assyrians go to the tent of Holofernes, they will find him dead, and this discovery will send them into a state of panic. Because of the ensuing frenzy, the Israelites will be able to destroy them easily. Of course, everything transpires according to the plan of Judith, and the Assyrians are defeated. Following this victory, we are told that the high priest and the elders of the Israelites from Jerusalem came to witness the victory and to praise Judith. As we saw earlier with the praise of Uzziah, the visitors from Jerusalem exalt Judith: "You are the glory of Jerusalem, you are the great boast of Israel, you are the great pride of our nation! You have done all this with your own hand; you have done great good to Israel, and God is well pleased with it. May the Almighty Lord bless you forever!" (15.9–10). Again, the people agree with the praise.

Following this second male praise of Judith, the women of Israel come together to bless her, and some of them even perform a dance in her honor. After these laudatory acts, Judith herself leads the women in a dance, and "all the men of Israel followed, bearing their arms and wearing garlands and singing hymns." Judith then sings a song of praise, found in 16.1–17, in which she not only reattributes her success to God (16.5), but also speaks of herself: "For she put away her widow's clothing to exalt the oppressed in Israel. She anointed her face with perfume; she fastened her hair with a tiara and put on a linen gown to beguile him. Her sandal ravished his eyes, her beauty captivated his mind, and the sword severed his neck!" After this hymn, the people arrive in Jerusalem, and Judith dedicates to the Lord all the possessions of Holofernes. They remain in Jerusalem for three months, praying, feasting, and celebrating.

When the people return to the city, Judith returns to her estate. She never remarries, but "for the rest of her life she was honored throughout the whole country . . . [and] she became more and more famous." Following her death, "the house of Israel mourned her for seven days." Finally, we are told, "No one ever again spread terror among the Israelites during the lifetime of Judith, or for a long time after her death."

THOMAS BAILEY ALDRICH'S "JUDITHS"

From this brief summary, it is easy to see why so many artists, writers, and librettists have been and continue to be drawn to the story of Judith.[2] The story contains religious piety, a brave and sexually appealing heroine, an "underdog" story line, and a gruesome beheading. With these characteristics, it is no small wonder it has proven fertile ground for artistic retellings. When Thomas Bailey Aldrich tried his hand at interpreting Judith, first in

---

2. For some of these interpretations, see Edna Purdie, *The Story of Judith in German and English Literature* (Paris: Librarie Ancienne Honoré Champien, 1927); Patricia Montley, "Judith in the Fine Arts: The Appeal of the Archetypal Androgyne," *Anima* 4 (1978): 37–42; Diane Apostolos-Cappadona, "'The Lord Struck Him Down by the Hand of a Woman': Images of Judith," in *Art as Religious Meaning* (ed. Diane Apostolos-Cappadona and Doug Adams; New York: Crossroad, 1987), 81–97; David A. Radavich, "A Catalogue of Works Based on the Apocryphal Book of Judith, from the Mediaeval Period to the Present," *Bulletin of Bibliography* 44 (1987): 189–92; Raymond J. Frontain, "The Price of Rubies: The Weight of Old Testament Women in Western Literature," in *Old Testament Women in Western Literature* (ed. R. Frontain and J. Wojcik; Conway, Ark.: University of Central Arkansas Press, 1991), 2–19; Elizabeth Philpot, "Judith and Holofernes: Changing Images in the History of Art," in *Translating Religious Texts: Translation, Transgression, and Interpretation* (ed. D. Jasper; Studies in Literature and Religion; New York: St. Martin's Press, 1993), 80–97; and, most recently, Stocker, *Judith, Sexual Warrior.*

poetic form in 1896 and then in dramatic form in 1904, the subject would have been well known.[3] As J. B. Kaufman notes, when Aldrich's play opened in Boston on 13 October 1904, it undoubtedly would have been guaranteed success not only by the subject matter, but also because of Aldrich's reputation: "Today Aldrich may be a forgotten literary figure, but in his own time he was considered the equal of such contemporaries as Mark Twain and Henry Wadsworth Longfellow."[4]

Aldrich's play alters the story of Judith—and Judith herself—in an attempt to add emotional and psychological depth. The poem even includes a prefatory note that states:

> In the following narrative the author has taken such liberties with the myth as suited his dramatic purpose. He has widely departed from precedent in his delineation of Judith, who moves through the Apocrypha a beautiful and cold-blooded abstraction, with scarcely any feminine attribute excepting her religious fervor . . . Judith's character throughout the ancient legend lacks that note of tenderness with which the writer has here attempted to accent her heroism.[5]

In Aldrich's work, Judith observes the suffering of her fellow townspeople from her tower, a common symbol of seclusion and chastity. Once Judith descends from her tower in Bethulia to travel to the Assyrian camp, she is thrust into an unknown and anxious environment. Renate Peters notes:

> Metaphorically speaking the descent from the tower indicates a descent from saintliness and moral superiority into moral confusion, from angelic neutrality into a flesh and blood existence, and from the light of faith into the darkness of doubt and death. Unlike the biblical Judith, Aldrich's hero is plagued by doubts as soon as she enters Holofernes's camp.[6]

The main source of Judith's doubt is her growing love and desire for Holofernes, who now no longer appears to be an anonymous tyrant, but rather a "gentle prince, with gracious words and ways."[7] By contrast, the apocryphal Judith is quite matter-of-fact about her relationship with Holofernes and even seems to relish making ironic puns about his eventual fate and her disdain for him (for example, 11.5–6, 16; 12.4, 14, 18).[8] By

---

3. See Thomas Bailey Aldrich, *Judith and Holofernes: A Poem* (Boston: Houghton, Mifflin and Company, 1896); and idem, *Judith of Bethulia: A Tragedy* (Boston: Houghton, Mifflin and Company, 1904).

4. J. B. Kaufman, "*Judith of Bethulia*: Un 'Piccolo' Film Epico / *Judith of Bethulia*: Producing the 'Little' Epic," *Griffithiana* 50 (1994): 179.

5. Aldrich, *Judith and Holofernes*, v–vi.

6. Renate Peters, "D. W. Griffith's Transformation of the Legend of Judith" (paper presented at the Canadian Comparative Literature Arts Conference, Ottawa, 30 May 1998), 5. I would like to thank Professor Peters for her graciousness in allowing me to use her unpublished work for this chapter.

7. Aldrich, *Judith of Bethulia*, 50.

8. See Carey A. Moore, *Judith* (AB 40; Garden City, N.Y.: Doubleday, 1985), 78–85 and passim. Moore views irony as being the key for interpreting Judith.

investing his Judith with doubt brought on by her desire for Holofernes, Aldrich is evidently trying to enhance the suspense and eroticism of the narrative. However, because Aldrich offers no internal motivation for Judith's temptation and her hesitation to kill Holofernes, his attempt fails. Judith pities Holofernes, yet she decapitates him; she is sure what she does is approved by God and therefore good, yet is not happy at the survival of her town.

At the end of the play, she refuses the honors her fellow Bethulians offer her and vows to "dwell apart, alone / In mine own house, where laughter may not come / Nor any light, vain voices of the world / Only the sorrowful shall find the door / Unbarred and open / In thy memory / Keep me as some beloved wife or child / Or sister that dies long and long ago!"[9] Her final words in the tragedy evidence the almost schizophrenic nature that Aldrich attributes to her: "Let no one born of woman follow me!"[10] Margarita Stocker comments on this ending: "This curiously redundant phraseology of childbirth provides the closing image because of Aldrich's subtext, which is intended to recuperate the independent virago for a lesson in woman's true destiny, marriage and motherhood, as her only route to fulfillment."[11] As we shall see, this lesson is also implied in Griffith's film. In sum, as Peters notes, Judith "remains an eminently incomprehensible and ambiguous figure in Aldrich's play," one who "remains the other for the others [in the play] and for herself," a woman who has "put herself outside humanity."[12]

D. W. GRIFFITH'S *JUDITH OF BETHULIA*

D. W. Griffith began filming *Judith of Bethulia* in June 1913, while still employed by Biograph Pictures. Ever the shrewd businessman, Griffith avoided any copyright infringement issues by purchasing a treatment of the subject from a writer named Grace A. Pierce in Santa Monica, even though he carried a copy of the Aldrich play on the set with him at all times.[13] During the month of June, Griffith and his Biograph troupe, including Blanche Sweet as Judith, Henry B. Walthall as Holofernes, and other minor players

---

9. Aldrich, *Judith of Bethulia*, 97.
10. Ibid., 98.
11. Stocker, *Judith, Sexual Warrior*, 185.
12. Peters, "D. W. Griffith's Transformation of the Legend of Judith," 6.
13. Evidently, Biograph purchased the treatment from Pierce in April 1913. Kaufman, "*Judith of Bethulia*," 179, raises the possibility that Pierce may have been a fictitious character, but quickly disproves the theory. See also Robert M. Henderson, *D. W. Griffith: The Years at Biograph* (New York: Farrar, Straus and Giroux, 1970), 151–52; and Richard Schickel, *D. W. Griffith: An American Life* (New York: Simon & Schuster, 1984), 191. Kaufman, "*Judith of Bethulia*," 189 n. 2, also notes the intriguing fact that there was a film version of Judith prior to Griffith's: in 1907 Cines Roma released a one-reel picture titled *Giuditta e Oloferne*, which was released in the United States in 1908, and as such Griffith may have been influenced by it as well.

who included Lillian and Dorothy Gish and Lionel Barrymore, shot the exterior scenes for the film in Chatsworth Park, near Los Angeles. At the beginning of July, the company returned to New York, where the interior scenes were shot at Biograph's studio in the Bronx. It was during this shooting period that Nance O'Neil, the first actress to play Aldrich's Judith, visited the set and gave Blanche Sweet (still only seventeen years old) some tips. While shooting in New York, Griffith's already strained relationship with Biograph took a turn for the worse. Biograph was in the habit of releasing only one-reel films, and Griffith's conscious defiance of this policy by shooting six unedited reels for *Judith*—at the outrageous cost of $36,000—was causing quite a stir. In response to Griffith's actions, Biograph informed him that he was to begin supervising other directors, but after *Judith* was completed he was not to direct any more films.[14] This proved to be too much for Griffith; at the end of September 1913, he left Biograph and took many of its best and brightest with him, thus sealing the fate of the company.[15] Nevertheless, Biograph finally released *Judith of Bethulia* in London in November 1913 to both commercial and critical acclaim. The picture was a hit again in March 1914 when it opened in New York, and the various editions of the film to appear later only testify to its popularity at the time.[16]

Summary of Griffith's *Judith of Bethulia*

In *Judith*, Griffith weaves together four interrelated story lines: the situation of the Bethulians, the relationship between the two young lovers Naomi and Nathan, the story of Judith, and the attack of the Assyrians led by Holofernes.[17] Of these plots, the story concerning Naomi and Nathan is the most abbreviated and rightly so considering its total absence from the apocryphal account and its marginal status in the Aldrich play. Even so, the character of Naomi is important in the film, for she provides a counter-example to Judith's character. Naomi is invested in her people; she is in love with Nathan, who loves her as well and who eventually saves her after the Assyrians capture her. Griffith takes pains to present Naomi's status after her capture; she is chained to a post and turned into a chaste spectacle. As

14. See Henderson, *D. W. Griffith: The Years at Biograph*, 154–55.
15. For a complete list, see ibid., 155–56.
16. Kaufman, *"Judith of Bethulia,"* 185, discusses the different versions of the film produced over the years. The version of the film used for this chapter is the Kino International version, which is drawn mainly from Biograph's 1917 elaboration of Griffith's film entitled *Her Condoned Sin*.
17. This juxtaposition of plots foreshadows his more successful attempt in *Intolerance* in 1916. For an excellent overview of *Intolerance*, see Scott Simmon, *The Films of D. W. Griffith* (Cambridge Film Classics; Cambridge and New York: Cambridge University Press, 1993), 137–60. For a discussion of the portrayal of Jesus in *Intolerance*, see W. Barnes Tatum, *Jesus at the Movies: A Guide to the First Hundred Years* (Santa Rosa, Calif.: Polebridge Press, 1997), 33–43.

Peters writes, Naomi "is the Victorian ideal, the normal woman, virtuous virgin, an object on display, to be gazed at, passive, helpless, bound and the object of sadistic men's desires."[18] In other words, Naomi is, for Griffith and his audience, the woman to be admired, the paradigmatic repository of appropriately womanly behavior and values. This characterization of Naomi is at odds with Griffith's use of dancing girls to entertain Holofernes, but, as I note above, Naomi's character can also be contrasted with that of Judith.

Judith's character in Griffith's film is similar to the character in Aldrich's play. Each Judith is somewhat isolated from her community in spite of (or perhaps because of) the Bethulians' reverence for her due to her status as a widow. In addition, Griffith's Judith is physically separated as well; she gazes on the Bethulians through a window in a large wall that marks off her space from theirs. Griffith also includes scenes of Holofernes looking out from his tent in an almost solitary visage, thus juxtaposing the two characters right from the start. After the Assyrians invade and cut off the town's water supply with a military frenzy Griffith would master one year later in his *The Birth of a Nation*, Judith receives a vision from God instructing her as to her mission.[19] This vision serves to downplay Judith's own initiative and creativity; in the apocryphal account it is Judith herself who devises the plan to kill Holofernes. Thus, not only is Judith separated from her townspeople, but Griffith, following Aldrich, has also diminished her as a moving force in the story. She becomes passive in her Bethulian context, even unable to offer any sympathy to a young mother who holds out her sick child for Judith to see.

Once Judith and her maid reach the Assyrian camp, though, the first of a number of reversals takes place, as they do in the apocryphal narrative. First, Holofernes is shown reclining on an enormous couch, which serves as his substitute throne. After Judith enters the Assyrian camp, Holofernes only gets off this couch once to inquire after Judith, thus indicating his almost total physical passivity. Indeed, most of the physical action after Judith arrives in the camp is performed by Holofernes's dancing girls and his main eunuch, Bagoas, who constantly seems delighted and amused by Judith's presence. The only time Holofernes engages in any leadership function is when a dissenter is brought in for punishment; the punishment for dissension in the film is crucifixion. By the inclusion of the troupe of dancing girls symbolizing an almost bacchanalian fury, as well as the allusion to the Roman crucifixion of Jesus, Griffith here seems to be foreshadowing his later and what most critics would consider to be his more successful film *Intolerance* of 1916.

Like Aldrich, Griffith tries to invest Judith with increased emotion by having her fall in love with Holofernes. Even before the decapitation

---

18. Peters, "D. W. Griffith's Transformation of the Legend of Judith," 8.
19. For an analysis of *The Birth of a Nation*, see Simmon, *The Films of D. W. Griffith*, 104–36.

scene, Judith is twice shown thinking of Holofernes and smiling, and then racked with guilt as she recalls her fellow townspeople. The titles for these scenes indicate her inner struggle: "Then did Judith wrestle with her heart, for Holofernes now seemed noble in her eyes. . . . Again Judith faltered for the love of Holofernes—yet struggles to cast away the sinful passion." In effect, the gulf between Judith and her townspeople now widens to separate Judith from her own feelings. That is, even though Judith does not feel at one with the other Bethulians, their suffering and God's plan for her conspire to alienate Judith from the first pangs of love she has felt since the death of her husband. This plot device finds its fullest expression in the penultimate scene in the film when Judith is invited to drink and feast with Holofernes.

The decapitation scene is actually quite brief. Judith enters Holofernes's tent and asks him to send Bagoas away so that she may serve him alone. She continues to force more and more drink on him, as well as cozying up to him, until he eventually passes out. Judith then picks up Holofernes's own sword. It is obvious that Griffith departs from the apocryphal narrative here, for Judith seems quite reluctant to grasp the sword, and one senses that she is perhaps too dainty to do so—which is in no way implied in the apocryphal story of Judith. She holds the sword aloft and then hesitates when Holofernes stirs; she is obviously racked with conflicting emotions. On the one hand, she loves Holofernes, but on the other hand, she is an instrument of God that will deliver her town from certain death. To help the viewer realize her inner conflict, Griffith shows us brief views of dead Bethulians at the town's well and starving people inside the town, including Nathan, who seems to be taking his last drink of water. Karl Brown, an assistant to Griffith's cameraman Billy Bitzer, later recalled the importance of this sequence:

> His [Griffith's] highest objective, as nearly as I could grasp it, was to photograph thought. He could do it, too. I'd seen it. In *Judith of Bethulia* there was a scene in which Judith stands over the sleeping figure of Holofernes, sword in hand. She raises the sword, then falters. Pity and mercy have weakened her to a point of helpless irresolution. Her face softens to something that is almost love. Then she thinks, and as she thinks the screen is filled with the mangled bodies of those, her own people, slain by this same Holofernes. Then her face becomes filled with hate as she summons all her strength to bring that sword whistling down upon the neck of what is no longer a man but a blood-reeking monster.[20]

Judith finally accepts her fate and cuts off Holofernes's head. She immediately seems sickened by the act and drops the sword in disgust— again, in contrast to the apocryphal story in which she is almost businesslike in her execution of Holofernes. After she and her maid retrieve

20. Karl Brown, *Adventures with D. W. Griffith* (New York: Farrar, Straus and Giroux, 1973), 21.

Holofernes's decapitated head, they return to Bethulia, where, miraculously, the Bethulian soldiers still have enough energy to rout the Assyrians, who retreat in a panic after discovering Holofernes's headless body. For her part, Judith immediately returns to her secluded space, and as she observes the soldiers rush out the city gates, she looks on in horror. Griffith even takes time to show Nathan rescuing Naomi, thus bringing closure to that story line as well. At the end of the film, Judith is shown leaving her secluded house and reveling in the adoration and praise of the Bethulians. If she has any regrets or is forlorn over killing Holofernes, she does not show it. Thus, Griffith embraces the apocryphal narrative's ending for Judith, in which she is lauded by all and shows no remorse, while abandoning Aldrich's ending, where Judith is racked with psychological and emotional distress over killing the man she loves. Nevertheless, one of the final gestures Judith makes in the film is to caress her own neck, and perhaps this is no accident; perhaps she is still thinking of Holofernes and her love for him.

Analysis of Griffith's *Judith of Bethulia*

In his work on Griffith's film, William Rothman singles out Judith's ambiguous sexuality for special discussion.[21] Here, more than in his other works, Griffith seems to focus on Judith as an embodied woman rather than an idealized one. In addition, Griffith presents Judith as being aware of her sexuality and as possessing desire, even sexual desire for Holofernes. Rothman claims, "The presentation of the good Judith drawn to the splendid yet brutal Holofernes is perhaps unique in all of Griffith's films in its acknowledgment, and acceptance, of the dark side of a woman's sexual desire."[22] However, the fact that Judith assumes a "man's role" in saving her town complicates her already ambiguous presentation in the film. In this respect, Griffith's Judith is similar to the apocryphal character, as Amy-Jill Levine notes: "Present in the public sphere, sexually active and socially involved, she endangers hierarchical oppositions of gender, race, and class, muddles conventional gender characteristics and dismantles their claims to universality, and so threatens the status quo."[23] Thus, in both the apocryphal story and Griffith's film, the character of Judith is one who questions assumptions of gender and appropriate behavior.

---

21. William Rothman, "D. W. Griffith's *Judith of Bethulia*," *Twentieth-Century Literary Criticism* 68 (1997): 213–20. See also Rothman's "*Judith of Bethulia*," in his *The "I" of the Camera: Essays in Film Criticism, History, and Aesthetics* (2nd ed.; Cambridge: Cambridge University Press, 2003), 17–28.

22. Rothman, "D. W. Griffith's *Judith of Bethulia*," 217.

23. Amy-Jill Levine, "Sacrifice and Salvation: Otherness and Domestication in the Book of Judith," in *A Feminist Companion to Esther, Judith, and Susanna* (ed. Athalya Brenner; FCB 7; Sheffield: Sheffield Academic Press, 1995), 209.

Based on the provocative nature of Judith's character, Rothman addresses the intersection between the almost hermaphroditic or bisexual nature of Judith and Griffith's more conventional perceptions and subsequent presentations of women, like that of Naomi:

> *Judith of Bethulia* centers on the dramatic struggle within Judith—spiritual, yet imaged in sexual terms and mirrored by the armed struggle between the Bethulians and the Assyrians—to perform an act that appears to deny her womanly nature. How can this struggle, and specifically its triumphant and liberating resolution, be reconciled with the affirmation, fundamental to Griffith's work, of an order in which sexuality can be fulfilled naturally only through love within a marriage?[24]

Rothman posits that Griffith, in a complicated and mainly symbolic fashion, allows Judith to be fulfilled as a woman (in his view), yet still perform her violent, "manly" act. Briefly, since Judith is a widow, her womanhood has already been achieved, but, in Griffith's view, she would still need a man to fulfill her role as a woman by providing a child. Because of her affection for Holofernes, the viewer may suspect that he is the one who will "fulfill" her. However, because of his failure to capture Bethulia, as well as his willingness to become overly intoxicated, Judith realizes that she actually has power over him and is thus free to carry out the vision presented to her by God, a properly "womanly" role given her relationship with God. Rothman comments on this process:

> When she displays the severed head in the marketplace, she acts as Bethulia's triumphant leader, revealing—to her people and to us—that she has assumed her dead husband's place. . . . The moment at which she unmasks Holofernes, the moment at which she gives herself completely to this higher power, is the moment of her fulfillment as a woman. Yet, paradoxically, this is also the moment at which she performs a man's act, is transformed into a man. This paradox is fundamental to Griffith's understanding of what it is to be a woman. When her trust is threatened, a true woman reveals that she possesses a man within her.[25]

Finally, in terms of fulfilling her role as mother, Rothman claims that since Judith restores life to Bethulia, she can be seen as the mother of the city. Thus, according to Rothman's analysis, Griffith's gender ideology is still present in the film, albeit in a muted fashion. However, the presence of these assumptions does not, in my opinion, diminish the power and impact of Judith's character; that is, even though Griffith's ideas about gender and appropriately "womanly" roles may still be present, Judith's story can still affect the way viewers and readers imagine gender relationships, as Levine writes: "Each time her story is told, this woman

---

24. Rothman, "D. W. Griffith's *Judith of Bethulia*," 218.
25. Ibid., 219.

who represented the community as well as exceeded that representation will both reinforce and challenge Bethulia's—and the reader's—gender-determined ideology."[26]

As I note above, the portrait of Judith in Griffith's film has received little scholarly attention, perhaps because of the perceived status of the film in the context of Griffith's work. For instance, at the end of the film, Griffith seems to give up his attempt to psychologize Judith, as Aldrich does, and simply allows the character to relish the praise of her townspeople without trying to delve more deeply into her emotional state. This reticence on his part is not in keeping with his earlier attempt to flesh out Judith's character and as such represents a significant weakness in the film.[27] In fact, over the years many critics have commented on the film's shortcomings. Richard Schickel, one of Griffith's most important biographers, remarks:

> The film is, on the whole, unsuccessful. . . . What one applauds here is a noble ambition, not a fully realized one. . . . Compared with the spectacles from abroad, *Judith* was perhaps superior. But compared with the standards Griffith had set in his shorter films and would shortly establish in his longer works, it cannot be judged as more than a most interesting transitional film.[28]

Edward Wagenknecht and Anthony Slide disagree with Schickel's overall disapproval of the film, yet still critique Griffith's work: "The battle scenes in *Judith* are, perhaps, the biggest disappointment. The staging is quite frankly a mess, and there is every sign of a small group of people desperately pretending to be a crowd."[29] However, I agree with Robert M. Henderson and Rothman in their positive appraisal of the film. Henderson describes the film as "the crowning achievement of Griffith's career at Biograph, not for its length alone. *Judith* makes use of almost all the cinematic advances that Griffith had perfected in his shorter films."[30] In turn, Rothman notes, "Everything points to the conclusion that *Judith of Bethulia* is a key film in Griffith's career. Indeed, it is a film of considerable compositional complexity, thematic directness, and cinematic artistry."[31]

CONCLUSIONS

In sum, *Judith of Bethulia* is more than just a transition piece in Griffith's early output. It shows Griffith pushing the boundaries of early cinema,

26. Levine, "Sacrifice and Salvation," 222–23.
27. For this position, see Robert M. Henderson, *D. W. Griffith: His Life and Work* (New York: Oxford University Press, 1972), 129–30.
28. Schickel, *D. W. Griffith*, 192.
29. Edward Wagenknecht and Anthony Slide, *The Films of D. W. Griffith* (New York: Crown Publishers, 1975), 29.
30. Henderson, *D. W. Griffith*, 127.
31. Rothman, "D. W. Griffith's *Judith of Bethulia*," 215.

perhaps in response to new, longer films from Europe like *Quo Vadis?* released in April 1913. It also foreshadows some of Griffith's most important work, like his controversial masterpiece *The Birth of a Nation* and his cinematic response to his critics, *Intolerance*. Placing the film in its historical and literary context, as well as understanding what Aldrich and Griffith are trying to accomplish, might allow us as viewers and readers to understand the story of Judith in a more profound way than before. The importance of this understanding lies in the recognition that the biblical text is not static, and that artistic interpretations, like Aldrich's and Griffith's, deserve to be taken seriously. Once we, as "interested parties," accept the validity of artistic interpretations, we might be able to use them to elucidate unwritten undercurrents in the biblical text, so that the story world of the text becomes more alive to us. It might even allow us to approach the text with fresh eyes, fresh ears, and even fresh minds.

STUDY QUESTIONS

1. Griffith's film is the only cinematic version of Judith that I know of, but for centuries artists have reveled in depicting Judith.[32] The artistic tradition in the West overwhelmingly focuses on Judith's beheading of Holofernes. As such, she is most often rendered engaging in an act of violence. However, artists must also contend with the image of Judith in the narrative as a beautiful woman, desired by nearly all of the male Assyrians. As such, Judith "is doomed to be presented in one of two ways: as a brutish woman who readily embraces her role in the killing; or a highly feminized figure who looks as if she couldn't possibly partake in this murderous act."[33] For example, Caravaggio and Artemisia Gentileschi both produced quite violent Judiths, complete with what my *CSI*-minded students term "arterial splatter"; but artists like Botticelli and Giorgione rendered Judith as a slim, feminine women who does not seem the least bit bloodthirsty. See for yourself: go online and hunt for images of Judith. See how she is portrayed and ask yourself if the woman you see could be capable of deceiving a powerful man, getting him drunk, and then beheading him. If so, how does the artist accomplish this? If not, how is she portrayed? How do the images you find affect the way you imagine Judith? Do they make her appear heroic? Cold-blooded? If so, why?

---

32. Those interested in Judith in art should consult Apostolos-Cappadona, "'The Lord Struck Him Down by the Hand of a Woman'"; and Philpot, "Judith and Holofernes."

33. Lynn Huber, Dan W. Clanton Jr., and Jane Webster, "Biblical Subjects in Art," in *Teaching the Bible through Popular Culture and the Arts* (ed. Mark Roncace and Patrick Gray; SBLRBS 53; Atlanta: Society of Biblical Literature, 2007), 205.

2. Judith has also enjoyed quite an afterlife in music.[34] In the twentieth century alone, two major vocal works have taken up the subject and have produced quite different results. Listen to Arthur Honegger's *Judith: Biblical Music Drama* of 1925 and the opera of 1985 by the German composer Siegfried Matthus. How do the pieces differ in terms of sound and compositional technique? How is Judith imagined in both pieces? Keep in mind that Matthus's piece is based on the nineteenth-century play by Friedrich Hebbel, and Hebbel rendered Judith in quite an idiosyncratic fashion.[35] What images are brought to mind through the combination of music and voice in both of these pieces? Does either interpretation of Judith render her as a hero? If not, how is she portrayed, and why? How do these portrayals overlap with, contrast with, or affect your reading of Judith?

3. In order to understand Judith better, compare and contrast her with Delilah in chapter 3. How would you describe the respective social statuses of both women? What is their motivation for their action—that is, why do they do what they do? How do they view Samson and Holofernes? What are the results of their actions? What ultimately happens to each of them as a result of their plans? After answering these questions, ask yourself if Delilah and Judith are similar to or different from each other, and why.

4. Certainly Judith is a violent narrative, and the standard portrayal of Judith in art does little to temper the violence in the story. Think about how Judith's violent act affects how you understand her as well as the praise she receives at the end of the narrative. Does her act of violence bother you? If so, why? If not, why not? How do the other characters in the story respond to her beheading of Holofernes—positively or negatively? Now think about the violence at the end of the book of Esther. How does the violence in Judith compare with this large-scale act of violence? Is either justified? If so, what does it mean to claim that these acts of violence were sanctioned or approved by God? Is it significant that these acts of violence were perpetrated or inaugurated by women? What sorts of issues does that raise for you? How do these issues affect the way you understand Esther and/or Judith?

---

34. For Judith in music, see Linda Bennett Elder, "Virgins, Viragos, and Virtuo(u)si among Judiths in Opera and Oratorio," *Journal for the Study of the Old Testament* 92 (2001): 91–119. Elder claims that more than sixty-five oratorios were based on Judith in the eighteenth and nineteenth centuries (93).

35. See Elder, "Virgins," 104–9. Elder discusses Matthus's opera in detail on 109–12.

7

"Susie-Q, Baby, I Love You"*

Susanna and Art in the Renaissance

AS I HAVE ARGUED ELSEWHERE, the customary artistic interpretation of Susanna during the Renaissance was a sexual, eroticizing one.[1] This trend resulted from patrons and artists focusing on the sexual, voyeuristic aspects of the plot. Mary D. Garrard agrees with this position, writing, "In art, a sexually exploitative and morally meaningless interpretation of the [Susanna] theme has prevailed, most simply, because most artists and patrons have been men, drawn by instinct to identify more with the villains than with the heroine."[2] That is, most portrayals of Susanna focus on the sexually charged and abusive encounter between Susanna and the elders in lieu of highlighting the thematic emphasis on faith in God found in the story. I will argue that representations of this sort seek to coerce the viewer into complicity with the elders in terms of their desire for Susanna and thus render their sexually aggressive actions less reprehensible. Because of this tendency, these interpretations are harmful ideologically in that they portray the desire to possess Susanna via rape as a natural result of viewing female beauty.

However, there are also counterreadings to the standard renderings of Susanna during the Renaissance. These interpretations seek to challenge or alter the customary presentation of the Susanna theme by altering conventional arrangements of figures or by investing Susanna with more of the thematic qualities, such as piety, found in the apocryphal narrative, as I will

---

*This chapter contains excerpts from my *The Good, the Bold, and the Beautiful: The Story of Susanna and Its Renaissance Interpretations* (Library of Hebrew Bible/Old Testament Studies 430; New York and London: T & T Clark, 2006).

1. See my *The Good, the Bold, and the Beautiful*, 121–39.

2. Mary D. Garrard, "Artemesia and Susanna," in *Feminism and Art History: Questioning the Litany* (ed. Norma Broude and Mary D. Garrard; New York: Harper & Row, 1982), 153.

note below. By their imaginative challenge to the more sexualizing trend of interpretation, these renderings can provide a model for modern readers to emulate in order to resist an erotically focused reading of the story or similarly shaped aesthetic renderings.

In what follows, I will summarize the story of Susanna and then examine examples of both trends of artistic interpretation.[3] First, I will discuss Tintoretto's sexual, voyeuristic renderings and will then explore Rembrandt's two Susannas, which I argue represent attempts to focus on the more pious, religious aspects of the story. By juxtaposing these two artists, I hope to show the divergent trends of the history of interpretation of Susanna, as well as illuminate how readers can approach these aesthetic interpretations as models for understanding different levels of the apocryphal narrative.

SUMMARY OF SUSANNA

The story of Susanna is part of three Greek additions to the book of Daniel, most likely composed in the first century B.C.E.[4] It is set in a Jewish community in Babylon during the exilic period (sixth century B.C.E.) and tells the story of a beautiful, virtuous woman named Susanna, who is the wife of Joakim, one of the most prominent judges of this community. The narrative claims that all the Jews would come to Joakim's house for his judgments. In v. 5, we are introduced to two other elders of the people, and the narrator immediately associates them with evil and lawlessness. We learn quickly that this assessment is accurate, as we are told in vv. 7–12 that these elders secretly watch Susanna as she walks through her garden during the heat of midday. They lust for her, but neither of them knows the other is watching. In v. 14, though, they bump into one another as they leave the garden, and after admitting their lust to one another, both men agree to confront Susanna as soon as possible.

Verses 15–18 recount Susanna preparing to bathe in her garden, and the elders are naturally spying on her. When she sends her servants away for bathing accoutrements, the elders make their move. They say, "Look, the doors of the garden have been closed and no one can see us. We are lusting for you; agree to be with us! But if [you do] not, we will testify against you, that a young man was with you and because of this you sent the girls away from you" (vv. 20–21).[5] Susanna seems to be faced with an untenable choice: she can either acquiesce and allow herself to be raped, or she can refuse and face certain death as a result of the elders' accusation. She says, "It is narrow for me on all sides! For if I do this, it is death for me, but if I do not, I will not escape your hands. It is chosen for me: I cannot do

---

3. For a more comprehensive reading of Susanna, see my *The Good, the Bold, and the Beautiful*, 44–93.

4. I argue for this date in ibid., 9–43.

5. All translations from Susanna are my own. For a complete translation, see ibid., 183–86.

it; I will fall into your hands rather than sin before the Lord!" (vv. 22–23). Following this, Susanna screams out loud, causing her servants to rush in, whereupon the elders tell everyone their false story. Susanna is then placed on trial, at which the elders order her to unveil herself so "that they might have their fill of her beauty" (v. 32). Clearly, these men are more interested in satiating their lustful desires than in dispensing justice.

The elders deliver their testimony in vv. 36–41 while Susanna remains silent. The narrator assures the audience that "her heart trusted in the Lord" (v. 35), and because of her faith she offers no defense. She is convicted and is sentenced to be stoned. As she is being led away, she prays in vv. 42–43: "O God, the eternal, the one who knows hidden things, seeing all things before their beginning, you know that they [the elders] have borne false witness against me. Now, I am about to die even though I have done none of these [things] of which they wickedly accused me." The Lord hears her prayer and rouses the spirit of a young Daniel, who stands to defend Susanna.

Daniel, even though he is a young man, challenges the verdict and asks the community to allow him to separate the elders so he can cross-examine them. It should be clear that the elders have rehearsed their stories, but the genius of Daniel's cross-examination is that he zeroes in on a seemingly trivial detail on which to question them. In vv. 52–55 he interrogates the first elder and asks him under which tree he saw Susanna and the young man making love. The elder's answer is the mastic tree, which in Greek is related to the word Daniel uses in v. 55 to describe the divinely ordained punishment for the elder's evil actions: "Already an angel of God has received the sentence from God and will split you in two!" Verses 56–59 narrate his examination of the second elder, and this elder claims that the tree was an evergreen. Daniel again uses wordplay in v. 59 to specify the elder's penalty. All the community witnesses the conflicting testimony, and in vv. 61–62 the narrator recounts, "The assembly then did to them the same wicked thing [they were going to do] to their neighbor; acting according to the Law of Moses, they killed them. Thus, innocent blood was saved in that day." Susanna is saved, and the stage is set for Daniel's future exploits in his eponymous book.

TINTORETTO

Tintoretto's career is intimately bound up with the city in which he spent his entire life: Venice. Born Jacopo Robusti, he was the son of a cloth dyer, thus his nickname Tintoretto, meaning "the little dyer." Little is known about his training, but early sources report that he worked briefly in Titian's workshop before being expelled prior to 1539.[6] It was his painting titled

---

6. See, for example, the testimony of Carlo Ridolfi from 1642, now available in *The Life of Tintoretto* (trans. Catherine and Robert Enggass; University Park, Pa., London: Pennsylvania State University Press, 1984), 15.

St. Mark Rescuing the Slave (1547/8) that brought him widespread recognition in Venice.[7] Because of this painting, he began to receive more prestigious commissions. Even though his family did not enjoy higher citizen status (*cittadino originario*), by 1553 Tintoretto had married the daughter of an important member of the Scuola Grande di S. Marco and thus was initiated into the "pious, civic-minded and essentially conservative world of the non-noble confraternities."[8] The *scuole* in Renaissance Venice were upper-class, yet not noble, devotional groups that were active in terms of both charitable causes and the arts.[9] These confraternities would figure prominently in Tintoretto's life. He was admitted to the Scuola Grande di S. Rocco; in circa 1565 and would spend the remainder of his life decorating their meetinghouse. The last two decades of his life were the most prolific. He not only did extensive work at the Scuole Grande di S. Rocco, he was also involved in redecorating the Doge's Palace after two fires caused considerable damage in 1574 and 1577. After Titian's death in 1576, Tintoretto received court commissions from abroad, including Prague. He also completed Paolo Veronese's commission for the Doge's Palace between 1588 and 1590 after Veronese's death in 1588, and did several large, important works for the church of S. Giorgio Maggiore between 1591 and his death in 1594, among them his last rendition of the Last Supper.

Over the course of his career, Tintoretto produced four different renditions of the Susanna story. His most famous version is his *Susanna and the Elders* (1555/6) found in the Kunsthistorisches Museum in Vienna, which I will discuss below. In the early to mid-1550s, Tintoretto engaged in what Terisio Pignatti terms "an undisguised ideological and stylistic confrontation" with his major contemporaries, Titian and Veronese.[10] Basically, Tintoretto took up either techniques or subjects utilized by the older, more established artists in order both to challenge himself and to present his talent comparatively.

One of the fruits of this confrontation was his first known *Susanna and the Elders*, now housed in the Louvre. In this work, Tintoretto shows Susanna being attended to by her servants, a scene not present in the apocryphal narrative. In the story, Susanna sends her maids to retrieve olive oil and ointment so that she may bathe. The servants only return later when one of the elders shouts out after Susanna refuses their advances. Also, the elders are rather inconspicuously rendered in the far upper right corner of

7. For a discussion of this work, see David Rosand, *Painting in Sixteenth-Century Venice: Titian, Veronese, Tintoretto* (rev. ed.; Cambridge: Cambridge University Press, 1997), 134–39.

8. Tomas Nichols, "Jacopo Tintoretto," *The Grove Dictionary of Art Online* (1998), n.p.; online: *http://www.groveart.com/index.html*.

9. For a brief discussion of *scuole*, see Peter Humfrey, *Painting in Renaissance Venice* (New Haven, Conn., and London: Yale University Press, 1995), 28.

10. See Terisio Pignatti, "Life and Works," in *Tintoretto* (by Francesco Valcanover and Terisio Pignatti; trans. Robert Erich Wolf; Library of Great Painters Series; New York: Harry N. Abrams, 1985), 27.

the piece, so they have not confronted Susanna yet. Since most interpretations of Susanna during the Renaissance choose to depict the encounter between Susanna and the elders, this choice seems odd. Finally, Susanna herself is looking directly at the viewer, again an uncommon iconographical choice during this time period. Based on these brief observations, we may ask what Tintoretto's intention(s) may have been in rendering Susanna in this fashion. Gail A. Bonjione offers the following answer to the question:

> In this work, two servants attend to her grooming needs, either combing her long tresses or manicuring her toes. Because of this attention to her body, which displays the muscular style of Michelangelo, Susanna appears somewhat vain. The mirror beneath her extended leg reinforces this *vanitas* element.[11] . . . Tintoretto obviously intended to focus on the figure of Susanna and her vanity and not on the actions of the Elders. The notion of Susanna as a victim is diminished because she is actively enticing the spectator with her direct gaze. She does not seem vulnerable at all.[12]

In this work, then, Tintoretto seems to be rendering Susanna in such a way that would allow the viewer to take part, both visually and psychologically, in the elders' lust for Susanna.

In his second painting of Susanna, commonly known as the Viennese *Susanna* (1555/6), Tintoretto portrays the heroine in much the same fashion. In this work, the figure of Susanna dominates the frame. She is sitting comfortably behind a wall in her garden with one foot dangling carelessly in her bath, gazing at herself in a mirror. She seems totally at ease, not knowing that the two elders are spying on her while she, in turn, looks at herself. One elder is in the foreground, lying on the ground in an attempt to watch unnoticed, while the other maneuvers around the far edge of the wall. As one gazes at the elders gazing at Susanna who is gazing at herself, a problem arises. If Susanna is so involved with her beauty—and the placement of oil and other items implies the *vanitas* element already present in the Louvre *Susanna*—then one might wonder how *this* Susanna would respond to the elders' advances. That is, because of the way in which Susanna exhibits her sexuality and her self-admiration, the viewer is led to the conclusion that she is open to a sexual encounter with the elders.

The key to this line of investigation is the gaze of Susanna into her mirror. John Berger, in an oft-quoted analysis, comments on the function of the mirror:

> Susannah is looking at herself in a mirror. Thus she joins the spectators of herself. The mirror was often used as a symbol of the vanity of woman. The moralizing,

---

11. This term refers to items that reinforce the concept of vanity, in this case, the items of self-beautification Susanna brings with her to the bath. Images that reinforce the element of *vanitas* could be claiming that Susanna is as interested in her appearance as the elders are, and as such raise questions about Susanna's behavior in response to their sexual advances.
12. Gail A. Bonjione, "Shifting Images: Susanna through the Ages" (Ph.D. diss., Florida State University, 1997), 91.

however, was mostly hypocritical. You painted a naked woman because you enjoyed looking at her, you put a mirror in her hand and you called the painting *Vanity*, thus morally condemning the woman whose nakedness you had depicted for your own pleasure. The real function of the mirror was otherwise. It was to make the woman connive in treating herself as, first and foremost, a sight.[13]

As I show above, this auto-voyeurism is not present in the apocryphal narrative. Why then would Tintoretto have incorporated it into his work and heightened the erotic presence in the picture as a result? Garrard provides a possible answer:

Renaissance and Baroque artists, however, like the early church fathers, ignored the fundamental moral point concerning the discovery of truth and the execution of justice, to focus instead upon the secondary plot devices of temptation, seduction, and the erotic escapades of the Elders. . . . Both the patristic and the artistic conceptions of Susanna, whether as an Eve triumphant over her own impulses or as a voluptuous sex object who may not bother to resist, are linked by the same erroneous assumption: that Susanna's dilemma was whether or not to give in to her sexual instincts.[14]

Along with this factor, one of the main reasons for this heightened sense of the erotic in sixteenth-century interpretations of Susanna was that many artists used Venus and Lucretia as models for rendering Susanna.[15] Garrard notes:

The frequent echo of these antique prototypes in paintings of the Susanna theme underlies their use as a device to evoke erotic recollections, in the classic formulation of having it both ways: adhering superficially to the requirement that Susanna be chaste, while appealing subliminally to the memory of the Venus archetype, whose gestures of modesty call attention to what she conceals.[16]

In her examination of nakedness in the West, Margaret R. Miles agrees with Garrard's analysis. She writes that Tintoretto's work attempts

to reproduce, in the eyes of an assumed male viewer, the Elders' intense erotic attraction, projected and displayed on Susanna's flesh. The Elders, placed in crepuscular shadows, do not bear the weight of communicating the urgency of their active desire; rather, her body represents that desire. Viewers are directed—trained—by the management of light and shadow and by the central position of Susanna's body to see Susanna as object, even as cause, of male desire. In the painting, Susanna's innocence becomes guilt as her body communicates and explains the Elders' lust. As this visual narration indicates, female

---

13. John Berger, *Ways of Seeing* (London: BBC and Penguin, 1972), 50–51.
14. Garrard, "Artemesia and Susanna," 152–53.
15. For a survey of portrayals of Venus, see Kenneth Clark, *The Nude: A Study in Ideal Form* (Garden City, N.Y.: Doubleday, 1956), 109–232. See also the critique of Clark's work by Lynda Nead in her *The Female Nude: Art, Obscenity, and Sexuality* (London and New York: Routledge, 1992).
16. Garrard, "Artemesia and Susanna," 154.

nakedness has received its symbolic representation, in the societies of the Christian West, from "the Elders." Female nakedness has a range of meanings assigned by voyeurs for whom female bodies represented simultaneously threat, danger, and delight.[17]

Thus, because of the use of antique models for the depiction of Susanna, the gendered material conditions of production of artistic works based on Susanna during the Renaissance, and the gendered position of viewers, Susanna is somehow forced to identify with a position that results in harmful views and actions against herself. That is, due to the interests and needs of those producing and financing interpretations of the story of Susanna, the figure of Susanna as presented in the story is twisted into a figure who not only causes male desire, but is open to it as well.

Not long after he painted the Viennese *Susanna*, perhaps even in the same year, Tintoretto produced a series of ceiling paintings in which he again mimicked the style of Veronese. The seven works in this cycle include *Joseph and Potiphar's Wife*, *Judith and Holofernes*, and *Esther and Ahasuerus*. The cycle also includes a small *Susanna and the Elders*, now housed in Madrid at the Museo del Prado, in which Tintoretto seems to reference his previous Viennese work. Specifically, the two elders seem to be almost identical in both works, and the garden wall in both is remarkably similar. However, the placement of the subjects has been altered considerably. In accordance with the standard rendering of the theme during the Renaissance, the elders are confronting Susanna. One stands to the right of her and assumes a gesture of speaking softly to her, while the other on her left is clutching her breast. Certainly we are never told of any physical contact between the elders and Susanna in the apocryphal story, but this did not stop artists from embellishing the story to heighten the erotic overtones. Thus, by adding a sexually explicit scene not found in the apocryphal narrative, Tintoretto, like other artists throughout the ages, is calling into question Susanna's willingness to refute the advances of the elders.

There is one final painting of Susanna and the elders by Tintoretto to consider: the print circa 1575 in the National Gallery in Washington, D.C. Even more than the Viennese *Susanna*, the figure of Susanna dominates this work. She is shown in the very center of the foreground with one foot in the water, like in the Viennese piece, receiving what presumably is oil for her bath from a servant. Unlike Tintoretto's first two efforts, here Susanna's partial nakedness is on direct display to the viewer. However, like his Louvre print, Tintoretto places the elders off in the far distance; indeed, they appear to be almost in a fog. Even so, they can easily see Susanna, for the foliage close to them is shaped like an arch, thus allowing them to see Susanna, and the viewer to see them. One possible reason for the difference in presentation here could be biographical. By circa 1575, Tintoretto was

---

17. Margaret R. Miles, *Carnal Knowing: Female Nakedness and Religious Meaning in the Christian West* (Boston: Beacon Press, 1989), 123–24.

beginning his intensive work on the Scuole Grande di S. Rocco, as well as starting work on the Doge's Palace. As such, he might have relied on his workshop apprentices—including his son Domenico and daughter Marietta—to help him complete many works around this time. Tintoretto had always used a workshop like other artists of the period, but his swiftness in completing paintings had always necessitated a heightened reliance. Humfrey acknowledges this increased dependence on his apprentices toward the end of his life and comments that "the inevitable result was a decline in quality in most of Tintoretto's late works."[18] In fact, Nichols writes, "After 1580 relatively few paintings can be attributed to Tintoretto alone."[19] Was this growing reliance on his apprentices behind the different view of the theme in this work? Perhaps, but the important point to make is that here again we see the theme of *vanitas* and the presentation of Susanna as a sumptuous nude. Ellen Spolsky writes concerning these issues:

> At the same time the painting itself is an *objet d'art*, the painted woman is also an object, available to the viewer's gaze. His stare might be illicit, but the painter helps him over his guilt, as it were, by picturing her nudity as vanity; her preening legitimates his gaze, and she is thus made accessible to the viewer.[20]

Given the presence of these elements, the concerns I raise above with regard to the three earlier works also apply here.

Tintoretto's interpretations of Susanna have, by and large, been praised for their technique and atmosphere, but they have also been critiqued for their assumptions and presentation of Susanna as perhaps more involved in the advances of the elders than the apocryphal story implies. However, none of the analyses of the Susanna paintings tries to understand them in light of the religious nature of Tintoretto's work. He was, after all, a native of Venice and a member of one of the religiously conservative *scuole*, and as such he would have brought a sense of devotion, perhaps even piety, to his work. Certainly the sheer number of religious paintings in his vast output testifies to his preoccupation with religious themes; for example, he painted works based on the Last Supper at least eight different times. In his analysis of Tintoretto's religious works, David Rosand reaches the following conclusion regarding Tintoretto's expression(s) of piety:

> It would seem more appropriate to talk about the fundamentalism of Tintoretto's Christian faith—or at least the faith that is figured in his paintings. . . . Tintoretto's own religious vision is neither mystical nor exclusively personal; rather, it is open and popular, common in the sense of shared conviction.[21]

---

18. Humfrey, *Painting in Renaissance Venice*, 236.
19. Nichols, "Jacopo Tintoretto," n.p.
20. Ellen Spolsky, "Law or the Garden: The Betrayal of Susanna in Pastoral Painting," in *The Judgment of Susanna: Authority and Witness* (ed. Ellen Spolsky; SBLEJL 11; Atlanta: Scholars Press, 1996), 102–3.
21. Rosand, *Painting in Sixteenth-Century Venice*, 159.

In a similar vein, Humfrey even goes so far as to analyze Tintoretto's religious works theologically: "By setting his biblical stories in humble, mundane and shadowy surroundings, and then illuminating them with sudden pools and shafts of light, Tintoretto triumphantly succeeds in conveying a sense that the world of ordinary sinful humanity is subject to workings of divine providence."[22] However, one finds no trace of an emphasis on divine providence in his interpretations of Susanna—a remarkable fact given the intervention of God via Daniel in the story. Based on Tintoretto's religious paintings, one could argue—as Rosand does—that his religiosity was so generic that he had no proverbial ax to grind, in contrast to other interpreters, as I will show below. It is possible, of course, that Tintoretto held strong religious beliefs and that these beliefs influenced his work, but nothing in his Susanna paintings attests to that theory. Instead, I find it more likely that in the case of his Susanna paintings, Tintoretto was following standard artistic conventions established by masters like Titian and Veronese and decided to depict Susanna as a sexually aware, attractive nude figure, perhaps in the hopes of receiving further commissions. As such, his Susanna oeuvre in no way constitutes a statement on his religious proclivities, but rather a more common desire to paint an inviting nude. As Garrard notes:

> Few artistic themes have offered so satisfying an opportunity for legitimized voyeurism as Susanna and the Elders. The subject was taken up with relish by artists from the sixteenth through eighteenth centuries as an opportunity to display the female nude, in much the same spirit that such themes as Danae or Lucretia were approached, but with the added advantage that the nude's erotic appeal could be heightened by the presence of two lecherous old men, whose inclusion was both iconographically justified and pornographically effective. It is a remarkable testament to the indomitable male ego that a biblical theme holding forth an exemplum of female chastity should have become in painting a celebration of sexual opportunity, or, as Max Rooses enthusiastically described Rubens's version, a "gallant enterprise mounted by two bold adventurers."[23]

Thus, Tintoretto's depictions of Susanna have no religious significance or theological message. Rather, the theme is simply a vehicle for the pornographic display of the female nude and an increased opportunity for biblically sanctioned voyeurism.

REMBRANDT

The counterreadings of the standard rendering of the Susanna theme in the Renaissance I wish to discuss are also arguably the most famous, namely, the two Susannas of Rembrandt. Owing to the massive biographical literature

---

22. Humfrey, *Painting in Renaissance Venice*, 234.
23. Garrard, "Artemesia and Susanna," 149–50.

available on Rembrandt, I will only mention data of that nature to enhance my examination of his interpretations of Susanna. Following this examination, I will offer some concluding remarks to this chapter.

In the early 1630s, Rembrandt moved from Leiden to Amsterdam, and there he worked for and lived with an art dealer named Hendrik van Uylenburgh. He married in 1634 and spent most of his time painting commissioned portraits that van Uylenburgh arranged for him. During this time, though, he still managed to work on various historical and biblical subjects, and in circa 1636 painted his first *Susanna and the Elders*.

Almost all scholars agree that one of Rembrandt's primary models for this work was Pieter Lastman's oil of 1614 on the same subject. This influence should come as no surprise; when Rembrandt was nineteen years old, he began a six-month apprenticeship with Lastman in Amsterdam. When Lastman died in 1633, Rembrandt made several drawings of his former master's paintings, among them a Susanna. In Lastman's *Susanna*, the two elders are in plain view, surrounded by lush foliage, and in the midst of attempting to persuade Susanna to let them rape her. Susanna appears in the classic *Venus pudica* pose, trying to conceal her genitalia and looking toward heaven, as if she is already entreating God for help. The tone of the picture is somber, with the landscape predominantly dark and only Susanna shown in full light. In sum, Lastman's interpretation of Susanna is idiosyncratic in that the mood of the painting is solemn; yet by adopting the Venus pose for Susanna and portraying her exposed breasts, it stands in the long line of eroticizing and voyeuristic readings of the apocryphal story.

Rembrandt's work based on Lastman's oil exhibits many of the same characteristics. Here, too, we see Susanna in the Venus pose covering not only her genitalia but also her breasts.[24] The landscape of the piece is also similar in that it is dark, even more so than Lastman's work, and Susanna occupies almost all of the visual field. However, there are at least two striking innovations in this painting not found in Lastman's. First, the elders are almost completely hidden from sight. In fact, only one elder is detectable, and only after serious study of the dense foliage to the right of Susanna.[25] The effects of this (dis)placement of the elders, usually considered to be a cipher for the male viewer, will be discussed below. The second innovation is Susanna herself; that is, her position, sense of movement, and direct gaze out of the frame all represent a new wrinkle in the standard renderings of the theme.[26]

---

24. Contra this statement, see Mieke Bal, "Between Focalization and Voyeurism: The Representation of Vision," in *Reading "Rembrandt": Beyond the Word-Image Opposition* (Cambridge New Art History and Criticism Series; Cambridge: Cambridge University Press, 1991), 170: "In terms of iconographic traditions, the pose of Susanna is less strictly tied to the Medici Venus, and thus there is a less direct evocation of a traditionally erotic meaning."

25. Mieke Bal, "The Elders and Susanna," *Biblical Interpretation* 1 (1993): 2, notes that the visible elder in this work is "assumed to be a later addition."

26. Tintoretto's *Susanna and the Elders* in the Louvre also portrays Susanna gazing out of the frame, but, as I will note below, the two works differ in their overall portrayal of Susanna.

In an interesting article, Eric J. Sluijter argues that Rembrandt knowingly altered the conventional treatment of the Susanna theme, especially regarding those works that might have influenced his interpretations, including the works of Lastman, Cornelius van Haarlem, Peter Paul Rubens (ca. 1606), Lucas Vorsterman (ca. 1620; after Rubens's ca. 1606 piece), and perhaps even the work of Annibale Carracci.[27] Sluijter notes that Rembrandt tries both to involve the viewer and to depict Susanna's state of mind. He does so, as I note above, by adopting Lastman's use of the *Venus pudica* pose, as well as alluding to another classical model, the *Venus Doidalsas*, or the Crouching Venus, thus heightening Susanna's erotic appeal.[28] However, the most important advance according to Sluijter is Rembrandt's choice of which moment to represent. As we have seen, almost all of the Renaissance interpretations of Susanna depict the moment when the elders confront Susanna in her garden, and as such are able to represent a naked woman in a sexual situation. In Rembrandt's first *Susanna*, though,

> what the viewer sees is a Susanna who suddenly realizes that she is being watched—one could imagine that she has just heard a twig snap. She starts in fear and begins to rise from a sitting position. Her weight is already on her feet, which emphasizes the agitated suddenness of her reaction and gives a suggestion of wavering unbalance. . . . In the process she steps on her slipper; thus Rembrandt stressed the abrupt clumsiness of her spontaneous movement, which is at the same time brilliantly used as a metaphoric motif referring to her chasteness. Slightly turning away her upper body from the onlooker, trying to hide her secret parts, her large dark eyes look intensely at the viewer. It is the viewer she confronts as the intruder who made her start in fear.[29]

The simulated movement of Susanna suggests clumsy movement in response to a presence, real or imagined, and as viewers we expect that presence to be filled by the elders. However, their almost total absence from this painting means that presence is filled by another party, namely, the viewer of the work, the recipient of Susanna's pleading and fearful gaze. Both Sluijter and Mieke Bal agree that this gaze, as well as the position of the viewer, serves to heighten the erotic appeal of the work:

> It is the gaze of the viewer to which she reacts so forcefully. Unlike Rubens's *Susanna*, her reaction is not ambiguous: the viewer is recognized as the intruder and primary offender. Susanna is trapped by the beholder's gaze, which becomes explicitly the illicit gaze of the voyeur. At the same time this makes the image more intensely erotic. In this very erotically charged moment, the engaged viewer experiences, as it were, the rush of being caught in an illicit act

---

27. See Eric J. Sluijter, "Rembrandt's Early Paintings of the Female Nude: *Andromeda* and *Susanna*," in *Rembrandt and His Pupils* (ed. Görel Cavalli-Björkman; Uddevalla, Sweden: Risbergs Tryckeri, 1993), 31–54.
28. Ibid., 41.
29. Ibid., 41–42.

by the source of his sensual enjoyment. In this way the moral and erotic tension are linked as never before.[30]

Bal argues that since the gaze of Susanna has no connection to any internal narrative structure, it represents a de-narrativized look directed at the viewer of the work, and as such it engages the spectator in an act of uninvited voyeuristic pleasure.[31] This pleasure can even be seen as malicious. Spolsky writes, "It is difficult not to see the painter's choice of this moment as sadistic; the viewer is allowed to enjoy her [Susanna's] shock and fear."[32] Thus, many interpreters argue that even though Rembrandt alters the traditional iconographic topos of the Susanna theme in this work, he does so in a way that heightens the erotic and voyeuristic undertones present in other interpretations of the story.

The 1640s were not as kind to Rembrandt as the previous decade had been. In 1642, his wife, Saskia, died of tuberculosis, leaving him alone with their young son, Titus. Not long after her death, Rembrandt hired a nurse named Geertge Dircx, with whom he became sexually involved. By 1649, though, he wished to dispense with her to take up with a twenty-three-year-old named Hendrickje Stoffels. Evidently, Geertge was unhappy with her severance allowance, and a court case began, which she later won. Following the trial, Rembrandt started publicly to defame her, to the point that she was consigned to a reformatory, where she remained for five years. Thus, his second *Susanna and the Elders*, painted circa 1647 and often referred to as the Berlin *Susanna*, was created in a stressful period of conflicting personal commitments. Owing to his personal problems, it was actually one of the last pieces he painted in the 1640s.

The two works are obviously similar in many respects. The landscape and foliage are alike; both are dark and foreboding, as is typical of Rembrandt. The shading of both works highlights the figure of Susanna, which is roughly the same in both paintings. In the Berlin *Susanna* she is more stylized; that is, there is less sense of movement and almost no awkwardness, and her shoe is missing. Even so, she still is positioned in the Venus pose, and her body and features are almost identical. The most noticeable difference between the two works is the presence of the elders. Whereas in the piece of 1636 they are hidden for the most part, here they are both fully represented on the same visual plane as Susanna. The elder on the left takes up a familiar position in representations of the theme: he is trying to disrobe Susanna and could be whispering in her ear. The second elder is approaching the pair on the far right, grasping what appears to be a staff. The presence of the elders echoes earlier treatments of the story and could be seen as an adoption of the more traditional presentation of Susanna in art during this period.

---

30. Ibid., 44.
31. Bal, "Elders and Susanna," 14.
32. Spolsky, "Law or the Garden," 104.

However, in her work, Bal disagrees and argues that the differences introduced in the Berlin *Susanna* actually resist the voyeuristic aspects of the piece from 1636.[33] She focuses her attention first on Susanna's left hand, which alludes to the Venus pose. Bal claims that at the same time this intertextual citation is made, the citation is also undermined by the defensive posture of Susanna's figure.[34] Furthermore, as I note above, the elder on the left is attempting to disrobe Susanna and as such could be taken as a cipher for male desire in and from the painting. Bal, though, notes:

> Syntactically, in combination with Susanna's appeal to the viewer to turn his eyes away if the undressing eventually occurs, it [the elder's action] can simultaneously be taken to criticize the gesture: It says, the body may be naked in a moment, but please don't look. The vulnerability of this young, helpless female figure is certainly a possible occasion for voyeurism in its sadistic variant. But this *ideologeme* is counterbalanced by the opposite *ideologeme*, the strongly active look.[35]

Finally, in order to read against the interpretation of this work that sees continuity present with other eroticizing renderings of the theme, Bal focuses on the elders themselves as potential imitative examples. She argues that the presentation of the elders in the painting vitiates against any potential wish viewers might have to emulate their gaze, or possibly even their actions. Such presentation includes

> the ridiculous overdressing of the men, with their pompous mantles and hats, the staff and seat for the one, the chain referring to his honorable function for the other. These elements hamper the viewer's gaze in that they activate the narrative of abuse of power with which most viewers will not automatically wish to identify. The position the viewer is invited to share, that of the Elder at the right of the painting, is thereby just too uncomfortable to allow the viewer to take up his objectifying, abstract, and delectating gaze very easily.[36]

Thus, Bal's reading of Rembrandt's Berlin *Susanna* claims that the eroticism and voyeurism present in other works depicting this theme are undermined by the particulars of the painting. Put another way, both Sluijter and Bal agree that Rembrandt altered the traditional representation of Susanna in pictorial art during the Renaissance; they simply differ on the results of that alteration.

In sum, Rembrandt's two Susannas represent sites of competing claims as to their functions and effects on viewers. Sluijter argues that Rembrandt's

---

33. See Bal, "Between Focalization and Voyeurism," 167–68.
34. Kathleen P. McClain, "Seeing Beyond the Traditional Image of Susanna and the Elders" (M.A. thesis, University of Alabama, Birmingham, 2000), 58 n. 94, agrees with Bal's assessment, even though she does not cite Bal. She notes that if Rembrandt's original vision for the Berlin *Susanna* was to have one elder groping Susanna, then this would move Susanna away from the Venus tradition, which emphasizes concealment, not sexual contact.
35. Bal, "Between Focalization and Voyeurism," 167.
36. Ibid., 168.

piece of 1636 furthers the eroticizing tendencies of earlier Susannas by focusing on her individual figure and psychological state. Bal, in contrast, claims that the Berlin *Susanna* resists these tendencies, even though it may appear to embrace them. In my opinion, both of the works resist the traditional iconographic meanings found in traditional renderings due to the figure of Susanna. As Bonjione notes in her work, the Medici Venus in the *Venus pudica* pose "does not invite voyeurism and appears quite uncomfortable with the fact that anyone is observing her naked body."[37] However, unlike the classical Medici Venus and other renderings of Susanna, Rembrandt paints Susanna looking directly at the viewer, and this gaze, I would argue, contains no trace of erotic appeal or sexual suggestion.[38] If there is any acquiescence to the eroticizing tradition of other Susannas, I agree with Bal and Spolsky that it is of the sadistic variant; that is, one would have to enjoy terror, confusion, and the potential of domination in order to find this Susanna sexually appealing. Thus, Rembrandt, like Gentileschi, resists the standard interpretations of Susanna as a sexual object and instead presents the viewer with a young woman shocked and horrified to find that she is being watched, one who appeals to the viewer both to turn away and to help her. In this regard, Rembrandt's Susannas build on the eroticizing tendencies I discussed above with regard to Tintoretto, but they do so in order to critique them.

CONCLUSIONS

We can approach the story of Susanna as a piece of literature by examining two different levels in the story's narrative. On the one hand, there is the surface level, the level that attempts to reproduce reality. At this level, Susanna is described as beautiful, fearful of the Lord, educated in the Law, a daughter, a wife, and a mother. She also speaks and performs a few actions. On the other hand, there is the thematic level, the level that contains a larger message or moral to the story. In my opinion, it is the thematic level of the narrative that is dominant, in that the story seems to focus on these issues and themes more so than it does on descriptions and insights into characters and their actions.

Given the descriptive, surface-level portrait of Susanna in the story, the thematic dimensions of her character are easily identified. Susanna is described as beautiful, religious, and God-identified in explicit contrast to the elders. Because Susanna's attributes, speech, and actions all point to her religious identity, it is likely that the author is using her to make a comment on righteous, religious persons who suffer. That is, Susanna can be

---

37. Bonjione, "Shifting Images," 114.

38. In Tintoretto's *Susanna and the Elders* in the Louvre, Susanna's gaze out of the frame is not pleading or fearful. Due to the excessive presence of *vanitas* elements, as well as the fact that she is unaware of the presence of the elders, her gaze cannot be taken as a cry for help.

seen as standing for all of the righteous Jews who suffer. In that capacity, the outcome of the story would be an incentive for continued belief; if Susanna can keep her faith in God throughout her trial and ultimately be vindicated, then the readers of her story can as well. Put another way, the story develops the thematic dimensions of Susanna's character, and the progression of the narrative ultimately develops a thematic function for her character. That is, her actions and beliefs serve to make a larger thematic point, or to establish a moral to the story. In my opinion, the proposition put forth by the thematic level of Susanna's character seems clear. Her refusal to be affected by social shame, her unwillingness to be a passive participant in her own rape because of the resultant sin, and her willingness to allow God to defend her all highlight her religious identity in contrast to the elders' (mis)conception of God. Because of Susanna's ultimate acquittal and the elders' executions, the author is using Susanna's character to persuade the reader that Susanna's faith and idea of God are better than those of the elders. Thus, the overall theme/moral of the story that centers on Susanna's character leads the reader to identify with and wish to imitate Susanna's religiosity.

However, as I note above, the artistic tradition (and to some extent the musical and literary traditions) that has grown up around the story of Susanna interprets it in two main fashions. On the one hand, the dominant rendering of Susanna in Renaissance art specifically asks viewers to assume the position of watcher or voyeur. That is, when we view interpretations of this story by such artists as Tintoretto, we are being asked to take on the very role and perform the very action that we are asked to condemn when we read about the elders and their actions. Thus, there is cognitive dissonance in the act of interpretation between what we know of the story and what we are being asked to do when we view artwork based on the story. In my opinion, the reason for the dissonance is that these eroticizing interpretations focus only on the surface level of the story's rhetoric; that is, they are concerned solely with portraying the encounter between Susanna and the elders in a way that highlights the erotic and voyeuristic traits of the story. On the other hand, there are Renaissance renderings of the narrative by such artists as Rembrandt who emphasize the message the story endorses. That is, these interpretations privilege the theme and moral of the story, and as such they provide models for readers to emulate in resisting the surface level of the story and interpretations, both scholarly and aesthetic, based on that level.

Based on this reading of the narrative, the rhetoric in the story seems unambiguous and focused almost totally on the themes of piety and religious identity. The author shows Susanna facing social shame, personal danger, and religious sin with fear tempered by an all-encompassing trust in God and God's judgment. Readers are shown the elders' behavior toward God, Susanna, and their own people. Finally, we see Daniel enter the narrative as a result of Susanna's faith, and we see how he saves Susanna and convicts the elders. The end of the story illustrates whose values and actions the story endorses (Susanna's and Daniel's) and which characters suffer because of the views and exploits the narrative condemns. This all seems clear from the story. Thus, the story is a thematic one that endorses piety and religiosity while condemning lust and corruption of power.[39]

However, as Erich S. Gruen notes, there is more to the story than this straightforward message:

> To read this yarn simply as a religious fable displaying God's protection of the innocent and punishment of the wicked misses much. The tale directs its mockery at a range of community failings: hypocrisy, false religiosity, inverted values, and unprincipled vacillation. . . . The exposure of pomposity in the leadership and gullibility in the rank and file supplied a pointed reminder to the nation: Jews need to look to their own shortcomings. That such a message could be inserted into the text of Daniel is quite striking. It attests to a notable self-assurance on the part of Hellenistic Jews who exposed the foibles of fellow Jews to public scrutiny. It recalled to mind the basic principles of justice and morality that needed to be observed, especially in Jewish communities that governed their own activities. And it provided a subtle reminder that lapses in adherence to those principles could divide Jews internally, thus setting them up for victimization by greater powers.[40]

Thus, Susanna's story carries in it not only a sense of religious triumphalism, but also a tone of self-criticalness. It may have served as a reminder to form more moral communities or risk being fragmented and possibly dispersed again. In her work, Marti J. Steussy concludes with a similar note:

> At various times throughout history—in Israel's expansion to an empire under Solomon, in Judea's misadventures under Hellenistic and Roman overlords, in rural America's observations of cosmopolitan New York and San Francisco— devout religious people trained in the "good old traditions" have suspected their leaders of personal and public perversion, private licentiousness and corruption in office. They have asserted, against those fears, that God will not long tolerate such lawlessness. The Susanna story plays well to such an audience. But such disaffection is generally not revolutionary. Whether through fear of anarchy or because a basic identification with the rulers remains, suspicion expresses itself in calls for pious government and private restraint, rather than in attempts to overturn the order. So too with our versions of Susanna.[41]

Thus, the story of Susanna is not a radical call to arms, but more of a hearkening back to some of the basic emphases of Judaism: religiosity and

---

39. For a similar reading of the story, see R. A. F. MacKenzie, "The Meaning of the Susanna Story," *Canadian Journal of Theology* 3 (1957): 211–18.

40. Erich S. Gruen, *Heritage and Hellenism: The Reinvention of Jewish Tradition* (Hellenistic Culture and Society Series 30; Berkeley: University of California Press, 1998), 176–77.

41. Steussy, *Gardens in Babylon: Narrative and Faith in the Greek Legends of Daniel* (SBLDS 141; Atlanta: Scholars Press, 1993), 142–43.

faith in God. Similarly, it is not a story focused on the physical aspects and actions of characters portrayed "realistically." Rather, Susanna is a narrative whose moral is overriding; it is a story that emphasizes a certain message—namely, those who have faith in God will be rewarded.

In conclusion, the importance of identifying different levels of rhetoric in Susanna and distinct interpretive trends that take up those different levels of rhetoric is twofold. First, this identification allows us to be more accurate historically in identifying the ideological bases of an interpreter's rendering of the story. That is, if we are more aware of the view of women an interpreter holds, based on his or her reading of the narrative, then we can have a better handle on the ideology behind a certain interpretation. Second, more specificity in terms of the ideology of images of women will hopefully allow us to develop more means to resist harmful images of this sort in our own time.

STUDY QUESTIONS

1. In addition to artistic renderings, Susanna has been rendered musically often through the centuries. The most important recent interpretation is Carlisle Floyd's opera *Susannah*, which premiered in 1955. Floyd transplants Susanna's story to the rural South in the period just after World War II. His is not a literal rendering of the biblical story, though. Daniel is morphed into the Reverend Olin Blitch, who after saving Susanna begins to lust for her as well. Listen to Floyd's opera and ask how the changes he has made affect your understanding of the story of Susanna. Specifically, how does Floyd alter the desires and motivations of Susanna? Next, listen to other key musical renderings of Susanna, for example, Orlando Lassus's setting of "Susanne un jour," William Byrd's "Susanna Fair," and the oratorio of 1681 by Alessandro Stradella. How do these interpretations adapt or retell the narrative? Which level of the narrative do they privilege: the sexual or the pious? How do they compare with Floyd's opera? And how and why do all of these musical interpretations affect your understanding of Susanna?

2. One of the components of the surface level of the narrative is the voyeurism of the elders and how it leads to their lust and ultimately their attempted rape of Susanna. The issue of sexual violence in the story is an important one, and some interpreters have focused their attention on it.[42] I would like you also to think about how reading about—and in the case of this chapter, viewing examples of—sexually aggressive behavior may affect you. Clearly, the narrator wants to draw readers into the story, because only by arousing their interest will the ideas the narrator is expressing be noticed. If we have to adopt the

---

42. See, for example, Carey A. Moore, "Susanna: A Case of Sexual Harassment in Ancient Babylonia," *Biblical Research* 8 (1992): 20–29, 52.

outlook of the elders, at least momentarily, for the story to function, what could be the result of that act? Could we be placing ourselves in a position analogous to that of the elders? Are we guilty of voyeurism by dint of our adoption of the perspective of the elders? If so, what is the effect of our gazing at Susanna? And could it be harmful for us to gaze at all the nude Susannas the history of art offers us? Are we then susceptible to the same urges and lusts that corrupted the elders?[43] On a related topic, how could Susanna's story affect and/or help victims of sexually aggressive behavior today?

3. Obviously, this chapter does not exhaust the depictions of Susanna in art. It does not even exhaust the Susannas created during the Renaissance. As such, play art critic and gather more images of Susanna via the websites I mention in study question 6 on page 27. Try to align the images you find with the levels of rhetoric in the narrative I discuss above. Where do the images fit, and why? What scene do they choose to render? How is Susanna portrayed? Pay special attention to twentieth-century artists like Roux Michel (*http://www.artfigurative.com/ GALLERIES/COMPOSIZIONI/index. html*), Rogier Willems (*http:// www.rogierwillems.nl/Nederlands/portretten-suzanna.htm*), and Alexander Gurevich (*http://www.antho.net/english/museum/gurevich/pic16.html*). How do these images compare to the more familiar-looking pieces from the Renaissance? Are there any images you find to be disturbing? If so, why? Finally, how do these visual interpretations of Susanna affect your understanding of the apocryphal narrative?

---

43. See my *The Good, the Bold, and the Beautiful*, 178–80.

8

Why We Should Care about the History of Interpretation

WE HAVE COVERED A LOT OF GROUND in the preceding chapters. We have examined primary biblical texts as well as the ways later authors, composers, artists, and interpreters have retold, expanded, and/or reimagined female characters from the Hebrew Bible and the Apocrypha. The question of significance, though, may still loom large for some readers. That is, why is it important to examine the history of interpretation? Why should we care about the ways in which these female characters have been portrayed in later retellings and interpretations?

The answer lies in the ways in which traditions develop and stories morph from context to context. Every time a story is told in a different context, it takes on the contours and assumptions found therein, so that additional meanings and insights become part of the developing tradition. The reason that examining the history of interpretation is integral for understanding themes and issues within a religious tradition is that at any given time the common understanding of a particular issue "emerges in the interplay of Bible readers, textual clues, interpretive traditions, and contemporary social realities."[1] To study the history of interpretation, then, is to study the ways in which real people appropriate and utilize sacred texts to explain themselves to themselves as well as justify their current contexts. The importance of examining the ways in which these characters have been portrayed in various genres or interpretations—what I call the interpretive tradition—is twofold. First, showing that this tradition is not univocal allows us to question why certain readings have been allowed to dominate the discussion. Second, and more importantly, by tracing these characters'

---

1. Stephen R. Haynes, *Noah's Curse: The Biblical Justification of American Slavery* (Oxford: Oxford University Press, 2002), 187.

journeys through these sources, we can show that the popular understandings of them are not givens; rather, they are constructed from disparate sources, not all of which agree. This awareness allows us to appreciate the role aesthetic and religious interpretations play in our understandings of biblical texts. And if we can see how these popular understandings have been constructed, then we can begin to deconstruct them in order to allow ourselves to come to the Bible anew.

ℭ BIBLIOGRAPHY

Aberbach, Moses, and Bernard Grossfeld. *Targum Onkelos to Genesis: A Critical Analysis Together with an English Translation of the Text*. Denver: KTAV Publishing and Center for Judaic Studies, University of Denver, 1982.

Abugideiri, Hibba. "Hagar: A Historical Model for 'Gender Jihad.'" Pages 81–107 in *Daughters of Abraham: Feminist Thought in Judaism, Christianity, and Islam*. Edited by Yvonne Yazbeck Haddad and John L. Esposito. Gainesville, Fla.: University Press of Florida, 2001.

Adams, Anne Tyra. *Beauty in the Fields: The Diary of Ruth's Fellow Harvester*. Promised Land Diaries Series. Grand Rapids, Mich.: Baker Books, 2005.

Agourides, S. "Apocalypse of Sedrach: A New Translation and Introduction." Pages 605–13 in vol. 1 of *The Old Testament Pseudepigrapha*. Edited by James H. Charlesworth. 2 vols. New York: Doubleday, 1983, 1985.

Aldrich, Thomas Bailey. *Judith and Holofernes: A Poem*. Boston: Houghton, Mifflin and Company, 1896.

———. *Judith of Bethulia: A Tragedy*. Boston: Houghton, Mifflin and Company, 1904.

Alter, Robert. "Biblical Type-Scenes and the Uses of Convention." Pages 47–62 in *The Art of Biblical Narrative*. New York: Basic Books, 1981.

———. *The Five Books of Moses: A Translation with Commentary*. New York and London: W. W. Norton, 2004.

———. *Genesis: Translation and Commentary*. New York and London: W. W. Norton, 1996.

Anderson, Gary A. "The Culpability of Eve: From Genesis to Timothy." Pages 233–51 in *From Prophecy to Testament: The Function of the Old Testament in the New*. Edited by Craig A. Evans. Peabody, Mass.: Hendrickson, 2004.

———. *The Genesis of Perfection: Adam and Eve in Jewish and Christian Imagination*. Louisville, Ky.: Westminster John Knox Press, 2001.

Apostolos-Cappadona, Diane. "'The Lord Struck Him Down by the Hand of a Woman': Images of Judith." Pages 81–97 in *Art as Religious Meaning*. Edited by Diane Apostolos-Cappadona and Doug Adams. New York: Crossroad, 1987.

Baetzhold, Howard G., and Joseph B. McCullough, eds. *The Bible According to Mark Twain*. New York: Simon & Schuster, 1996.

Bal, Mieke. "Between Focalization and Voyeurism: The Representation of Vision." Pages 138–76 in *Reading "Rembrandt": Beyond the Word-Image Opposition.* Cambridge New Art History and Criticism Series. Cambridge: Cambridge University Press, 1991.

———. "The Elders and Susanna." *Biblical Interpretation* 1 (1993): 1–19.

———. *Lethal Love: Feminist Literary Readings of Biblical Love Stories.* Indiana Studies in Biblical Literature. Bloomington: Indiana University Press, 1987.

Barrett, Rebecca Kaye. "Higher Love: What Women Gain from Christian Romance Novels." *Journal of Religion and Popular Culture* 4 (2003). Online: *http://www.usask.ca/relst/jrpc/art4-higherlove.html.*

Baruch, Elaine Hoffman. "Forbidden Words—Enchanting Song: The Treatment of Delilah in Literature and Music." Pages 239–49 in *To Speak or Be Silent: The Paradox of Disobedience in the Lives of Women.* Edited by Lena B. Ross. Wilmette, Ill.: Chiron Publications, 1993.

Beal, Timothy K. *The Book of Hiding: Gender, Ethnicity, Annihilation, and Esther.* London and New York: Routledge, 1997.

———. "The Passion: They Know Not What They Watch." *Chronicle of Higher Education* (19 March 2004): B, pp. 14–15.

Bechtel, Carol M. *Esther. Interpretation: A Bible Commentary for Teaching and Preaching.* Louisville, Ky.: John Knox Press, 2002.

Berger, John. *Ways of Seeing.* London: BBC and Penguin, 1972.

Berlin, Adele. *Esther.* Jewish Publication Society Bible Commentary Series. Philadelphia: Jewish Publication Society, 2001.

Berquist, Jon L. "Role Dedifferentiation in the Book of Ruth." *Journal for the Study of the Old Testament* 57 (1993): 23–37.

Bickerman, Elias. "The Colophon of the Greek Book of Esther." *Journal of Biblical Literature* 63 (1944): 339–62.

———. "The Scroll of Esther, or Esther and Mordecai." Pages 171–240 in *Four Strange Books of the Bible: Jonah, Daniel, Koheleth, Esther.* New York: Schocken Books, 1967.

Big Idea, Inc. Product information for *Esther: The Girl Who Became Queen.* Online: *http://bigidea.com/products/shows/shows_content.aspx?pid=43.*

Blidstein, Gerald J. "Eve: The Fear and the Loneliness." Pages 43–51 in *In the Rabbis' Garden: Adam and Eve in the Midrash.* Northvale, N.J.: Jason Aronson, 1997.

Boling, Robert G. *Judges.* Anchor Bible 6A. Garden City, N.Y.: Doubleday, 1975.

Bonjione, Gail A. "Shifting Images: Susanna through the Ages." Ph.D. diss., Florida State University, 1997.

Bos, Johanna W. H. "Out of the Shadows: Genesis 38; Judges 4:17–22; Ruth 3." *Semeia* 42 (1988): 37–67.

Bowman, Donna. "The Bible-Shaped Mirror: Biblical Women and Contemporary Culture in Recent Film." *SBL Forum.* No pages. Cited June 2008. Online: *http://sbl-site.org/Article.aspx?ArticleID=778.*

Brayford, Susan. *Genesis.* Septuagint Commentary Series. Leiden: Brill, 2007.

———. "The Taming and Shaming of Sarah in the Septuagint of Genesis." Ph.D. diss., Iliff School of Theology and the University of Denver, 1998.

———. "To Shame or Not to Shame: Sexuality in the Mediterranean Diaspora." *Semeia* 87 (1999): 163–76.

Broch, Yitzhak I. *Ruth: The Book of Ruth in Hebrew and English with a Talmudic-Midrashic Commentary.* 2nd ed. Jerusalem and New York: Feldheim, 1983.

Brown, Howard M., and Louise K. Stein. "The Music of the Reformation and the Council of Trent." Pages 273–80 in *Music in the Renaissance*. 2nd ed. Prentice Hall History of Music Series. Upper Saddle River, N.J.: Prentice-Hall, 1999.

Brown, Karl. *Adventures with D. W. Griffith*. New York: Farrar, Straus and Giroux, 1973.

Brown, Raymond E. *The Birth of the Messiah: A Commentary on the Infancy Narratives in the Gospels of Matthew and Luke*. Updated ed. Anchor Bible Reference Library. New York: Doubleday, 1993.

Browne, E. Martin, ed. "The Fall of Man, from the York Cowper's Play." Pages 37–44 in *Religious Drama 2: Mystery and Morality Plays*. Cleveland: Meridian Books, 1958.

Campbell, Edward F., Jr. *Ruth*. Anchor Bible 7. Garden City, N.Y.: Doubleday, 1975.

Card, Orson Scott. *Sarah*. Women of Genesis Series. New York: Forge Books, 2000.

Carruthers, Jo. *Esther through the Centuries*. Blackwell Bible Commentaries. Oxford: Blackwell, 2008.

Charlesworth, James H., ed. *The Old Testament Pseudepigrapha*. Vol. 1. Anchor Bible Reference Library. New York: Doubleday, 1983.

Chu, Julie Li-Chuan. "The Inspiration of the Role Dedifferentiation in the Book of Ruth for Taiwanese Women." *Semeia* 78 (1997): 47–54.

Clanton, Dan W., Jr. "The Bible and Graphic Novels: A Review and Interview with the Authors of *Marked* and *Megillat Esther*." *SBL Forum* 4, no. 1 (2006). Online: *http://www.sbl-site.org/Article.aspx?ArticleID=477*.

———. "Cartoons and Comics." Pages 329–34 in *Teaching the Bible through Popular Culture and the Arts*. Edited by Mark Roncace and Patrick Gray. Society of Biblical Literature Resources for Biblical Study 53. Atlanta: Society of Biblical Literature, 2007.

———. *The Good, the Bold, and the Beautiful: The Story of Susanna and Its Renaissance Interpretations*. Library of Hebrew Bible/Old Testament Studies 430. New York and London: T & T Clark, 2006.

———. "Judy in Disguise: D. W. Griffith's Judith of Bethulia." Pages 119–30 in *Studies in Jewish Civilization 14: Women and Judaism*. Edited by Leonard J. Greenspoon, Ronald A. Simkins, and Jean Axelrad Cahan. Omaha, Neb.: Creighton University Press, 2003.

———. "(Re)Dating the Story of Susanna: A Proposal." *Journal for the Study of Judaism in the Persian, Hellenistic, and Roman Periods* 34, no. 2 (2003): 121–40.

———. "*Samson et Dalila*: What French Opera Reveals about the Biblical Duo." *Bible Review* 20, no. 3 (June 2004): 12–19, 44–46.

———. "Trollops and Temptresses: Delilah(s) in 20th-Century Popular Music." *SBL Forum* 3, no. 3 (2005). Online: *http://www.sbl-site.org/Article.aspx?ArticleID=391*.

Clanton, Dan W., Jr., and Bryan Bibb. "Classical Music." Pages 53–83 in *Teaching the Bible through Popular Culture and the Arts*. Edited by Mark Roncace and Patrick Gray. Society of Biblical Literature Resources for Biblical Study 53. Atlanta: Society of Biblical Literature, 2007.

Clanton, Dan W., Jr., and Mark Roncace. "Animated Television." Pages 343–52 in *Teaching the Bible through Popular Culture and the Arts*. Edited by Mark Roncace and Patrick Gray. Society of Biblical Literature Resources for Biblical Study 53. Atlanta: Society of Biblical Literature, 2007.

Clark, Kenneth. *The Nude: A Study in Ideal Form.* Garden City, N.Y.: Doubleday, 1956.

Collet, Henri. *"Samson et Dalila" de C. Saint-Saëns: Étude historique et critique Analyse Musicale.* Les Chefs-d'Œuvre de la Musique Series. Paris: Librarie Delaplane, 1922.

Collins, John J. "Before the Fall: The Earliest Interpretations of Adam and Eve." Pages 293–308 in *The Idea of Interpretation: Essays in Honor of James L. Kugel.* Edited by Hindy Najman and Judith H. Newman. *Journal for the Study of Judaism in the Persian, Hellenistic, and Roman Periods*: Supplement Series 83. Leiden and Boston: Brill, 2004.

———. "Sibylline Oracles: A New Translation and Introduction" Pages 317–472 in *The Old Testament Pseudepigrapha.* Vol. 1, *Apocalyptic Literature and Testaments.* Edited by James H. Charlesworth. New York: Doubleday, 1983.

Corley, Kathleen E. *Private Women, Public Meals: Social Conflict in the Synoptic Tradition.* Peabody, Mass.: Hendrickson, 1993.

Crawford, Sidnie White. "The Additions to Esther." Pages 970–72 in vol. 3 of *The New Interpreter's Bible.* Edited by Leander Keck et al. 12 vols. Nashville: Abingdon Press, 1994–2002.

Crenshaw, James L. "A Monstrous Test: Genesis 22." Pages 9–29 in *A Whirlpool of Torment: Israelite Traditions of God as an Oppressive Presence.* Overtures to Biblical Theology. Philadelphia: Fortress, 1984.

Cunningham, Philip A., ed. *Pondering the Passion: What's at Stake for Christians and Jews?* Lanham, Md.: Rowman & Littlefield, 2004.

Danby, Herbert, trans. *The Mishnah.* Oxford: Oxford University Press, 1933.

Darr, Katheryn Pfisterer. *Far More Precious Than Jewels: Perspectives on Biblical Women.* Gender and the Biblical Tradition Series. Louisville, Ky.: Westminster John Knox Press, 1991.

———. "More Than Just a Pretty Face: Critical, Rabbinical, and Feminist Perspectives on Esther." Pages 164–202 in *Far More Precious Than Jewels: Perspectives on Biblical Women.* Gender and the Biblical Tradition Series. Louisville, Ky.: Westminster John Knox Press, 1991.

———. "More Than a Possession: Critical, Rabbinical, and Feminist Perspectives on Hagar." Pages 132–63 in *Far More Precious Than Jewels: Perspectives on Biblical Women.* Gender and the Biblical Tradition Series. Louisville, Ky.: Westminster John Knox Press, 1991.

———. "More Than the Stars of the Heavens: Critical, Rabbinical, and Feminist Perspectives on Sarah." Pages 85–131 in *Far More Precious Than Jewels: Perspectives on Biblical Women.* Gender and the Biblical Tradition Series. Louisville, Ky.: Westminster John Knox Press, 1991.

Day, Linda. *Esther.* Abingdon Old Testament Commentary Series. Nashville: Abingdon Press, 2005.

De Lench, Charles H. *The Love Story of Ruth and Boaz: A Dramatic Verse Version of the Biblical Story.* New York: Exposition Press, 1966.

Denzy, Nicola, and Patrick Gray. "The Bible in Film." Pages 97–118 in *Teaching the Bible through Popular Culture and the Arts.* Edited by Mark Roncace and Patrick Gray. Society of Biblical Literature Resources for Biblical Study 53. Atlanta: Society of Biblical Literature, 2007.

Eisner, Will. *The Plot: The Secret Story of "The Protocols of the Elders of Zion."* New York and London: W. W. Norton, 2005.

Elder, Linda Bennett. "Virgins, Viragos, and Virtuo(u)si among Judiths in Opera and Oratorio." *Journal for the Study of the Old Testament* 92 (2001): 91–119.

Evans, J. M. *Paradise Lost and the Genesis Tradition*. Oxford: Oxford University Press, 1968.

Exum, J. Cheryl. *Plotted, Shot, and Painted: Cultural Representations of Biblical Women*. Journal for the Study of the Old Testament: Supplement Series 215 / Gender, Culture, Theory Series 3. Sheffield: Sheffield Academic Press, 1996.

————. "Is This Naomi?" Pages 129–74 in *Plotted, Shot, and Painted: Cultural Representations of Biblical Women*. Journal for the Study of the Old Testament: Supplement Series 215 / Gender, Culture, Theory Series 3. Sheffield: Sheffield Academic Press, 1996.

————. "Samson's Women." Pages 61–93 in *Fragmented Women: Feminist (Sub)Versions of Biblical Narratives*. Valley Forge, Pa.: Trinity Press, 1993.

————. "Why, Why, Why, Delilah?" Pages 175–237 in *Plotted, Shot, and Painted: Cultural Representations of Biblical Women*. Journal for the Study of the Old Testament: Supplement Series 215 / Gender, Culture, Theory Series 3. Sheffield: Sheffield Academic Press, 1996.

Fewell, Danna Nolan. "Judges." Pages 73–83 in *The Women's Bible Commentary*. Edited by Carol A. Newsom and Sharon H. Ringe. Expanded ed. with Apocrypha. Louisville, Ky.: Westminster John Knox Press, 1998.

Fewell, Danna Nolan, and David M. Gunn. *Compromising Redemption: Relating Characters in the Book of Ruth*. Literary Currents in Biblical Interpretation Series. Louisville, Ky.: Westminster John Knox Press, 1990.

————. *Gender, Power, and Promise: The Subject of the Bible's First Story*. Nashville: Abingdon Press, 1993.

————. "'A Son Is Born to Naomi!': Literary Allusions and Interpretation in the Book of Ruth." Pages 233–39 in *Women in the Hebrew Bible: A Reader*. Edited by Alice Bach. New York and London: Routledge, 1999.

Finkel, Avraham Yaakov. *The Torah Revealed: Talmudic Masters Unveil the Secrets of the Bible*. San Francisco: Jossey Bass, 2004.

Forshey, Gerald E. *American Religious and Biblical Spectaculars*. Media and Society Series. Westport, Conn.: Praeger, 1992.

Foucault, Michel. *The History of Sexuality*. Vol. 1, *An Introduction*. Translated by R. Hurley. New York: Random House, 1978.

————. "Method." Pages 92–102 in *The History of Sexuality*. Vol. 1, *An Introduction*. Translated by R. Hurley. New York: Random House, 1978.

————. "Power and Sex." Pages 110–24 in *Politics, Philosophy, Culture: Interviews and Other Writings, 1977–1984*. Edited by Lawrence D. Kritzman. Translated by A. Sheridan et al. New York and London: Routledge, 1988.

————. "Power and Strategies." Pages 134–45 in *Power/Knowledge: Selected Interviews and Other Writings, 1972–1977*. Edited by Colin Gordon. Translated by Colin Gordon et al. New York: Pantheon Books, 1980.

Fox, Michael V. *Character and Ideology in the Book of Esther*. 2nd ed. Grand Rapids, Mich.: Eerdmans, 1991.

Friedman, Richard Elliott. *Who Wrote the Bible?* New York: Summit Books, 1987.

Frontain, Raymond J. "The Price of Rubies: The Weight of Old Testament Women in Western Literature." Pages 2–19 in *Old Testament Women in Western Literature*. Edited by R. Frontain and J. Wojcik. Conway, Ark.: University of Central Arkansas Press, 1991.

Gallaudet, T. H. *Scripture Biography for the Young with Critical Illustrations and Practical Remarks: Ruth.* New York: American Tract Society, 1839.

Garrard, Mary D. "Artemisia and Susanna." Pages 146–71 in *Feminism and Art History: Questioning the Litany.* Edited by Norma Broude and Mary D. Garrard. New York: Harper & Row, 1982.

Ginzberg, Louis. *Legends of the Jews.* Vol. 2, *Bible Times and Characters from Moses in the Wilderness to Esther.* JPS Classic Reissues Series. Philadelphia: Jewish Publication Society, 2003.

Gitay, Zefira. "Hagar's Expulsion: A Tale Twice-Told in Genesis." Pages 73–91 in *Abraham and Family: New Insights into the Patriarchal Narratives.* Edited by Hershel Shanks. Washington, D.C.: Biblical Archaeology Society, 2000.

Goldin, Judah, trans. *The Fathers According to Rabbi Nathan.* New York: Schocken Books, 1955.

Goldstein, Rabbi Elyse. "Male and Female Were They Created: Eve, Lilith, and the Snake." Pages 44–58 in *ReVisions: Seeing Torah through a Feminist Lens.* Toronto: Key Porter Books, 1998.

Gray, John. *Joshua, Judges, Ruth.* New Century Bible Commentary. Grand Rapids, Mich.: Eerdmans, 1986.

Greenberg, Rabbi Irving. "Confronting Jewish Destiny: Purim." Pages 224–57 in *The Jewish Way: Living the Holidays.* New York: Simon & Schuster, 1988.

Gruen, Erich S. *Heritage and Hellenism: The Reinvention of Jewish Tradition.* Hellenistic Culture and Society Series 30. Berkeley: University of California Press, 1998.

Gunn, David M., and Danna Nolan Fewell. *Narrative in the Hebrew Bible.* New York and Oxford: Oxford University Press, 1993.

Hassan, Riffat. "Islamic Hagar and Her Family." Pages 149–67 in *Hagar, Sarah, and Their Children: Jewish, Christian, and Muslim Perspectives.* Edited by Phyllis Trible and Letty M. Russell. Louisville, Ky.: Westminster John Knox Press, 2006.

Hastings, Selena. *The Illustrated Jewish Bible for Children.* New York: DK Publishing, 1994.

Haynes, Stephen R. *Noah's Curse: The Biblical Justification of American Slavery.* Oxford: Oxford University Press, 2002.

Henderson, Robert M. *D. W. Griffith: His Life and Work.* New York: Oxford University Press, 1972.

———. *D. W. Griffith: The Years at Biograph.* New York: Farrar, Straus and Giroux, 1970.

Herford, R. Travers, trans. *Pirkē Aboth: The Tractate "Fathers," from the Mishnah, Commonly Called "Saying of the Fathers."* New York: Jewish Institute of Religion, 1945.

Hill, Paul. "I Shot an Abortionist." No pages. Online: *http://www.armyofgod.com/PHill_ShortShot.html.*

Horowitz, Elliott. *Reckless Rites: Purim and the Legacy of Jewish Violence.* Princeton, N.J., and Oxford: Princeton University Press, 2006.

Huber, Lynn, Dan W. Clanton Jr., and Jane Webster. "Biblical Subjects in Art." Pages 187–228 in *Teaching the Bible through Popular Culture and the Arts.* Edited by Mark Roncace and Patrick Gray. Society of Biblical Literature Resources for Biblical Study 53. Atlanta: Society of Biblical Literature, 2007.

Humfrey, Peter. *Painting in Renaissance Venice.* New Haven and London: Yale University Press, 1995.

Isaacs, Ronald H. "Hospitality." Pages 15–21 in *A Taste of Text: An Introduction to the Talmud and Midrash*. New York: UAHC Press, 2003.

Jeansonne, Sharon Pace. *The Women of Genesis: From Sarah to Potiphar's Wife*. Minneapolis: Fortress, 1990.

Kahl, Brigette. "Hagar between Genesis and Galatians: The Stony Road to Freedom." Pages 219–32 in *From Prophecy to Testament: The Function of the Old Testament in the New*. Edited by Craig A. Evans. Peabody, Mass.: Hendrickson, 2004.

Kamlin, Richard. "Levirate Law." Pages 296–97 in vol. 4 of *The Anchor Bible Dictionary*. Edited by David Noel Freedman et al. 6 vols. New York: Doubleday, 1992.

Kates, Judith A. "Women at the Center: Ruth and Shavuot." Pages 187–98 in *Reading Ruth: Contemporary Women Reclaim a Sacred Story*. Edited by Judith A. Kates and Gail Twersky Reimer. New York: Ballantine Books, 1994.

Kaufman, J. B. "*Judith of Bethulia*: Un 'Piccolo' Film Epico / *Judith of Bethulia*: Producing the 'Little' Epic." *Griffithiana* 50 (1994): 176–91.

Kessler, Edward. *Bound by the Bible: Jews, Christians, and the Sacrifice of Isaac*. Cambridge: Cambridge University Press, 2004.

———. "The Sacrifice of Isaac (the *Akedah*) in Christian and Jewish Tradition: Artistic Interpretations." Pages 74–98 in *Borders, Boundaries, and the Bible*. Edited by Martin O'Kane. *Journal for the Study of the Old Testament*: Supplement Series 313. Sheffield: Sheffield Academic Press, 2002.

Klein, Lillian R. "Honor and Shame in Esther." Pages 149–75 in *A Feminist Companion to Esther, Judith, and Susanna*. Edited by Athalya Brenner. Sheffield: Sheffield Academic Press, 1995.

Klijn, A. F. J. "2 (Syriac Apocalypse of) Baruch: A New Translation and Introduction." Pages 615–652 in *The Old Testament Pseudepigrapha, Volume 1: Apocalyptic Literature and Testaments*. Edited by James H. Charlesworth. New York: Doubleday, 1983.

Knight, Douglas A. "The Pentateuch." Pages 263–96 in *The Hebrew Bible and Its Modern Interpreters*. Edited by Douglas A. Knight and Gene M. Tucker. Philadelphia: Fortress; Decatur, Ga.: Scholars Press, 1985.

Kramer, Phyllis Silverman. "The Dismissal of Hagar in Five Art Works of the Sixteenth and Seventeenth Centuries." Pages 195–217 in *Genesis: A Feminist Companion to the Bible*. Edited by Athalya Brenner. Sheffield: Sheffield Academic Press, 1998.

Kravitz, Leonard, and Kerry M. Olitzky. *Pirke Avot: A Modern Commentary on Jewish Ethics*. New York: UAHC Press, 1993.

———. *Ruth: A Modern Commentary*. New York: URJ Press, 2005.

Kugel, James L. *The Bible as It Was*. Cambridge, Mass., and London: Harvard University Press, 1999.

Kvam, Kristin E., Linda S. Schearing, and Valarie H. Ziegler, eds. *Eve and Adam: Jewish, Christian, and Muslim Readings on Genesis and Gender*. Bloomington: Indiana University Press, 1999.

LaCocque, André. "Esther." Pages 49–83 in *The Feminine Unconventional: Four Subversive Figures in Israel's Tradition*. Overtures to Biblical Theology. Minneapolis: Fortress, 1990.

———. *The Feminine Unconventional: Four Subversive Figures in Israel's Tradition*. Overtures to Biblical Theology. Minneapolis: Fortress, 1990.

————. "Ruth." Pages 84–116 in *The Feminine Unconventional: Four Subversive Figures in Israel's Tradition*. Overtures to Biblical Theology. Minneapolis: Fortress, 1990.

————. *Ruth: A Continental Commentary*. Translated by K. C. Hanson. Minneapolis: Fortress, 2004.

Landres, J. Shawn, and Michael Berenbaum, eds. *After "The Passion" Is Gone: American Religious Consequences*. Walnut Creek, Calif.: AltaMira Press, 2004.

Laniak, Timothy S. *Shame and Honor in the Book of Esther*. Society of Biblical Literature Dissertation Series 165. Atlanta: Scholars Press, 1998.

Leibowitz, Nehama. *Studies in Bereshit (Genesis) in the Context of Ancient and Modern Jewish Bible Commentary*. 2nd rev. ed. Translated by Aryeh Newman. Jerusalem: World Zionist Organization Department for Torah Education and Culture, 5734/1974.

Leneman, Helen. "Portrayals of Power in the Stories of Delilah and Bathsheba: Seduction in Song." Pages 227–43 in *Sacred Text, Secular Times: The Hebrew Bible in the Modern World*. Edited by Leonard Jay Greenspoon and Bryan F. LeBeau. The Klutznick Chair in Jewish Civilization Center for the Study of Religion and Society Studies in Jewish Civilization 10. Omaha, Neb.: Creighton University Press, 2000.

Lerner, Anne Lapidus. *Eternally Eve: Images of Eve in the Hebrew Bible, Midrash, and Modern Jewish Poetry*. HBI Series on Jewish Women. Waltham, Mass., and London: Brandeis University Press/University Press of New England, 2007.

Lerner, Gerda. *The Creation of Patriarchy*. New York and Oxford: Oxford University Press, 1986.

Levenson, Jon D. *Esther*. Old Testament Library. Philadelphia: Westminster, 1997.

Levine, Amy-Jill. "Matthew." Pages 339–49 in *The Women's Bible Commentary*. Edited by Carol A. Newsom and Sharon H. Ringe. Expanded ed. with Apocrypha. Louisville, Ky.: Westminster John Knox Press, 1998.

————. "Ruth." Pages 84–90 in *The Women's Bible Commentary*. Edited by Carol A. Newsom and Sharon H. Ringe. Expanded ed. with Apocrypha. Louisville, Ky.: Westminster John Knox Press, 1998.

————. "Sacrifice and Salvation: Otherness and Domestication in the Book of Judith." Pages 208–33 in *A Feminist Companion to Esther, Judith, and Susanna*. Edited by Athalya Brenner. Feminist Companion to the Bible. Sheffield: Sheffield Academic Press, 1995.

————. "Settling at Beer-lahai-roi." Pages 12–34 in *Daughters of Abraham: Feminist Thought in Judaism, Christianity, and Islam*. Edited by Yvonne Yazbeck Haddad and John L. Esposito. Gainesville, Fla.: University Press of Florida, 2001.

Lieber, David L., ed. *Etz Hayim: Torah and Commentary*. New York: The Rabbinical Assembly, 2001.

Linafelt, Tod. "Ruth." Pages 1–90 in *Ruth and Esther* by Tod Linafelt and Timothy K. Beal. Berit Olam. Collegeville, Minn.: Liturgical Press, 1999.

Linafelt, Tod, and Timothy K. Beal. *Ruth and Esther*. Berit Olam. Collegeville, Minn.: Liturgical Press, 1999.

Locke, Ralph P. "Constructing the Oriental 'Other': Saint-Saëns's *Samson et Dalila*." *Cambridge Opera Journal* 3 (1991): 261–302.

Lomax, John A., and Alan Lomax, collectors and compilers. *Our Singing Country: A Second Volume of American Ballads and Folksongs*. New York: Macmillan, 1941.

Luttikhuizen, Gerard P. *The Creation of Man and Woman: Interpretations of the Biblical Narratives in Jewish and Christian Traditions.* Themes in Biblical Narrative 3. Leiden and Boston: Brill, 2000.

MacKenzie, R. A. F. "The Meaning of the Susanna Story." *Canadian Journal of Theology* 3 (1957): 211–18.

MacMaster, Eve B. *God Gives the Land: Stories of God and His People; Joshua, Judges, and Ruth.* Scottdale, Pa., and Kitchener, Ont.: Herald Press, 1983.

Marzollo, Jean. *Ruth and Naomi.* New York: Little, Brown and Company, 2005.

Mbuwayesango, Dora Rudo. "Childlessness and Woman-to-Woman Relationships in Genesis and in African Patriarchal Society: Sarah and Hagar from a Zimbabwean Woman's Perspective (Gen 16:1–16; 21:8–21)." *Semeia* 78 (1997): 27–36.

McClain, Kathleen P. "Seeing Beyond the Traditional Image of Susanna and the Elders." M.A. thesis, University of Alabama, Birmingham, 2000.

Menn, Esther Marie. *Judah and Tamar (Genesis 38) in Ancient Jewish Exegesis: Studies in Literary Form and Hermeneutics.* Supplements to the *Journal for the Study of Judaism* 51. Leiden: Brill, 1997.

Meyers, Carol. *Discovering Eve: Ancient Israelite Women in Context.* New York: Oxford University Press, 1988.

Miles, Margaret R. *Carnal Knowing: Female Nakedness and Religious Meaning in the Christian West.* Boston: Beacon Press, 1989.

Milgrom, Jo. *The Binding of Isaac: The Akedah—A Primary Symbol in Jewish Thought and Art.* Berkeley: BIBAL Press, 1988.

Milton, John. *Paradise Lost.* Norton Critical Edition. Edited by Gordon Teskey. New York and London: W. W. Norton, 2005.

Montley, Patricia. "Judith in the Fine Arts: The Appeal of the Archetypal Androgyne." *Anima* 4 (1978): 37–42.

Moore, Carey A. *Esther.* Anchor Bible 7B. Garden City, N.Y.: Doubleday, 1971.

———. *Judith.* Anchor Bible 40. Garden City, N.Y.: Doubleday, 1985.

———. "Susanna: A Case of Sexual Harassment in Ancient Babylonia." *Biblical Research* 8 (1992): 20–29, 52.

Mosala, Itumeleng J. "The Implications of the Text of Esther for African Women's Struggle for Liberation in South Africa." *Semeia* 59 (1992): 129–37.

Nadar, Sarojini. "Gender, Power, Sexuality, and Suffering Bodies in the Book of Esther: Reading the Characters of Esther and Vashti for the Purpose of Social Transformation." *Old Testament Essays* 15, no. 1 (2002): 113–30.

———. "A South African Indian Womanist Reading of the Character of Ruth." Pages 159–75 in *Other Ways of Reading: African Women and the Bible.* Edited by Musa W. Dube. Atlanta: Society of Biblical Literature, 2001.

Nayap-Pot, Dalila. "Life in the Midst of Death: Naomi, Ruth, and the Plight of Indigenous Women." Pages 52–65 in *Vernacular Hermeneutics.* Edited by R. S. Sugirtharajah. Sheffield: Sheffield Academic Press, 1999.

Nead, Lynda. *The Female Nude: Art, Obscenity, and Sexuality.* London and New York: Routledge, 1992.

Neeman, Rachel. "Esther." Pages 56–61 in *The Films of Amos Gitai: A Montage.* Edited by Paul Willemen. London: British Film Institute, 1993.

Neusner, Jacob. "*Genesis in Genesis Rabbah*: Recasting the Patriarchs into the Models for Israelite Conduct." Pages 30–45 in *Judaism and the Interpretation of Scripture: Introduction to the Rabbinic Midrash.* Peabody, Mass.: Hendrickson, 2004.

————. *Genesis Rabbah: The Judaic Commentary to the Book of Genesis; A New American Translation.* Vol. I, *Parashiyyot One through Thirty-three on Genesis 1:1 to 8:14.* Brown Judaic Studies 104. Atlanta: Scholars Press, 1985.

————. *Genesis Rabbah: The Judaic Commentary to the Book of Genesis; A New American Translation.* Vol. 2, *Parashiyyot Thirty-four through Sixty-seven on Genesis 8:15 to 28:9.* Brown Judaic Studies 105. Atlanta: Scholars Press, 1985.

————. "*Genesis Rabbah.*" Pages 355–81 in *Introduction to Rabbinic Literature.* Anchor Bible Reference Library. New York: Doubleday, 1994.

Nichols, Tomas. "Jacopo Tintoretto." In *The Grove Dictionary of Art Online* (1998). No pages. Online: *http://www.groveart.com/index.html.*

Nickelsburg, George W. E., and James C. VanderKam, trans. *1 Enoch: A New Translation.* Minneapolis: Fortress, 2004.

Niditch, Susan. "The Three Wife-Sister Tales of Genesis." Pages 23–69 in *A Prelude to Biblical Folklore: Underdogs and Tricksters.* Urbana: University of Illinois Press, 2000.

Nielsen, Kirsten. *Ruth. Old Testament Library.* Philadelphia: Westminster, 1997.

Noort, Ed, and Eibert Tigchelaar, eds. *The Sacrifice of Isaac: The Aqedah (Genesis 22) and Its Interpretations.* Leiden and Boston: Brill, 2002.

O'Kane, Martin. "The Bible and the Visual Imagination." Pages 1–33 in *Painting the Text: The Artist as Biblical Interpreter.* The Bible in the Modern World Series 8. Sheffield: Sheffield Phoenix Press, 2007.

Pasachoff, Naomi, and Robert J. Littman. "The Protocols of the Elders of Zion." Pages 265–68 in *Jewish History in 100 Nutshells.* Lanham, Md.: Jason Aronson, 1995.

Peters, Renate. "D. W. Griffith's Transformation of the Legend of Judith." Paper presented at the Canadian Comparative Literature Arts Conference, Ottawa, 30 May 1998.

Petersen, David L. "A Thrice-Told Tale: Genre, Theme, and Motif." *Biblical Research* 18 (1973): 30–43.

Petersen, John. "Redeeming a Patriarch: Plotting in the Tale of Judah and Tamar." Pages 119–64 in *Reading Women's Stories: Female Characters in the Hebrew Bible.* Minneapolis: Fortress, 2004.

Petersham, Maud, and Miska Petersham. *Ruth.* New York: Macmillan, 1938.

Phillips, John A. *Eve: The History of an Idea.* San Francisco: Harper & Row, 1984.

Philpot, Elizabeth. "Judith and Holofernes: Changing Images in the History of Art." Pages 80–97 in *Translating Religious Texts: Translation, Transgression, and Interpretation.* Edited by D. Jasper. Studies in Literature and Religion. New York: St. Martin's Press, 1993.

Pignatti, Terisio. "Life and Works." Pages 9–56 in *Tintoretto* by Francesco Valcanover and Terisio Pignatti. Translated by Robert Erich Wolf. Library of Great Painters Series. New York: Harry N. Abrams, 1985.

Plate, S. Brent, ed. *Re-viewing "The Passion": Mel Gibson's Film and Its Critics.* New York: Palgrave Macmillan, 2004.

Plaut, W. Gunther, ed. *The Torah: A Modern Commentary.* Rev. ed. New York: Union for Reform Judaism, 2005.

Purdie, Edna. *The Story of Judith in German and English Literature.* Paris: Librarie Ancienne Honoré Champien, 1927.

Radavich, David A. "A Catalogue of Works Based on the Apocryphal Book of Judith, from the Mediaeval Period to the Present." *Bulletin of Bibliography* 44 (1987): 189–92.

Reinhartz, Adele, and Miriam Simma Walfish. "Conflict and Coexistence in Jewish Interpretation." Pages 101–25 in *Hagar, Sarah, and Their Children: Jewish, Christian, and Muslim Perspectives*. Edited by Phyllis Trible and Letty M. Russell. Louisville, Ky.: Westminster John Knox Press, 2006.

Ridolfi, Carlo. *The Life of Tintoretto* [1642]. Translated by Catherine and Robert Enggass. University Park, Pa., and London: Pennsylvania State University Press, 1984.

Rivers, Francine. *Unshaken*. Wheaton, Ill.: Tyndale House Publishers, 2001.

Robinson, S. E. "Testament of Adam: A New Translation and Introduction." Pages 989–95 in the *Old Testment Psudepigrapha, Volume 1: Apocalyptic Literature and Testaments*. Edited by James M. Charlesworth. New York: Doubleday, 1983.

Rosand, David. *Painting in Sixteenth-Century Venice: Titian, Veronese, Tintoretto*. Rev. ed. Cambridge: Cambridge University Press, 1997.

Rothman, William. "D. W. Griffith's Judith of Bethulia." *Twentieth-Century Literary Criticism* 68 (1997): 213–20.

———. "Judith of Bethulia." Pages 17–28 in The "I" of the Camera: Essays in Film Criticism, History, and Aesthetics. 2nd ed. Cambridge: Cambridge University Press, 2003.

Rushkoff, Douglas. *Testament: West of Eden*. New York: DC Comics, 2007.

Russell, Letty M. "Twists and Turns in Paul's Allegory." Pages 71–97 in *Hagar, Sarah, and Their Children: Jewish, Christian, and Muslim Perspectives*. Edited by Phyllis Trible and Letty M. Russell. Louisville, Ky.: Westminster John Knox Press, 2006.

Sakenfeld, Katharine Doob. *Ruth*. Interpretation: A Bible Commentary for Teaching and Preaching. Atlanta: John Knox Press, 1999.

Samuels, *Ruth*. Bible Stories for Jewish Children. Jersey City, N.J.: KTAV Publishing House, 1973.

Sarna, Nahum M. *Genesis*. Jewish Publication Society Bible Commentary Series. Philadelphia: Jewish Publication Society, 1989.

Sasson, Jack M. *Ruth: A New Translation with a Philological Commentary and a Formalist-Folklorist Interpretation*. 2nd ed. Sheffield: Sheffield Academic Press, 1995.

Scherman, Rabbi Nosson, and Rabbi Meir Zlotowitz. *The Chumash*. Artscroll Series. Brooklyn: Mesorah Publications, 2001.

Schickel, Richard. *D. W. Griffith: An American Life*. New York: Simon & Schuster, 1984.

Schneider, Tammi J. *Sarah: Mother of Nations*. New York and London: Continuum, 2004.

Schur, Maxine Rose. *The Story of Ruth*. Minneapolis: Kar-Ben Publishing, 2005.

Simmon, Scott. *The Films of D. W. Griffith*. Cambridge Film Classics. Cambridge and New York: Cambridge University Press, 1993.

"The Simpsons Archive." Online: *http://www.snpp.com*.

Skinner, John. *Genesis*. International Critical Commentary. 2nd ed. Edinburgh: T & T Clark, 1930.

Sluijter, Eric J. "Rembrandt's Early Paintings of the Female Nude: Andromeda and Susanna." Pages 31–54 in *Rembrandt and His Pupils*. Edited by Görel Cavalli-Björkman. Uddevalla, Sweden: Risbergs Tryckeri, 1993.

Sly, Dorothy. *Philo's Perception of Women*. Brown Judaic Studies 209. Atlanta: Scholars Press, 1990.

Soloveitchik, Rabbi Joseph B. *Abraham's Journey: Reflections on the Life of the Founding Patriarch*. Edited by David Shatz, Joel B. Wolowelsky, and Reuven Ziegler. *MeOtzar HoRav* Series: Selected Writings of Rabbi Joseph B. Soloveitchik 9. Jersey City, N.J.: Toras HoRav Foundation/KTAV Publishing House, 2008.

Speiser, E. A. *Genesis: A New Translation with Introduction and Commentary*. Anchor Bible 1. Garden City, N.Y.: Doubleday, 1977.

Spiegel, Shalom. *The Last Trial: On the Legends and Lore of the Command to Abraham to Offer Isaac as a Sacrifice; The Akedah*. Translated by Judah Goldin. New York: Jewish Theological Seminary of America, 1950. Repr., Woodstock, Vt.: Jewish Lights Publishing, 1993.

Spolsky, Ellen. "Law or the Garden: The Betrayal of Susanna in Pastoral Painting." Pages 101–17 in *The Judgment of Susanna: Authority and Witness*. Edited by Ellen Spolsky. Society of Biblical Literature Early Judaism and Its Literature 11. Atlanta: Scholars Press, 1996.

Sprague, Ruth L., and Margaret Nixon. *People of the Old Testament*. Boston: United Church Press, 1964.

Steinberg, Naomi. *Kinship and Marriage in Genesis: A Household Economics Perspective*. Minneapolis: Fortress, 1993.

Steinsaltz, Adin. "Sarah." Pages 21–31 in *Biblical Images*. Northvale, N.J., and London: Jason Aronson, 1994.

Steussy, Marti J. *Gardens in Babylon: Narrative and Faith in the Greek Legends of Daniel*. Society of Biblical Literature Dissertation Series 141. Atlanta: Scholars Press, 1993.

Stocker, Margarita. *Judith, Sexual Warrior: Women and Power in Western Culture*. New Haven, Conn., and London: Yale University Press, 1998.

Storr, Catherine. *Ruth's Story*. Milwaukee: Raintree Publishers, 1986.

Swann, Mona. "Ruth the Gleaner." Pages 15–28 in *At the Well of Bethlehem: A Narrative Drama in Three Parts*. Boston: Baker's Plays, 1937.

Tatum, W. Barnes. *Jesus at the Movies: A Guide to the First Hundred Years*. Santa Rosa, Calif.: Polebridge Press, 1997.

Thompson, John L. "Hagar: Abraham's Wife and Exile." Pages 17–99 in *Writing the Wrongs: Women of the Old Testament among Biblical Commentators from Philo through the Reformation*. Oxford and New York: Oxford University Press, 2001.

Trible, Phyllis. "Genesis 22: The Sacrifice of Sarah." Pages 271–90 in *Women in the Hebrew Bible: A Reader*. Edited by Alice Bach. New York and London: Routledge, 1999.

———. "Hagar: The Desolation of Rejection." Pages 9–35 in *Texts of Terror: Literary-Feminist Readings of Biblical Narratives*. Overtures to Biblical Theology. Philadelphia: Fortress, 1984.

———. "A Human Comedy." Pages 166–99 in *God and the Rhetoric of Sexuality*. Overtures to Biblical Theology. Philadelphia: Fortress, 1978.

———. "A Love Story Gone Awry." Pages 72–143 in *God and the Rhetoric of Sexuality*. Overtures to Biblical Theology. Philadelphia: Fortress, 1978.

———. "Ominous Beginnings for a Promise of Blessing." Pages 33–69 in *Hagar, Sarah, and Their Children: Jewish, Christian, and Muslim Perspectives*. Edited by Phyllis Trible and Letty M. Russell. Louisville, Ky.: Westminster John Knox Press, 2006.

Trible, Phyllis, and Letty M. Russell, eds. *Hagar, Sarah, and Their Children: Jewish, Christian, and Muslim Perspectives*. Louisville, Ky.: Westminster John Knox Press, 2006.

Tuchman, Shera Aranoff, and Sandra E. Rapoport. *The Passions of the Matriarchs*. Jersey City, N.J.: KTAV Publishing House, 2004.

Valcanover, Francesco, and Terisio Pignatti. *Tintoretto*. Translated by Robert Erich Wolf. Library of Great Painters Series. New York: Harry N. Abrams, 1985.

van Dyk, Alta C., and Peet J. van Dyk. "HIV/AIDS in Africa: Suffering Women and the Theology of the Book of Ruth." *Old Testament Essays* 15, no 1 (2002): 209–24.

Van Seters, Jon. "The Pentateuch." Pages 3–49 in *The Hebrew Bible Today: An Introduction to Critical Issues*. Edited by Steven L. McKenzie and M. Patrick Graham. Louisville, Ky.: Westminster John Knox Press, 1998.

Visotzky, Burton L. *Reading the Book: Making the Bible a Timeless Text*. New York: Schocken Books, 1996.

von Rad, Gerhard. *Genesis*. Rev. ed. Translated by John H. Marks. *Old Testament Library*. Philadelphia: Westminster, 1972.

Vos, Catherine F. *The Child's Story Bible*. 5th ed. Revised by Marianne Catherine Vos Radius. Grand Rapids, Mich.: Eerdmans, 1983 [1934].

Wadud, Amina. "In the Beginning, Man and Woman Were Equal: Human Creation in the Qur'an." Pages 15–28 in *Qur'an and Woman: Rereading the Sacred Text from a Woman's Perspective*. New York and Oxford: Oxford University Press, 1999.

Wagenknecht, Edward, and Anthony Slide. *The Films of D. W. Griffith*. New York: Crown Publishers, 1975.

Waldman, J. T. *Megillat Esther*. Philadelphia: Jewish Publication Society, 2005.

Waters, John W. "Who Was Hagar?" Pages 187–205 in *Stony the Road We Trod: African American Biblical Interpretation*. Edited by Cain Hope Felder. Minneapolis: Fortress, 1991.

Wegner, Judith Romney. *Chattel or Person? The Status of Women in the Mishnah*. Oxford and New York: Oxford University Press, 1988.

Weinberg, Jennifer Liberts. *What Is a Princess?* New York: Random House, 2004.

Westermann, Claus. *Genesis 12–36: A Commentary*. Translated by John J. Scullion, S.J. Minneapolis: Augsburg, 1985.

Wiesel, Elie. "Esther." Pages 133–51 in *Sages and Dreamers: Biblical, Talmudic, and Hasidic Portraits and Legends*. New York: Summit Books, 1991.

———. "Ishmael and Hagar." Pages 3–22 in *Wise Men and Their Tales: Portraits of Biblical, Talmudic, and Hasidic Masters*. New York: Schocken Books, 2003.

———. "The Sacrifice of Isaac: A Survivor's Story" and "Parables and Sayings III." Pages 69–102 in *Messengers of God: Biblical Portraits and Legends*. Translated by Marion Wiesel. New York: Summit Books, 1976.

White, Sidnie Ann. "Esther: A Feminine Model for Jewish Diaspora." Pages 161–77 in *Gender and Difference in Ancient Israel*. Edited by Peggy L. Day. Minneapolis: Fortress, 1989.

Willemen, Paul, ed. *The Films of Amos Gitai: A Montage*. London: British Film Institute, 1993.

Wills, Lawrence M. "Esther and Greek Esther." Pages 93–131 in *The Jewish Novel in the Ancient World*. Myth and Poetics Series. Ithaca, N.Y., and London: Cornell University Press, 1995.

Wintermute, O. S. "Jubilees: A New Translation and Introduction." Pages 35–142 in *The Old Testament Pseudepigrapha*, volume 2. Edited by James H. Charlesworth. 2 vols. New York: Doubleday, 1985.